The Middle Class in Mozambique

In recent years, the growth of a middle class has been a key feature of the 'Africa Rising' narrative. Here, Jason Sumich explores the formation of this middle class in Mozambique, answering questions about the basis of the class system and the social order that gives rise to it. Drawing extensively on his fieldwork, Sumich argues that power and status in dominant party states such as Mozambique derive more from the ability to access resources than from direct control of the means of production. By considering the role of the state, he shows how the Mozambican middle class can be both bound to a system it benefits from and alienated from it at the same time, as well as exploring the ways in which the middle class attempts to reproduce its positions of privilege and highlighting the deeply uncertain future that it faces.

Jason Sumich is a lecturer in the department of sociology at the University of Essex. He is a political anthropologist who works on issues of class formation, the state, hegemony, citizenship, and the politics of enclaving in Southern Africa, primarily Mozambique. He holds a PhD from the London School of Economics (2006) and an MA from the University of Cape Town (2001). His current research explores new forms of urban governance and control as a member of the project 'Enclaving: Patterns of Global Futures in Three African Cities', funded by the Research Council of Norway.

T0370770

THE INTERNATIONAL AFRICAN LIBRARY

General Editors

LESLIE BANK, *Human Sciences Research Council, South Africa*
HARRI ENGLUND, *University of Cambridge*
ADELINE MASQUELIER, *Tulane University, Louisiana*
BENJAMIN SOARES, *University of Florida, Gainesville*

The International African Library is a major monograph series from the International African Institute. Theoretically informed ethnographies, and studies of social relations 'on the ground' which are sensitive to local cultural forms, have long been central to the Institute's publications programme. The IAL maintains this strength and extends it into new areas of contemporary concern, both practical and intellectual. It includes works focused on the linkages between local, national and global levels of society; writings on political economy and power; studies at the interface of the socio-cultural and the environmental; analyses of the roles of religion, cosmology and ritual in social organisation; and historical studies, especially those of a social, cultural or interdisciplinary character.

For a list of titles published in the series, please see the end of the book.

The Middle Class in Mozambique

The State and the Politics of Transformation in Southern Africa

Jason Sumich

University of Essex

International African Institute, London

and

 CAMBRIDGE
UNIVERSITY PRESS

CAMBRIDGE
UNIVERSITY PRESS

University Printing House, Cambridge CB2 8BS, United Kingdom

One Liberty Plaza, 20th Floor, New York, NY 10006, USA

477 Williamstown Road, Port Melbourne, VIC 3207, Australia

314-321, 3rd Floor, Plot 3, Splendor Forum, Jasola District Centre, New Delhi - 110025, India

79 Anson Road, #06-04/06, Singapore 079906

Cambridge University Press is part of the University of Cambridge.

It furthers the University's mission by disseminating knowledge in the pursuit of education, learning and research at the highest international levels of excellence.

www.cambridge.org
Information on this title: www.cambridge.org/9781108460712
DOI: 10.1017/9781108659659

First published 2018
First paperback edition 2020

A catalogue record for this publication is available from the British Library

Library of Congress Cataloging in Publication data
Names: Sumich, Jason, author.
Title: The middle class in Mozambique : the state and the politics of
    transformation in southern Africa / Jason Sumich.
Other titles: International African library ; 57.
Description: New York, NY : Cambridge University Press, 2018. | Series:
    International African library ; 57 | Includes bibliographical references
    and index.
Identifiers: LCCN 2018024267 | ISBN 9781108472883 (hardback : alk. paper)
    | ISBN 9781108460712 (pbk. : alk. paper)
Subjects: LCSH: Middle class–Mozambique. | Mozambique–Economic
    conditions–21st century. | Mozambique–Social conditions–21st century. |
    Mozambique–Politics and government–21st century.
Classification: LCC HT690.M85 S86 2018 | DDC 305.5/509679–dc23
LC record available at https://lccn.loc.gov/2018024267

ISBN   978-1-108-47288-3   Hardback
ISBN   978-1-108-46071-2   Paperback

To Afia and my parents.

Contents

Figures

Maps

Acknowledgements

This book is the product of an extremely long gestation period, and the list of people to thank and the debts I have accumulated at this point are almost endless. That being said, there are some people I would like to especially mention. First and foremost, I wish to thank everyone with whom I have spent time in Maputo over the past 16 years. I am continually amazed by people's warmth, generosity, and patience, especially with a foreigner who always wanted to tag along and ask endless, often artless, questions. I would specifically like to thank the following who have inspired me and have tremendously shaped my thinking, and for their friendship and support: Gilda Acubo, Dino and their family, Jose Adalima, Isabel Casimiro, João Trindade and family, Jaime Comiche, Paulo Ezquiel, Euclides Gonçalves, Amílcar Geraldo, Katya Hassan, Mayisha Mangueira, Sandra Manuel and Helder, Patricia Nicolau, Carmeliza Rosário, Sónia Romão, Margarida Paulo and Jonas Pohlmann, and Rita, who, on top of everything else, so often gave me a place to stay!

Over the years, various institutions in Mozambique graciously gave me an institutional home during fieldwork. I am very grateful to the Centro de Estudos Africanos (CEA) at the Eduardo Mondlane University in Maputo. I would like to warmly thank the members of CEA for their time, help, guidance, and advice, particularly Teresa Cruz e Silva, João Paulo Coelho, David Hedges, João Pereira, and Amelia Neves do Souto. I would also like to thank the Instituto de Estudos Sociais e Económicos (IESE), which so kindly offered me a desk and let me pester its staff. Thanks to all, and especially to Sérgio Chichava, Luís de Brito, António Francisco, and Salvador Forquilha.

I – and this book – have benefited greatly from numerous discussions with the following people; these have been consistently challenging and stimulating, and their friendship kept me going. Thanks to Julie Archambault, Jo Beall, Bjørn Enge Bertelsen, Maxim Bolt, Lorenzo Bottos, Katrin Bromber, Jan Budniok, Lars Buur, Henrike Donner, Sean Fox, Paolo Gaibazzi, Eric Morier-Genoud, Paulo Granjo, Tom Goodfellow, Keith Hart, Casey High, Joe Hanlon, Alcinda and João Honwana, Deborah James, Helen Kyed, Carola Lentz, Fraser McNeill, Oscar Monteiro, Henrietta Moore, Morten Nielsen, Andrea Noll, James

Putzel, Jon Schubert, Edward Simpson, John Sharp, Martin Thomassen, and Linda Van de Camp.

The fieldwork I have conducted over the last 16 years has been financially supported by numerous institutions. My PhD fieldwork was made possible through the financial assistance of the University of London Central Research Fund, the British Institute in Eastern Africa Fieldwork Grant, four research studentships from the Department of Anthropology at the London School of Economics, the Malinowski Award from the London School of Economics, and the Radcliffe-Brown Award from the Royal Anthropological Institute. Further research was supported by the Crisis States Research Centre, London School of Economics, the Norwegian University of Science and Technology (NTNU), the Research Council of Norway, and the German Institute of Global and Area Studies (GIGA). I would like to especially thank Melissa Nelson at GIGA for her editorial assistance. Versions of various parts of this book have appeared in the following journals: *Análise Social*, *Cambridge Journal of Anthropology*, *Development and Change*, *Ethnos*, *Journal of Southern African Studies*, and *Social Analysis*.

I benefited greatly from the help, direction, and advice of Leslie Bank, Judith Forshaw, Niranjana Harikrishnan, Stephanie Kitchen, Maria Marsh, Cassi Roberts, and Abigail Walkington as this book, ever so slowly, inched along the long march towards publication. I also would like to thank the two anonymous reviewers whose insightful and constructive comments definitely improved this book.

Finally, I would like to thank my wife and best friend, Afia, and my parents. My debt to them for all their support and encouragement is incalculable. I would like to particularly thank my father, who, through his generous offers of editing, has read this book more times than any human being should ever have to.

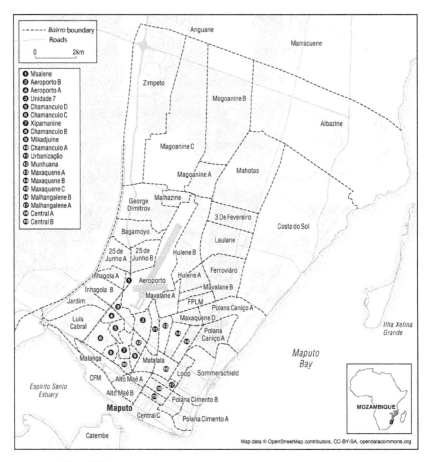

Map 1 Maputo

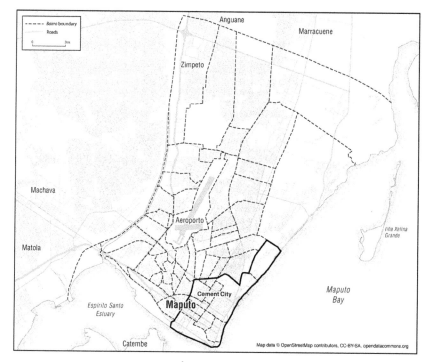

Map 2 The old 'cement city'

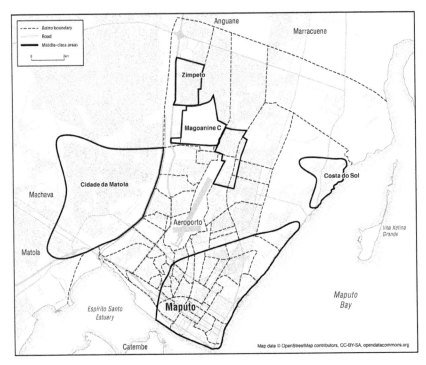

Map 3 New middle-class areas

1   Introduction

> All human history is nothing but a continuous transformation of human
> nature.
> (Karl Marx, quoted in Cheng 2009: 1)

Tiago[1] joined the Front for the Liberation of Mozambique (Frelimo)
during the liberation struggle against the Portuguese (1964–75). He and
his wife, Flora, have served the party loyally their entire adult lives, and
now enjoy a comfortable middle-class existence in the capital. They were
radicalised by the example of the 1968 rebellions in France and were
forced to flee Mozambique due to their political activities. While in exile
in Europe, they met representatives of Frelimo and returned to take part
in the struggle. Tiago and his wife worked for Frelimo in offices in Africa
and Europe and then with a ministry in Maputo. They have served
Frelimo throughout its over four decades of political and social contor-
tions, from socialism at independence to Marxist-Leninism, from gradual market reforms during the darkest days of the civil war to the
adoption of multiparty capitalism. The party has rewarded them for their
loyalty, as can be seen by their transition from revolutionaries to
members of the urban middle class. Like many in the capital, Tiago,
Flora and their children often take advantage of the lunch siesta and
come home to eat together. During one lunch, they began to argue about
a scandal involving Tiago's boss, the minister, who had been implicated
in appropriating money from a non-governmental organisation (NGO).
Tiago's son began attacking the alleged corruption of the minister and
the government in general. Tiago half-heartedly defended his minister,
while his children laughed. His son remarked bitterly, 'Come on, Dad,
you know he did it, they always do, but you constantly defend them.
Samora Machel [Mozambique's first president and a socialist icon] is
dead and things have changed. You know how it is now.' Tiago took
offence and stated, 'Yes, I defend them; look at what they have done for
this country!' He paused, trying to think of a policy that he supported and
that was still in place. Finally, he said, 'The emancipation of women!

---

[1] All of the names of my interlocutors used in this book are pseudonyms, although I have
used the real names of public figures.

That is what Frelimo has done. I will continue to support the party, which has accomplished that in this country!'

Tiago's argument with his son illustrated a dilemma that would be familiar to many of those who supported Frelimo during the socialist period. Frelimo had advocated gender equality not as an end in itself, but as one step, albeit a fundamental step, according to Samora, in the revolution.[2] To build the nation, the party first had to create national citizens. The goals of Mozambican socialism were to abolish patriarchy, selfish individualism, tribalism, rural feudalism, superstition, obscurantism, and other 'backward' cultural practices through a grand project of social engineering. In their place, a homogenised, 'rational' citizen who selflessly strove for the collective good would emerge (Vieira 1977). The cultural transformation of the populace was supposedly the precondition for progress, which would ultimately lead to the 'end of exploitation of man by man' (Hall and Young 1997: 89). This did not come to pass. The only thing Tiago could claim as an unambiguous success of the revolution to which he had dedicated his life was something that was supposed to be a 'mere' stepping stone towards the brave new world. Tiago and Flora have comfortable lives, but the revolution they fought had far grander goals than the creation of small middle-class islands floating on a sea of poverty. Their privilege is tainted with unease at the death of the project that once gave it meaning.

Studies of privileged social categories, such as the middle class, are still comparatively rare in anthropology, despite decades of calls to 'study up' (Errington and Gewertz 1997; Nader 1972; Shore 2002). This is beginning to change in African studies, especially as the supposed growth of a middle class has become a central component of the 'Africa Rising' narrative of dramatic transformation and potential, a more liberal version of the East Asian tigers, after decades when the continent was consigned to the bottom of the world's politico-economic hierarchy (Lentz 2015; Schubert 2016; Sumich 2016). While the middle class as a social category is usually defined in strictly economic terms, there is an implicit ideological subtext, a narrative of 'middle-classness', which concerns its social role in the discourse of powerful institutions such as the World Bank and the International Monetary Fund (IMF) (Heiman, Liechty, and Freeman 2012; Kalb 2014). This discourse provides a teleological story of what the new middle class of Africa and the Global South more generally should be, creating a tale of their emergence as politically independent actors from the combination of market reforms, sustained

---

[2] The degree to which women in contemporary Mozambique are emancipated, and what that means in practice, is debatable. The party championed gender equality during the liberation struggle and the socialist period, but this goal was frequently undermined in practice (Manuel 2014).

economic growth, and efforts at democratisation (Melber 2016). This group, then, through professional and educational achievement combined with growing political and economic clout, will, hopefully, entrench liberal values and act as a counterweight to the authoritarian ambitions of overweening states.

In many ways, Mozambique, with its adoption of multiparty elections, its rising literacy rate, and an impressive period of economic growth that lasted for more than a decade, served as a poster child for the Africa Rising narrative, despite the fact that the majority of the nation's citizens are still mired in the persistent and dire poverty that has grown more severe during the last few years of economic crisis. The idea of the middle class as a watchful guardian of the state depends on autonomy and a clear demarcation between the state and society. In his work on state formation in Egypt, Mitchell argues, 'One has to take the distinction between state and society not as a starting point of the analysis, but as an uncertain outcome of the historical process' (2002: 74). This uncertain outcome is evident in much of Africa, and especially in Mozambique. I argue that the middle class in Mozambique is shaped by past and present power relationships, and its origins, autonomy, social role, and relationship to the party state are consequently far more ambiguous than is typically portrayed in the Africa Rising narrative.

What is rarely clear in the optimistic accounts of many champions of the discourse of middle-classness is what a middle class would actually be in a specific social context. What is the basis of the class system and of the social order that gives rise to it and binds the two together? An attempt to answer such questions must go beyond selective statistics and 'just so' stories and examine how such a group sees itself, what created it, how stable it is, and what are the limitations and constraints it faces. With this book, I attempt to answer such questions through the discussion of a specific social context, Mozambique. In classic anthropological fashion, my goal is to explore the ways in which local understandings of what it means to be middle class can challenge prevailing general assumptions. I argue that, for dominant party states such as Mozambique, and perhaps for much of Africa as well, power and status tend to derive more from the ability to access resources rather than from direct control of the means of production (Sumich 2008). In the following, I explore the ways in which the construction of political and social meaning, signification, and symbolic power shape and are shaped by the means of access, the kinds of relationships, and the forms of personhood necessary to acquire resources, and the moral basis of the system's legitimation. In Mozambique, a relationship with the party state and the legacy of a revolution help to define boundaries between social groups and shape the permeability of their borders. It is such symbolic resources that structure ideas of an 'us' and 'them', a corporate identity, or class consciousness, but a consciousness that is shaped by its particular history and context.

Places of privilege in the social hierarchy of Mozambique are often intimately connected to Frelimo's attempt to create a new kind of 'authentic' national citizen. The party leadership has had a high modernist mindset – drawing from the experiences of the liberation struggle, widespread intellectual currents, and their own idealised self-image – that has informed efforts to shape a new, national subject (Sumich 2009; 2013). In a similar manner to that described by Soares de Oliveira (2015) for Angola, Frelimo championed a form of citizenship that transcended ethnic and regional boundaries and would be free of what the party saw as the degradation of the past. During the socialist period, Frelimo based its claim to legitimacy on the idea that, for progress to occur, the population would have to be transformed into a new kind of subject under the direction of the party. Wedeen demonstrates that politics is not simply material; rather, it is a contest for control of the symbolic world and the appropriation of meaning (1999: 30). As we shall see throughout this book, the transformative project was central to the party's conceptual universe; it was a major component of the symbolic system of signification that attempted to structure power relations as the moral basis of the political order. One of the primary routes to accessing positions of privilege and status was the ability to understand this transformative vision and adapt oneself to it.

As Yurchak argues in his discussion of the last Soviet generation, the world view and values of a political project can continue to shape social life even after the system that enshrined them has collapsed (2006). When socialism in Mozambique was abandoned, its system of signification was not overturned as much as it was transformed. Frelimo continues to base its legitimacy on the claim that the party leadership is culturally 'above' the wider population; that they are the only ones who can arbitrate between supposedly less advanced, inherently conflictual social groups (Dinerman 2006: 273). Many members of Maputo's middle class also share Frelimo's symbolic world and vocabulary. They are deeply enmeshed in its system of domination, which sets out parameters of what constitutes a modern citizen and the ways in which privilege is legitimated, even if they have long lost faith in the party. This calls to mind what Wedeen has referred to as a 'lack of exteriority' in her work on the personality cult of Hafiz al-Assad in Syria (1999: 130). According to Wedeen, Syrians did not uncritically believe in the regime; in fact, many of its claims were viewed with ironic disdain. However, even when Syrians challenged, subverted, or repudiated the regime and its claims, they drew on its conceptual and moral universe and made use of its symbolic vocabulary, and they were therefore not entirely exterior to the state's political project even if they resisted it (ibid.).

Although many members of Maputo's middle class share the same conceptual universe as Frelimo and are among the primary beneficiaries of the post-independence order, they are increasingly alienated from the party. For them, Frelimo continually fails to implement its grand projects on its own terms due to a combination of corruption, malevolence, and incompetence, putting the very fabric of the nation at risk. However, their ability to occupy a privileged space in society stems, to varying degrees, from access based on their closeness to the powerful, in a political system jokingly referred to as a *ditadura de apelidos* – a dictatorship of surnames – referring to the party 'aristocracy'. This 'aristocracy' is composed of the top party leadership, past and present, their families, and their close business associates. The perks of its membership are unstable to some degree, with fortunes rising and falling depending on which party faction is currently ascendant. However, despite internal competition, it is this 'aristocracy' that monopolises power and, since the fall of socialism, economic opportunities, and its members are referred to as a generalised 'them' by the wider population.

The middle class in Mozambique, as elsewhere, can be seen as a broad sociological category encompassing many subject positions. It is primarily made up of those who see themselves as occupying an intermediate position in their immediate social world (Southall 2016: 176). In this book, I discuss those who understand themselves as being members of a middle class based on a variety of factors, including material power, political connections, status, and cultural behaviours. For the sake of simplicity, I will refer to them throughout the book as members of the middle class. Instead of devising ever more rigid definitions of the middle class, my primary goal is to examine it as an ongoing process and explore its relationship to the class structure of Mozambique and its underlying systems of signification and attempts at legitimating the social order.

For much of the postcolonial period, the privileged members of sub-Saharan African societies were often portrayed as 'problematic', as corrupt rent-seekers or neo-colonial compradors (Werbner 2004). This began to change with the Africa Rising narrative, if not for the ruling elite then at least for other privileged sectors of society. Now, instead of being the parasitical appendages of the pathologically corrupt state that haunted the Afro-pessimist portrayals of earlier decades, a new discourse of middle-classness has emerged with its connotations of aspiration, meritocracy, and autonomy. Building from theories that a middle class will punish political extremism, demand greater accountability from rulers, and contribute to democratisation (Southall 2016: 220), such people have a far more positive social role to play. This discourse of middle-classness provides a new vision of the social order; unlike earlier discussions of rent-seekers, privilege is recast as 'clean and modern', independent and autonomous, able to enact progressive social transformation. Bertelsen, in his discussion of the presumed dichotomy between 'tradition' and 'modernity', observes that 'the cleanliness of the modern is constantly made dirty by practices that were thought to be relegated to the undesirable residual category of the modern-tradition' (2016: 16). The relationship between a middle class and the state that created it has many similarities to Bertelsen's observation that are normally omitted in the discourse of middle-classness.

In Mozambique, elements of the discourse of middle-classness have a strong affinity with elements of the ideological rhetoric of Frelimo's earlier social-engineering projects regarding how to create a 'modern' citizenry for a 'modern' nation state. For the people I know, 'middle class' is a concept that draws from international discourses. It is often used as a shorthand to describe local forms of stratification, with the added moral benefit of allowing the privileged to distance themselves from a venal elite while building on conceptions of being 'socially advanced' in comparison to the wider population. Such ideas have served as symbolic ways to legitimate relationships of domination and inequality since independence. Most of my interlocuters have, as previously mentioned, a close relationship to the ruling party. However, viewing themselves as a separate 'middle class' helps them to understand why political initiatives that promised to usher in a period of generalised prosperity have descended into corrupt parody, concentrating power and wealth in narrow sectors of the population while not undermining the moral basis of their own privileged position. However, the level of privilege that underlies notions of oneself as a member of the middle class and as a modern citizen, in contradistinction to the wider population, is essentially dependent on frequently arbitrary relationships to party officials and the practices necessary to prosper in the social terrain of the party state. Rather than being an autonomous social category moulding the state into its own moderate image, the middle class of Maputo is in the difficult position of being dependent upon the political and ideological scaffolding of a system its members often despise, but, as we shall see, one that they also reproduce through their actions.

This book is based on fieldwork conducted with members of the middle class in Maputo between 2002 and 2016. There are many aspects of being a member of the middle class that have received significant attention in other studies, such as schooling, consumption, work, and family life.[3] While my account discusses many of these aspects, the central focus will be on the relationship between the middle class and

---

[3] A prime example of this is Roger Southall's (2016) wonderfully detailed and incisive account of the formation of the black middle class in South Africa, which explores everything from this group's political dependency on the ruling ANC to how it has been shaped by marketing strategies.

the party state that created it. Through such an examination, I discuss some of the apparent contradictions that characterise the country. The first is that a socialist, egalitarian revolution became an elitist project of social engineering. The second is that the adoption of aspects of liberalism, such as competitive elections, market reforms, and constitutionally mandated individual rights, has allowed a revitalised, elected, single-party state to preside over an exclusionary political order that even alienates the privileged. While the current state of affairs is a far cry from the utopian dreams of independence or the hopes that followed the end of the civil war, I do not view political projects in Mozambique simply as cynical ploys by entrenched elites, even if cynicism abounds. Nor are political projects an unchanging result of Mozambique's history, even if, as Marx so famously remarked, 'The tradition of all dead generations weighs like a nightmare on the brains of the living.' Instead, I argue that the Frelimo leadership and many members of Maputo's middle class, who have been closest to Frelimo's political project, share a conceptual universe and symbolic set of meanings from which they lack exteriority and which shapes the means of access to and the formation of privilege in Mozambique. This symbolic world is not static or entirely fixed; it can mean different things to different people at different times. The ways in which political projects are implemented, interpreted, manipulated, and resisted, however, take place within a similar set of references and understandings of the nation as a particular kind of moral community. While the state is an experiment in social engineering on a grand scale, it is not a linear, evolutionary process. Instead, it is a chaotic mixture of rupture and continuity. In the remainder of this chapter, I discuss the middle class of Mozambique and its origins, the 'new man', and the transformative project, briefly examining the ways in which African nationalism and state formation have been conceptualised in order to better understand the formation of a postcolonial, state-based middle class in Mozambique. I then discuss the importance of this book's setting, Maputo, and provide an outline of the following chapters.

The middle class of Mozambique

The middle class across the globe is often portrayed as the cornerstone of liberalism for its supposed role as the bastion of democracy and the consuming engine of global capitalism. This is the heart of the discourse of middle-classness (Heiman, Liechty, and Freeman 2012: 18). As mentioned earlier, proponents of the Africa Rising narrative assume that this emergent social category will play a similar role on the continent. The African Development Bank argues not only that the middle class is the future of the continent, but also that 34 per cent of Africa's population, or over 314 million people, are already members of it as they are capable of daily per capita expenditure of between US$2 and US$20 (Mubila et al. 2011). This definition negates the existence of categories such as the working class and much of the urban poor. As US $1.90 is the World Bank's definition of extreme poverty, there is basically nothing between destitution and the middle class (Sumich 2016). Membership of the middle class, as defined by the African Development Bank and several other leading international agencies, is predicated on 'an individual act of consumption' (Kalb 2014: 160). The overriding focus on individual consumption (with consumption portrayed by the African Development Bank as independent of the cost of living) completely ignores the social, political, and historical relations that structure inequality and form a middle class. In this book, I attempt to redress this imbalance by focusing specifically on the political underpinnings that give rise to a middle class.

The definition of middle class used by Mubila and his colleagues at the African Development Bank is vague enough to be sociologically meaningless. Being a member of a middle class means that one is not poverty-stricken by definition, but membership in this social category is not restricted solely to economic standing. More sociologically informed studies of classes tend to be based on the work of Marx, Weber, and Bourdieu. For Marx, classes are the emerging products of social relationships and the wider social structure, and they cannot be understood independently of other social groups (1983). In the Marxist conception, classes are defined and structured by their relationship to the means of production and by wider social relations based on labour and the control of economic resources (ibid.). While Weber and Bourdieu place great importance on economic power, their definitions of class also consider questions of lifestyle, cultural forms, status, and local specificity as the foundation of relationships of domination (Bourdieu 1984; Weber 1961). Marx, Weber, and Bourdieu highlight, to differing degrees, the ways in which the middle class has both quasi-universal and contextually dependent aspects. For my purposes, the middle class shares some general sociological characteristics that make this social category more or less recognisable across the globe. These characteristics include broad economic factors, such as a degree of material power, and social marks of distinction such as certain levels of formal education and cultural capital, employment in a professional capacity, and a largely urban-based lifestyle. Within these overarching borders, though, lie considerable variations that depend on the particular political and economic relationships that give rise to a middle class in a specific context. Central to this are the ways in which members of a middle class engage in what Lentz (2015) calls 'boundary work', the attempts to distinguish itself as a distinct entity from other social groups. These relationships and distinctions are rarely static; in this book, I trace the ways in which a privileged category is continually made and remade in relationship to wider political and economic transformations.

The middle class of the Africa Rising narrative is in many ways the latest iteration of modernisation theory, leading towards a fixed, pre-ordained outcome. This conceptualisation of middle-classness, with its discursive implications of upward mobility due to merit and achievement (Lentz 2015), can help explain the popularity of the term in Mozambique, despite questions about its exact meaning. The fact that the term is frequently used in Maputo, either as a self-description or a description of others, means that it is a locally significant category, and many members of this group have a lifestyle that, superficially at least, corresponds with what would be recognisably middle class globally. Statistical indicators in Mozambique can be vague and unreliable, but they perhaps serve to indicate some general socio-economic contours of a long-established, party-connected middle class. Out of Maputo's estimated population of 1.7 million, the members of the middle class are usually considered to be part of the 31 per cent who work in the formal sector of the economy (Andersen 2012). They are also part of the 14 per cent of the city's population who have had access to higher education (Paulo et al. 2007: 16). Most members of the middle class whom I know number among the estimated 60,000 or so people who have fixed-line internet in their homes (Pitcher 2012: 153).

The above indicators tell us that membership in Maputo's middle class is restricted to a small, privileged group, but little else. The Mozambican middle class occupies its place in the politico-economic hierarchy through its ability to utilise the means of access to power, often as a direct result of their relationship with the political structures of the country. It has been part and parcel of a series of modernising projects, the herald of a brave new world always on the verge of becoming, but still just out of reach. Its status as an adherent of various post-independence transformative projects has been a fundamental factor in drawing boundaries between the middle class and the wider population. In tracing the ways in which the Mozambican middle class is formed through particular political and economic relationships, I feel that it is best to follow the example set by Marcus (1983) and try to understand the composition of privileged groups from members' own points of view. While Mozambican definitions of the middle class take material factors into account, these definitions are often closer to Bourdieu's (1984) idea of 'distinction', as many focus on status, lifestyle, levels of education, mastery of Portuguese (and, increasingly, English), and relationships to the party and the state.

For example, one man from a powerful Frelimo family told me: 'The middle class is extremely vague; it's hard to give firm borders as it blends into the elite on the top and the petty bourgeois on the bottom. I guess it's a continuum and about social reproduction, especially through education for their children.' A university professor, on the other hand, gave a somewhat contrasting explanation:

I guess I am a member of the middle class, but it's different than in Europe, there is very little security. More than half of my salary goes to paying school fees for my kids; my car broke down and I can't afford to fix it. No, it's different than Europe; there are huge gaps between social groups, not gradients like Europe, very little connects us and if one falls, they fall all the way down.

Others were more concrete: 'The middle class is the state.' The university professor quoted above stated that the Mozambican middle class originated with those who were relatively privileged during the colonial period and took power after independence. This group was joined by those he referred to as *emergentes* (emergent), people who, through Frelimo, were able to access education and use party structures for their advancement (Sumich 2010).

While definitions differ, all of those to whom I have spoken feel that anything that could now be seen as the middle class has its origins in the political structures of the country and stems from a relationship with Frelimo, its projects, and the institutions the party controls. In other words, the middle class is a politically dependent category with little control over resources or the means of production in an economy that is largely dependent on access to the state (a point I discuss in more detail in Chapters 5 and 6). In the case of Luanda, Schubert argues that class stratification is just as intimately tied to expressions of cultural identities and behaviours long seen as markers of the elite as it is to strict material power (2014; 2016). While class relations and social stratification in Mozambique, and in the world more generally, are predicated on unequal access to resources, they are expressed through the mastery or lack of certain cultural forms (as argued by Udelsmann 2007 for Angola). These cultural behaviours, such as urban identification, forms of familial and romantic relationships, particular conceptions of gender roles, and an ambivalent stance towards 'tradition', are expressed in a variety of everyday settings as a claim to distinction. Of central concern to this book are the ways in which these cultural behaviours are intertwined with larger political projects and become fundamental to the creation of boundaries between social categories through concepts such as citizenship and status.

The category of the middle class is often portrayed as depoliticised and benign, both the cause and the result of capitalist, liberal democracy (Heiman, Liechty, and Freeman 2012). Membership in a middle class, however, is fundamentally political, based on forms of inequality in relationship to other social groups. Lentz argues for a conceptual division between the middle class of Africa and an elite, as many analysts draw little distinction between the two (2015). According to her, 'elite' refers to individuals or social groups who occupy specific positions of power, while 'middle class' can refer to the privileged more generally (ibid.). A strict divide between positions of authority and a more generalised privileged status tends to be far more contradictory and incomplete in Mozambique and in many other dominant or single-party states. The subjects of this book have either long-standing personal or familial connections with Frelimo. In fact, they and the party have long been mutually constitutive of each other. Many have careers in the professions with salaries that usually range between the equivalent of US$1,000 per month, ten times the minimum wage in Maputo, to US$5,000 at the upper levels (although in 2016 salaries had been effectively halved due to inflation). They are members of what could be termed an older, established middle class: those who are not part of the current national leadership but have occupied positions of privilege since the early independence period, and in some cases since the colonial period as well. There are other social groups that can claim middle-class status: examples would include high-ranking members of opposition parties, some businessmen, those who have risen through the opportunities afforded by the adoption of capitalism, and employees of international agencies, although they also often use political connections to bolster their position.

In many ways, my interlocutors resemble what was once termed the 'national bourgeoisie'. Access to political power and the opportunities for accumulation that come with it are central to the creation and reinforcement of economic and social power (Cohen 1982). A national bourgeoisie lacks autonomy, as privilege is based on a relationship to the nation's power structures and dominant political projects. Members of a national bourgeoisie are rarely characterised by their control of the means of production, but instead by their ideologies, cultural behaviours, and symbolic vocabularies and markers, which proclaim and attempt to legitimise their place in the hierarchy (Cohen 1974; 1981). As argued by Southall for Southern Africa, ruling national liberation movements act as party machines, 'providing avenues of recruitment, advancement and social class formation' (2013: 16). In Mozambique, capitalism created new opportunities, but it did not necessarily overturn the foundations of the party state or the political logic of privilege. In fact, the creation of a national bourgeoisie has been a central post-socialist goal of Frelimo, although the term is used by the party in the sense of a capitalist class that is both national and nationalist. Membership in this exalted social category, though, is usually restricted to the highest ranks of the party, their families, and close associates. The entanglement of political and economic power combined with elite monopolisation of opportunities means that the middle class is characterised by precariousness, ambivalence, and the delicate interplay between condemnation and complicity (as discussed in greater detail in Chapters 5 and 6). If the power structures that gave birth to the middle-class collapse, its ability to socially reproduce itself will become questionable.

The *homem novo* (new man) for a new Mozambique

If the foundation of nationalism is the 'imagined community', as Benedict Anderson (2006) argued, then the primary goal of a nationalist project is the creation of an identifiable community, or at least fixed social categories of people. In this book, I offer an anthropological analysis of Frelimo's attempts to create a new society through the total transformation of the Mozambican population into the *homem novo* (Vieira 1977; Zawangoni 2007) and how this has affected the formation of a middle class. To paraphrase Stalin's famous directive to Soviet authors, Frelimo attempted to act as 'engineers of the human soul'. The goal was to create a system of signification that would wipe the slate clean and enable new forms of consciousness, sociability, subjectivities, loyalties, gender relations, and economic and labour practices, and allow identification to take hold throughout the population, although in a manner incomparably less brutal than in Stalin's USSR.

Grand projects of political transformation require exemplars – those who embody the values enshrined in the political order. In his work about former officers of the now defunct East German army, Bickford argues that 'the soldier is the state ... Soldiers represent the imagined community of the state in living, active form; they are homogenized into a single identity of the state, and represent this imagined ideal of homogenization' (2011: 3). In this respect, soldiers embody the power of the state and its legitimacy, as they are theoretically willing, or at least obliged, to kill and die for it if necessary (ibid.). Cadres of the ruling party and the citizens who come the closest to, or most actively emulate, the subject the state holds as a normative ideal also become living embodiments of the social order. While less obvious than a uniformed military, they are symbolic of the desired national subject.

The military represents the power of sovereignty throughout the world, but the type of citizen that is privileged tends to be a more transitory embodiment of the state. As ideologies, political projects, key constituencies, and goals transform, and so can the categories of people who are the exemplars of such visions. In her work on Bolivia, Lazar argues that citizenship is not simply a juridical concept; it is also a relational process that is acted out between various subjects and wider social structures (2008). In a similar manner, social categories and the boundaries that demarcate positions of status and privilege are also processes, part of wider negotiations between subjects and those who man the state structures. While access to material resources is typically a fundamental factor of middle-class status, in Mozambique this group was formed through its relationship to the state and the progressive re-imaginings of grand political projects as previous versions became untenable. Due to their lack of control over the means of production, members of this group demonstrate relatively few features of a Marxist definition of the bourgeoisie (a point that is explained in more detail in Chapter 5), but the group's postcolonial formation is deeply intertwined with its involvement in a movement that once labelled itself as Marxist. Marxism in Mozambique, much like that in China and Cuba (see Cheng 2009), largely ignored Marx's focus on objective economic conditions. Socialism in Mozambique and many other nations in the Global South focused its efforts on creating a particular kind of social subject, which would then lead to the transformation of the economic superstructure, rather than the more orthodox version of Marxism where transforming the economic superstructure leads to a new kind of social subject (these points are dealt with in more detail in Chapter 3). More recently, the party state has adopted elements of liberal capitalism that, while diametrically opposed to socialism in theory, once again depend on the transformation of the populace to secure the new political order. Loyalty is often demonstrated and access to the powerful granted, as it was in the socialist period, through a willingness to master certain cultural forms that symbolise the boundaries of the category of the officially desired citizen.

It has been widely pointed out that the state is not a thing, a singular expression of will and control, but instead is a series of shifting, sometimes cooperating, sometimes conflicting institutions, assemblages, and discourses (Abrams 1988; Blom Hansen and Stepputat 2001; Williams 2012). The state exists as imaginaries, cultural practices, and a system of shared symbolic meanings between cadres and subjects that are maintained through practices that reaffirm its existence, both in occasional spectacular rituals and in day-to-day activities (Krohn-Hansen 2009). The Frelimo party state operates as a hub in which various actors, institutions, and modes of governance intersect, despite its projected image and long-standing Leninist pretensions of monolithic unity. In a similar manner to Welker's description of a corporation, the Frelimo party state acts as a nexus of institutions, structures, relationships, and ideas that 'hang together despite tensions and inconsistencies' (2014: 4). Much like Wedeen's (2008) description of political power in Yemen, Frelimo is powerful because of its ability to project an image of a singular, unified will, no matter the reality. As with Wedeen's (1999) description of Baathist rule in Syria, Frelimo's ability to appropriate meaning in order to influence and police the symbolic domain has long been a cornerstone of party rule.

One of the primary symbols of the Frelimo party state during the early independence period was *o homem novo*, the new man. It provided a normative vision of radical transformation, and was emblematic of the cultural practices and world view thought necessary to build the nation. To strive to be a new man was to demonstrate that one accepted the legitimacy and necessity of Frelimo's social revolution. The party's system of signification, centred on the new man, and the actual practices of the social revolution were by no means universally popular or legitimate. Lubkemann demonstrates that, in large areas of the country, the party's attempts to build the new society by replacing existing forms of social organisation and meaning failed and Frelimo was forced to rely on coercion to gain compliance (2008). Indifference to or disgust for the party's social revolution contributed to the civil war, insofar as they allowed foreign-created and foreign-funded rebels, the Mozambican National Resistance (Renamo), to take root in parts of the country (for a brief discussion of Renamo's ideological project, see Chapters 3 and 4).

Even if this transformative vision became impossible to realise and attempts to do so were the cause of growing repression, it remained central to a dominant system of signification. Power, as party cadres argued, was not simply the means to compel obedience; its use was necessary to achieve a larger moral end. Frelimo's attempts at social engineering did achieve a degree of hegemonic legitimacy among some sections of the population, although often in a variety of shifting and contradictory ways. This helps to explain an apparent paradox often encountered in modern-day Maputo. The socialist period is often referred to there as *o tempo de fome* (the time of hunger), as the utopian promise of the early years of independence was swamped by the devastation of the civil war, the fear of informers, repressive security services, state oppression, and economic crisis. At the same time, Samora, the public voice and symbolic embodiment of the revolution, the man who stood above the nation to direct the grand transformation of Mozambique and its people, retains his iconic posthumous status as a visionary leader who truly and selflessly wanted the best for the country. He is a symbol used with dubious success by Frelimo to bolster its legitimacy, while critics employ him as a counter-symbol demonstrating how the party has lost its way and has betrayed its founding principles. An apt example is the spread of T-shirts depicting Samora among urban youth. The political intention behind these party-produced symbols is to stress the link between Frelimo and its heroic roots, and thereby claim continuing legitimacy, but these T-shirts are also read as an affirmation of the Samora era and a critique of the present. In Wedeen's terms, this demonstrates the lack of exteriority, with the regime and its citizens employing the same symbolic vocabulary, even if they are making diametrically opposed points (1999). It is this ambiguity that characterises the relationship between my interlocutors and how they imagine the state. The transition to capitalism has brought most of them growing prosperity, and very few wish to return to socialism. However, the contemporary period is also marked by a social order that many see as morally bankrupt and deeply insecure, as privilege rests on a growing polarisation and there are few obvious answers to remedy the situation.

The middle class of Mozambique does not exist autonomously from the state, but instead was created by it; its members secured positions of privilege through their ability to understand and adapt themselves to Frelimo's transformative projects. Shortly after independence, the new man became the master symbol of socialism, with the transformation of the people being the necessary condition for progress to occur. Any privileges the new men received were simply a prelude to what the entire population would soon enjoy. For the subjects of this book, those who were the closest to this political project, the normative underpinnings of the new man demonstrated how exercises of power that were frequently brutal could also be seen as socially transformative.[4] The trope of the new man gradually collapsed during the civil war and was finally abandoned after the fall of socialism. It has been replaced by far more incoherent symbols, such as some form of development that will supposedly be brought about by the national/nationalist bourgeoisie, which in practice seems restricted to the upper echelons and the supposed growth of a middle class. The system of signification and symbolic vocabulary that gave birth to the new man lingers on, both in the ways in which leading cadres' claim legitimacy by being culturally above the wider population and in how these claims are viewed. Those who should be closest to the ideal of the new man, the current ruling elite and their families, are the ones who, through accusations of corruption and crass self-interest, seem to be the furthest away. In this case, a shared symbolic world does not necessarily breed support, but instead holds the moral bankruptcy of the capitalist era in stark relief.

Nationalist imaginings

In the 1960s and 1970s, the emerging independent states of Africa were the objects of optimistic celebration. For those on the right, there was Rostow's 'modernisation' thesis, where the evolution from a 'traditional' society to the age of mass consumption and 'Westernisation' might

---

[4] Here, I follow Verdery's groundbreaking work on the Securitate, the Romanian secret police, which argues that power in the communist period was not only repressive. The Securitate's methods of knowledge production 'were at the same time socially transformative, aiming to produce a new social landscape, with implications for creating the "new socialist person" and a new society' (Verdery 2014: 159).

finally be under way (1960). While movements such as Algeria's National Liberation Front (FLN) captured the world's imagination through the work of Frantz Fanon, South Africa's African National Congress (ANC), the Zimbabwe African National Union Patriotic Front (ZANU-PF), Frelimo, and the People's Movement for the Liberation of Angola (MPLA) also garnered considerable sympathy from the left. The contours and desired direction of change were fiercely debated, but many, both within Africa and beyond, seemed sure that the continent was on the cusp of dramatic transformation and that the state would be the driving force (Chipkin 2007). This certainty faded in the 1980s, and the African state has since been regarded by many scholars with considerable confusion as to its relevance, its form, and even its existence (Soares de Oliveira 2007). African nationalism, which once drew enthusiastic converts on the continent and beyond, has suffered a similar depreciation.

In recent years, one of the dominant forms of conceptualising African politics has been neo-patrimonialism (Pitcher, Moran, and Johnston 2009). This refers to a hybrid form of governance where institutional structures and the formal rule of law are subverted by informal, clientelist networks linking the highest to the lowest. With the rise of neo-patrimonial analysis, it has become common to view the ideological claims and projects of African political movements as a façade for the more important business of self-enrichment and the building of networks of clients by 'eating' the state: that is, the diversion of public resources to private hands (Bayart 1993; 2000; Chabal and Daloz 1999; Nugent 2010). Jean-François Bayart has argued that African politics are based on the 'rhizome state', where parties, ideologies, and institutions are really hollow shells that mask actual power relationships built on historical and cultural models (1993; 2000). Power, in this view, was only altered by colonialism rather than fundamentally transformed, and it remains personalised and built on shifting relationships among the elite. The cause of many internal crises in African states has been the elite's strategy of increasing the exploitation of dependants and the mobilisation for personal use of resources gained from the outside world. This strategy is not a new development, but is in fact part of a long-standing cultural practice of 'extraversion' that has historically enmeshed local African actors in worldwide networks (Bayart 1993; 2000).

For Bayart, the impact of colonialism, while considerable insofar as it has resulted in at least a formal attempt to create nation states based on the Western model, is far less important for understanding contemporary Africa than history in the *longue durée*, as he argues that the basis of African politics remains essentially unchanged. Other analysts, while agreeing with the importance of the *longue durée*, have taken issue with the apparent dismissal of the colonial period. For scholars such as

Mamdani (1996) and Mbembe (2001), colonialism is crucial for understanding Africa today. Mamdani has argued that colonialism was based
on 'decentralised despotism' where settlers had civil rights guaranteed by
the state, while 'indigenous' subjects were under the thumb of 'chiefs'
and ruled by so-called customary law (1996). Independence deracialised
this relationship but did not democratise it, and now urbanites are taking
the place of the former settlers with civil rights, while rural dwellers
continue to live under decentralised despotism. For Mbembe, the legacy
of colonialism is not restricted to the institutions of political power, but
rather its character: the arbitrariness, vulgarity, monstrousness, and buf-
foonery, and the complicity between the people and their predatory,
often ridiculous leaders (2001).

It is true that the legacies of the colonial period and the *longue durée* of
history have been deeply influential for society today. However, as noted
by Chipkin, there is the danger that postcolonial essentialism 'treats the
postcolony as a mere phenomenon of colonial power' (2007: 38). The
history of the colonial period becomes overdetermined and nothing
that has happened since can have any independent meaning (ibid.).
In this book, I follow Chipkin's call to treat African nationalism as more
than resistance against colonialism (ibid.), but also as an attempt to
articulate what a vision of a new social order would be.

Anticolonialism was a deeply important mobilising factor, but there is
a danger of simply understanding it by what it is not, as opposed to what
it was trying to create. The focus on anticolonialism misses the utopian
drive of many nationalist movements: the desire to tame nature and no
longer be at its mercy; to transform the economy, politics, social relations, and people themselves; to raise cities where there was only
bush – in short, to create a new and more perfect form of society (see
Buck-Morss 1995). This is especially the case for Southern Africa, where
the political landscape has been shaped by protracted, violent struggles
against colonialism and the promises of the new society to come (Israel
2013). While it is important to understand the ways in which the past
shapes the present, this does not mean that the desire to build the new
should be discounted.

In the following chapters, I intend to rectify this imbalance. In some
cases, the projects and ideologies championed at independence simply
became a façade for clientelism, neo-patrimonialism, and the accumulation of resources by cynical elites. This does not mean that the visions
promoted during independence struggles lack any social significance for
supporters, nor that they were not instrumental in shaping the post-
independence social order and the conflicts and solidarities upon which
it rests. The legacies of promised utopias and the goals, methods, cultural
practices, and hierarchies they engendered continue to inform the present, even if in a far different manner than originally intended. If, as

Bickford argues, politics is primarily an act of symbolism (2011: 29), then ideologies are signs saturated with meaning; they attempt to define and structure narratives and projects about the way life should be and what are the legitimate bases for power. Thus, ideologies are 'so potent because it becomes not only ours but us – the terms and machinery by which we structure ourselves and identify who we are' (Anne Allison quoted in Bickford 2011: 93; see also Laclau and Mouffe 1985; Žižek 1989). Systems of signification and symbolic productions form and maintain connections and bonds between leaders and followers (Wedeen 1999: 10). This is an especially salient point in Mozambique, as Frelimo's political project was and is premised on the idea that the previous social order, in both its colonial and traditional manifestations, was illegitimate; the party, through its unique access to knowledge of the masses and social organisation gained from the liberation struggle, was therefore the only legitimate alternative (Coelho 2004). Much like Donham's description of the Ethiopian revolution, this totalising, revolutionary logic was an attempt to 'cut history off at the pass' (1999: 127). It offered an explanation as to why Mozambique was poor and 'backward' that was not based on blatant racism, and it charted a course for the future that could supposedly be achieved in just a few short decades. Such symbols and projects, even those that are discredited, continue to shape the social world, if not always in the ways that were initially intended.

In Mozambique, Frelimo's attempts to create a brave new world and the perceived failure to meet this goal have received considerable attention. To mention a few examples, in the post-independence period sympathetic observers defended the party's attempts to create a socialist society (Isaacman and Isaacman 1983; Munslow 1983; Saul 1979). Others, more critically, demonstrated how Frelimo's programme of social engineering had caused growing discontent in some rural areas, especially in the centre and north of the country (Geffray 1991; Lubkemann 2008). West has analysed the ways in which Frelimo's image has been transformed in the Mueda Plateau, the cradle of the liberation struggle, evolving from 'sorcerers of construction' who protected the people from predation to become a predator itself (1997; 2001; 2005). Dinerman argues that Frelimo's revolution was never the dramatic transformation it pretended to be; instead, the 'great rupture' of independence was largely a myth (2006). Pitcher has also demonstrated that, despite the many radical changes in postcolonial Mozambique, there are many continuities in the realm of political economy and the nature of the ruling elite (2002). While it is debatable just how profoundly transformative Frelimo's social revolution really was, its underlying logic has had profound effects on understandings of privilege and power. The utopian visions Samora described in rallies held across the country and the history of the liberation struggle continue to be central to the party's systems of signification and dominate the symbolic vocabulary of contemporary politics. As Coelho insightfully argues, the liberation struggle in Mozambique gave birth to a particular narrative vocabulary of power, one that, despite the political transformations of the post-independence period, remains fundamental to this day. According to Coelho:

> the centrality of a specific account of the liberation ... codified as a script, became an instrument to legitimize that authority and render it unquestionable. In other words, the Liberation Script came to constitute what Michel Foucault, and Giorgio Agamben after him, would term an 'apparatus'; that is, a strategic discourse located at the intersection of power relations and relations of knowledge. (Coelho 2013: 21)

The liberation script in Mozambique is similar to what Malkki called 'mythico-histories': carefully crafted accounts acting as morality plays, which create collective histories that define self and other (1995: 54–5). Such expressions of systems of signification make a powerful claim that Frelimo upholds the heroic legacy of the liberation struggle, but they also cast light on the party's failures to achieve its goals in its own terms.

In the following chapters, I examine the legacy of a transformative project and its systems of signification, cultural practices, and ideologies for members of a group who have often secured positions of privilege through their connection to it. By using the word 'ideology', I do not mean false consciousness as such. Instead, like Verdery, I view it as a discourse, a world view, and a cultural construct that provide supporters with structures through which to experience human relations and ways in which they can act upon the world by facilitating the creation of new moral imaginaries (1991). These new moral imaginaries were, and continue to be, intimately connected with the political order. Žižek (1989) argues that the ideological basis of authoritarian collectivism is the idea that the party transcends the individual cadre and is therefore exempt from the blame of morally suspect individual representatives. The corrupt cadre comes to act as a fantasy means for ideology to take its own failure into account in advance. For many of the people in this book, the sanctity of the party, as a way to account for its own failure in advance, has long since eroded. The socialist period was characterised by hunger, economic collapse, and war. However, as with the last Soviet generation described by Yurchak (2006), many of the founding values of socialism – the vision for the future and the kind of citizenship, personhood, and national identification it promoted – are still cherished or, perhaps more accurately, nostalgically reimagined by many of those I know. As Krohn-Hansen argues: 'Memories give form to the practice of politics and the construction of the state in a deep sense. Ideas about the past shape political identities, preserve myths of authority, authorize claims, and provide political actors with a horizon and direction' (2009: 11).

Of major interest is how formal processes of democratisation affect the ways in which the state is imagined and what it means to be Mozambican. By examining these questions, I hope to leave behind the normative dimensions that often accompany a discussion of democratisation: either triumphalism or the bemoaning of its supposed deficits or weaknesses. Instead of arguing that democratisation is necessarily good or bad, I will explore what the Mozambican case has to say about democratisation as an unfolding and varied process. If politics is primarily an act of symbolism, one of the potent weapons in a state's arsenal is categorisation, or the ability to brand some as insiders while labelling others as excluded outsiders (Bickford 2011). While liberal democracy makes universalistic claims of an all-embracing set of human rights through strict legal equality, in practice such rights are rooted in national belonging and are dependent on a rigid division between insider and outsider (Mouffe 2005: 39; see also Schmitt 1985). Mouffe argues that democracy is always based on relationships of inclusion and exclusion. Democratic theory, however, seems unable to conceptualise its internal 'political limit' (2005; see also Chipkin 2007). In this book, I examine the way in which the state and the social order were imagined, who was to be included and who was to be excluded, and how efforts were made to legitimise these relationships. This question is perhaps especially acute for Maputo's middle class. While its members still occupy privileged places in society, the underlying meaning of their social position, their role as a vanguard of the future, and their relationship with the wider population have been radically transformed (these points are discussed in greater detail in Chapters 5 and 6).

Mozambique and Maputo

Frelimo has ruled Mozambique since winning independence in 1975 after an 11-year liberation struggle. This victory soon gave way to a 15-year civil war, which ended in 1992. In 1977, Frelimo moved away from a broad socialist orientation and declared itself a Marxist-Leninist vanguard party. Tentative attempts at market reform began in 1983 and gained force beginning in the mid-1980s as the party faced collapse. From the official abandonment of socialism in 1990 and the end of the civil war to 2013, Mozambique boasted an annual economic growth rate averaging at a little more than 7 per cent.[5] More recently, the country experienced an economic boom after large deposits of coal, natural gas,

---

[5] See the 2015 CIA World Factbook for Mozambique. Available at: <www.cia.gov/library/publications/the-world-factbook/geos/mz.html>.

oil, and various minerals were discovered, which, for a time, lessened its previous dependence on international donors. Mozambique has held five presidential elections without a return to full-scale hostilities, although the freeness and fairness of those elections are disputed. Frelimo retained power through the transition to democracy and achieved a position of outright electoral dominance. Recently, however, the post-war system has come under increasing strain. The global glut in commodities has highlighted the continuing fragility of the economy. Crime is rising and the capital has been plagued by a wave of kidnappings targeting the Indian business class and the privileged more generally. The security forces seem unable to stop this, and members of the police have been arrested as kidnappers themselves. In 2012, after growing tension and sporadic violence, Renamo tore up the 1992 peace treaty and engaged in sporadic attacks in the centre and north of the country before returning to contest elections in 2014. Skirmishes, ambushes, and assassinations continued as Renamo disputed the results of the election. Frelimo has probably never been as powerful as it is now, but the political order it presides over appears increasingly fragile, and Maputo seems to be a major fault line.

The city of Maputo is fundamental to the exploration of the major themes of this book. Maputo is Mozambique's capital and largest city. Much like Frelimo, Maputo operates as a nexus where national and transnational institutions, structures, and actors come into contact. It is the political, economic, and cultural centre, where both the opportunities of the capitalist period and its attendant social divisions are concentrated. Approximately 14 per cent of the city's population has received higher education versus close to 6 per cent for the country as a whole (Paulo, Rosário, and Tvedten 2007: 16). Mortality for children under five is slightly under 9 per cent versus slightly under 18 per cent nationally, and income is close to three times the national average (ibid.). Poverty in Maputo, however, increased from 47 per cent in 1997 to approximately 53 per cent in 2007, before dropping again slightly, and inequality has become deeply entrenched (ibid.: 12). While Maputo is the wealthiest city in the country by far, it is also perhaps the most polarised.

With the adoption of elements of liberal democracy and capitalism, Maputo has become a showcase for the party's transformation from austere socialism to a booming African, so-called leopard economy, at least until the recent financial crisis cast a dark shadow over the Mozambican 'economic miracle'. However, the building boom in the capital continues, new luxury hotels are opening, even if they are half full at best, and cafés and shops are springing up in the city centre with bewildering speed. Main streets are bursting with expensive restaurants and boutiques, and the billboards that once proclaimed the superiority of

Figure 1.1 An aerial view of Maputo

socialism have long given way to the ubiquitous images of consumerism, advertising everything from mobile phones to pasta. The once lightly travelled roads are now clogged with SUVs that pass through festering slums on the way to the bustling city. Despite pockets of prosperity, the past has not been banished in the face of a new capitalist society. Among the numerous divisions in Maputo, one of the most basic for much of the city's history has been that between the *cidade de cimento* (cement city) and the *cidade de caniço* (reed city). During the colonial period, the cement city was reserved for the settler population. It has European-style apartment blocks, houses, and municipal services. The reed city grew on the outskirts of the cement city and consists of dwellings built by the African population. After independence and the large-scale exodus of Portuguese settlers, the social makeup of the cement city was transformed. It was no longer a white preserve, but was settled by multiracial (although predominantly black) urbanites. The reed city was also transformed after independence, and grew dramatically, especially after the onset of the civil war, which drove large numbers of internal refugees to the capital in search of the relative security that could be found there.[6]

During the colonial period, Maputo, or Lourenço Marques as it was then known, was widely considered to be one of the most breathtaking cities in Africa, and while it suffered from years of neglect and a lack of funds during the civil war, it is reclaiming its title. Strolling down the wide, tree-lined avenues and gazing at the colonial art deco architecture and the frantic building spree of the past few years, one feels far away from the squalid realities of an African slum. I have conducted fieldwork in Maputo at various times since 2002, and, while I have travelled widely

---

[6] The term 'reed city' is also simply illustrative now, as most dwellings are largely cement.

in the city and its immediate environs, the centre is where both my informants and I worked and spent much of our leisure time. Although the slums in Maputo are just a short distance away, they do not belong to the world that most of the people I know normally inhabit. This sense of social distance, however, was severely challenged by riots in 2008, 2010, and 2012, as the urban poor violently protested about rises in the cost of living and transportation, largely shutting the city down and making the presence of the marginalised difficult to ignore.

The world of the city centre reminds me of a privileged version of the socially self-contained 'urban villages' studied by the Chicago school in the 1920s or William Whyte's Italian slum (Hannerz 1980; Whyte 1993). If it were not for the endless streams of workers pouring in from the *bairros* (outlying neighbourhoods) and the presence of *empregadas* (maids or servants) in the houses of the privileged, the city centre could easily pass for a self-contained bubble floating slightly above Mozambique, at least until the riots. Numerous things have changed since I began conducting research in 2002, including the more recent fragmentation of the once compact 'cement city' (see Maps 1–3). With skyrocketing housing costs, many members of the middle class have been forced out of the city centre to new developments and gated communities that spread like an archipelago through the city and its outskirts (see Chapter 6). While the cement city has lost its geographic centrality, fragmenting into a network of small, middle-class enclaves of social and infrastructural privilege, its symbolism remains (Bertelsen, Tvedten, and Roque 2014). Many of the fundamental divisions in Mozambique continue to be conceptualised as the gulf between the inhabitants of the cement city (wherever they may actually be) and those of the reed city. This divide speaks to the unravelling of Frelimo's legitimacy, which is a major focus of this book. While the party bases its claim to power on its self-portrayal as the creator and guardian of national unity, it appears that, rather than enforcing unity, Frelimo now presides over the creation of more and more social divisions, which are only too apparent in the glaring inequalities that characterise Maputo.

Chapter organisation

The book is organised chronologically. 'Origins', the second chapter, focuses primarily on the late colonial period. Specifically, I examine the formation of an emergent privileged African group and the ways in which members of this group became increasingly alienated from the colonial order. From there, I discuss the social basis for the growing nationalist movement, the liberation struggle, and the beginnings of Frelimo's transformative project.

'Ascendance', the third chapter, focuses on the early independence period. I analyse the ways in which Frelimo attempted to implement a grand transformative project, how this was expressed through economic relationships and concepts such as citizenship and education, and the limits of this project. Of major importance is a discussion of the newly dominant systems of signification and how they shaped the types of citizens that the party tried to create, which social groups were privileged, which were marginalised, and why.

'Collapse', the fourth chapter, examines the civil war and the economic chaos that followed. This chapter investigates the reactions to Frelimo's attempts to inaugurate a social revolution that would transform the country and create a new kind of citizen. In this chapter, I focus on the ways in which the party's transformative project and its associated symbols and practices eroded during the war and the ways in which this affected the material and symbolic basis of privilege.

'Democracy', the fifth chapter, explores the changes brought about by the abandonment of socialism and the end of the war, and how the legacy of previous political projects continued to shape Mozambique. I discuss the material basis for the post-war middle class and the growing social divisions between members of the middle class and the party elite. I then examine how democratisation has changed ideologies of inclusion and exclusion and the emerging systems of signification and moral imaginaries between the state and the middle class.

'Decay' is the sixth chapter. In it, I focus on the seeming paradox that, while Frelimo is probably more powerful than ever before in its existence, the social order over which it presides is increasingly fragile. I explore this through a discussion of Mozambique's growing social polarisation, changes to concepts of citizenship, and the growing economic insecurity and alienation of members of the middle class from the political system that has benefited them for so long.

The final chapter brings the book to its chronological end in 2016. I conclude with a discussion of the legacy of a revolution, its systems of signification, symbolic vocabulary, and access granted by a familiarity with these processes in creating the Mozambican middle class. I then return to the guiding questions of this book: what would a middle class actually be in a specific social context? What is the basis of the class system and the social order that gave rise to it, and what binds them together? What constraints and limitations does it face? Finally, I discuss some of the ways in which the specific case of Mozambique informs discussions of the emerging middle class of Africa and the Global South more generally.

2   Origins

> When the whites came to our country we had the land, and they had the
> bible; now we have the bible and they have the land.   (Popular saying,
> quoted in Mondlane 1969: 23)

Mozambique has been a laboratory for various ideological and political
experiments for much of the twentieth century. From the overthrow of
the Portuguese monarchy on 5 October 1910 to the steady strangulation
of Dr António de Oliveira Salazar's quasi-fascist *Estado Novo* (New
State), established in 1933, the policies of the metropole have attempted
to reshape life in the colonies. In the 1950s and 1960s the anticolonial
'winds of change' grew in intensity and Afro-nationalist currents grew in
influence. In the 1960s and 1970s, left-wing political thought gained
strength, and a form of liberal democracy became hegemonic in the
1990s. While power in Mozambique has been enacted through policies
that range across the political spectrum, the one thing that has been
consistent has been the need to create a political subject. Liberation
movements, postcolonial or otherwise, are, despite the rhetoric, rarely
about liberating the people as they are, but rather about creating the
conditions for what they are supposed to become. In the following,
I discuss how a particular transformative vision became central to postcolonial inequalities, and the challenges this brought.

Cohen, in his discussion of elite culture, argued that members of an
elite face a paradox (1981). To remain in power, they must serve their
own sectional interests, while also demonstrating that they legitimately
represent the universal good (ibid.). How this is done, the systems of
signification, and the mobilisation of symbolism and cultural resources
are central issues for anthropology despite the fact that elites are perenni-
ally understudied in the discipline (Cohen 1981; Shore 2002). One of the
central ideological claims of a single-party state (and also an implicit
claim of elected dominant-party states) is that the party embodies the
interests of the nation writ large, that there is no major difference
between the sectional interests of the elite as they stand with the people.
The party not only transcends the individual cadres in Žižek's terms
(1989), but transcends all individual citizens as well. In Mozambique,

the Frelimo leadership's power and claim to represent the universal good flowed from its portrayal of the liberation of the country and its members' identification as a certain kind of national subject, one that was still rare but was intended as a vanguard for the future. The characteristics and behaviours associated with this specific kind of personhood had to become generalised throughout the population as a necessary precondition for development. The sectional interests of the elite were to be universalised throughout the population through transformative political projects.[1] Those who intimately understood this project, or successfully appeared to adopt it, were well represented in privileged strata of the post-independence order. In the following, I examine the social origins of the contemporary cultural politics of privilege in Mozambique by focusing the majority of my account on the origins of privilege from 1850 to independence in 1975, primarily in the south of the country but with some attention also paid to theatres of the liberation struggle in the north. Through a discussion of the origins of the social revolution, I illustrate the basis for the post-independence systems of signification and the trajectory of middle-class formation.

The nucleus of much of the post-independence political elite in Maputo had its origins as an urban-based petty bourgeoisie. Despite the fact that many of Frelimo's leaders came from families that had connections with powerful or royal African families, their places of relative privilege often depended more on their access to the colonial system than on so-called traditional power structures, such as chiefdoms or lineage-based organisations. Members of the leadership often benefited from the educational facilities of Protestant Swiss missions (Cruz e Silva 2001). Many of those I have worked with in Maputo have their origins in the south and came from families that participated in an economic system firmly tied to that of the country's more powerful and industrialised neighbour, South Africa. The social basis of an emergent African elite was state employment, migratory labour, the service industry, and, more rarely, commercial farming. Examples of this particular social background in the Frelimo leadership abound. Raúl Honwana (a nationalist icon) was a farmer and colonial civil servant. Many of his children made up the post-independence revolutionary aristocracy, including Luís Bernardo Honwana (former Minister of Culture), João Honwana (former commander of the air force), Fernando Honwana (aid to the first president, Samora Machel), and Gita Honwana (appointed by

---

[1] A similar process occurred in Angola. Soares de Oliveira argues that the ruling MPLA's nation-building project drew heavily on the social backgrounds and interests of its *assimilado* and Creole leadership. With the seizure of power, what had once been the narrow interests of a very particular social group came to define the nation and what it means to be a 'modern' citizen (2015: 7).

Frelimo to be one of Mozambique's first female judges). The father of Joaquim Chissano (former Foreign Minister and later president of Mozambique) was a translator for the colonial civil service. The father of Marcelino dos Santos (the former vice-president) worked for the national railways under the colonial state. Samora Machel worked as a nurse in the capital, his father was a prosperous peasant, and most of his family was involved with migrant labour to South Africa.

Relatively privileged elites – such as disgruntled *assimilados* and small numbers of *mulatos*,[2] Mozambican Indians, and whites – became increasingly disgusted by the prevailing system. An example is Paulo. Paulo was born in Maputo (then Lourenço Marques) in the 1920s into a Portuguese working-class family. While vastly privileged in comparison to the majority, his background ensured that he would always be excluded from the pinnacle of colonial society. His father strongly opposed the dictatorship of António Salazar and Paulo became radicalised early in his life. As he told me: 'As a child I would see people send their servants to the police for some minor thing and the servant would have to hand a note to the police which would tell the officer how many times to flog the poor person. It was not hard to see that the system was wrong.' The future Frelimo leadership was influenced by intellectual currents that were prominent throughout the world; nationalism, anti-colonialism, and a sense that the capitalist world order served to entrench the interests of the few at the expense of the many. However, I argue that the specific social context of Mozambique and the background and origins of the elite during the colonial period were influential in the ways in which such broad ideologies were understood and put into practice, emphasising the high modernist, anti-rural, anti-ethnic, and anti-traditional strands of thought. To understand this background, we must first discuss Mozambique's colonial history.

The Portuguese Empire

The paradox of Portuguese imperialism was that, although it had one of the great colonial empires, it had limited effective rule for much of the colonial period. The formation of Portugal's colonial empire did not stem from the subordination of the colonies to supply resources for growing mercantile and later industrial strength, as may be argued for Great Britain, but from desperate attempts to compensate for internal weakness (Newitt 1995). The ruling clique of a small state that had difficulties in feeding its own population looked to foreign shores for

---

[2] The term *mulato* is a common description of a person of mixed race in Mozambican Portuguese and does not have derogatory connotations.

the resources necessary to enrich themselves while facing fierce military and economic competition (Alpers and Ehret 1975; Axelson 1967; Newitt 1981; 1995).

As the Portuguese arrived in Mozambique in 1498 and their empire expanded along the west and east African coast in the sixteenth century, they hoped to replicate the conquests made by Spain in the New World and find their own fabulous sources of wealth (Axelson 1967; Isaacman and Isaacman 1983; Newitt 1981; 1995). The societies that the Portuguese initially encountered in what was to become central and northern Mozambique were very different from those found in Central and South America. There was no unified empire which a small group of Portuguese soldiers could neutralise with a decisive blow to the capital, nor was there large-scale infrastructure or apparatus for administration and domination that could be co-opted for colonial rule. Instead, the Portuguese encountered a varied social mosaic of coastal merchant towns that were involved in long-standing Indian Ocean trade networks and often dominated by Arab, Indian, and Swahili traders who were connected to the inland, matrilineal polities through a complicated set of relationships involving intermarriage, trade, and patronage (Alpers and Ehret 1975; Metcalf 2007; Newitt 1981; 1995). The Portuguese king ordered that these networks be reformed and brought under imperial control. For agents actually tasked with carrying out the king's orders, it was far more feasible to focus on creating a niche in the existing system than to attempt outright domination.

Until very late in the nineteenth century, the Portuguese Empire in Mozambique was a ramshackle edifice (Atmore 1985; Smith and Clarence 1985). Imperial rule was limited to a few small isolated outposts and actual power and commerce were frequently in the hands of foreign capital; *sertanejos* (Portuguese hunters and rural traders); Swahili, Indian, and Arab merchants; African chiefs; and prominent Afro-Portuguese families (Alpers and Ehret 1975; Axelson 1967). Much of the territory that makes up the modern nation state of Mozambique was not brought fully under Portuguese government control until the establishment of the New State. For hundreds of years the Portuguese colonialists who settled in Mozambique were of limited number. They frequently married into locally powerful families and, unlike other colonial powers such as the British, they tended not to introduce new methods of production or technologies until very late in the colonial period; rather, they adapted themselves and made use of what was already there (Metcalf 2007; Newitt 1995: 29–30, 100). Portugal's style of colonialism, the brutality and lack of overall effective exploitation that accompanied their rule, the apparent permissiveness towards what was termed 'miscegenation', and the tendency for local officials to adopt African social practices caused widespread condemnation and contempt among the other colonial powers, particularly Great Britain (Chabal 2002; Fry 2000; Newitt 1995; Penvenne 1995).

This sense of siege combined with the political weakness in Portugal itself, its dependence on foreign capital, and numerous attempts by other colonial powers to seize territory claimed by Portugal gave rise to a sense of national humiliation in the metropole. This ultimately resulted in an aggressively nationalistic colonial policy that meant a peaceful process of decolonisation was unlikely, especially after the advent of *o Estado Novo* (the New State). The dictatorship's colonial policy consisted of attempts to draw the colonies ever more tightly within the Portuguese grip (they later became known as overseas provinces) and to use colonial resources and markets to try to modernise Portugal itself. Colonial possessions also became a symbol of Portuguese national pride, proof that Portugal was not just a small and poor country.

The founding of Delagoa Bay and colonialism in the south of Mozambique

During the first three centuries of the empire, Portuguese officials con-centrated their attention on the central and northern port cities of the area that would become Mozambique. As if to demonstrate their com-mitment to international trade and their lack of interest in the land itself, Mozambique was officially ruled from Goa until 1752. The capital was then moved to the Island of Mozambique, off the coast of the present-day province of Nampula in the north. Although the far south of Mozam-bique had a natural deep-water seaport in Delagoa Bay, contact was limited and most Portuguese in the area were survivors of shipwrecks. This gradually began to change with the expansion of the ivory trade. By 1589, the Portuguese had a limited official presence in the area that eventually became the colonial capital of Lourenço Marques and later the independent capital of Maputo. In addition to the Portuguese pres-ence, Delagoa Bay was already inhabited by African societies drawn to the area because of the abundant opportunities to engage in whaling (Newitt 1995: 160–2).

The Portuguese attempted to draw these societies and the groups inhabiting the hinterlands into their already existing trade networks and installed a barter system for ivory. While significant profits were made from the ivory trade, the populations the Portuguese encountered in the south were structurally very different from those in the other areas of Mozambique and were more difficult to incorporate into the existing system. Much of the south was semi-arid and lacked the rich agricultural land of the centre of the country. The area was sparsely populated by patrilineal societies, with wealth and political power concentrated in the ownership of cattle. Young men would work for elders to gain the cattle necessary for *lobolo* ('bridewealth' in many southern African languages). While Portuguese trade goods were in use, they did not gain the significance that they held in other parts of the country, and more attention was focused on the internal cattle economy (Feliciano 1998; Newitt 1995). Portuguese manpower was limited and most colonial governors found it more profitable to focus their attention on the slave trade, which was run from the port cities in the centre and north of the country.

Although the south of Mozambique may have initially been a backwater even by the standards of a ramshackle empire, it was by no means isolated. By the end of the eighteenth century, the town of Lourenço Marques, which had been founded on Delagoa Bay, was becoming an area of commercial importance. English ships from India were calling to trade for ivory and an Englishman in the service of Austria had set up a permanent trade factory (Atmore 1985; Newitt 1995). The Portuguese presence was still relatively weak, especially after the outbreak of the revolutionary wars in Europe. French ships often attacked the Portuguese in the area and local chiefs found that they could get higher prices from English and Dutch merchants. These cosmopolitan connections increased in the nineteenth century. South African labour recruiters were active in bringing southern Mozambican labour into the Transvaal Republic, and British Indian merchants dominated the local trade networks, dealing with and competing against *sertanejos*, local African leaders and prominent Afro-Portuguese families (Harries 1994; Penvenne 1995). The cosmopolitan makeup of Lourenço Marques and Britain's designs on the area worried the Portuguese administration. In addition to European threats, strong African polities had also established themselves in southern Mozambique.

The competition among colonial powers for African territories threatened to become dangerous and destabilising, and efforts were made to settle boundary disputes between European states at the Berlin Conference in 1884–5. Portugal came with the *mapa cor de rosa* (pink map), which stated the country's claims on a large swathe of Central Africa, from the Atlantic coast of Angola to the Mozambican coast on the Indian Ocean. Although Portuguese explorers had followed the tried and tested colonial formula of signing treaties with anyone who could pass as an African authority figure, many of Portugal's claims were rejected. At the Berlin Conference, it was decided that effective occupation would be one of the major criteria in assigning territories. While Portugal claimed that vast amounts of Africa were subject to its suzerainty, the reality was very different. The south was already being economically incorporated into neighbouring South Africa, and the central section of Mozambique was divided into *prazos*. *Prazos* were theoretically land grants, usually to Afro-Portuguese families that ruled in the name of the king, and were subject to royal renewal. In actuality, *prazos* tended to resemble personal fiefdoms, in which loyalty to the king operated in name only and the actual power was that of the 'feudal lords' backed by personal slave armies. Other territories in the centre and north of the country were held by chartered companies that effectively wielded the powers of a government (Roberts 1986). The companies had their own police forces, they printed their own currencies, and they profited through the extraction of taxes. Many of these companies were owned by foreign capital. For example, the Niassa Company in the far north was around 80 per cent British owned (Newitt 1995). Portugal's grand claims were rejected and envious eyes were cast towards their remaining territory. Britain and Germany had long considered dividing Mozambique between them. However, Portugal's diplomatic defeat at the Berlin Conference unleashed a wave of colonial nationalism among the metropolitan population and the government tried with renewed vigour to extend effective control over its remaining possessions.

One of the targets for suppression was the Gaza Empire in the south of Mozambique. The Gaza Empire had grown out of the series of regional conquests and disturbances known as the Mfecane, unleashed by the growth of the Zulu Empire. Renegade Zulu generals had fled into Mozambique and used their disciplined armies and new tactics to establish their hegemony over local groups (Feliciano 1998; Newitt 1995; Smith and Clarence 1985). By 1894, the Portuguese had decided that the Gaza Empire had to be destroyed. Although the then emperor, Gungunhana, had officially aligned himself with the Portuguese, he had allowed Swiss Protestant missionaries from across the border with South Africa in his court, and the Portuguese colonial establishment suspected him of favouring the British and Kruger's *Zuid-Afrikaanse Republiek*. With the Portuguese government aware of the fragility of its empire after the Berlin Conference and with the temptation of securing the valuable commerce flowing through Lourenço Marques for its cash-strapped operations, the threat of a strong, independent African polity that could possibly side with colonial rivals was simply too much. Following the example of the recent military victory by Cecil Rhodes in Southern Rhodesia, the Portuguese government declared war on the Gaza Empire in 1895 and resistance was completely crushed by 1897.

The Gaza Empire had internal weaknesses that the Portuguese could turn to their advantage Its rulers had exploited and dominated other ethnic groups, subjecting them to repeated raids and obliging them to pay tribute (Feliciano 1998; Honwana 1988; Newitt 1995). The Portuguese sent a relatively strong force of European soldiers to forge military alliances with the disaffected groups who had suffered under Gaza rule. When war broke out, the Gaza Empire had some successes and even managed to infiltrate and attack Lourenço Marques, but the superior firepower of the Portuguese and their allies soon brought the war to a close. In 1895, Gungunhana was defeated, captured, and then exiled to the Azores. One of Gungunhana's chief commanders, Maguinuana, continued the fight against the Portuguese, but he was captured in 1897 and beheaded, thus ending not only the Gaza Empire, but also any significant, independent African polity in the south of Mozambique.

The Gaza wars were to have great significance for the future forms of Portuguese colonialism. The victory restored Portuguese pride in their colonial empire, after the humiliation at the Berlin Conference and military setbacks in other parts of Mozambique. The Portuguese commander, António Ennes, became a national hero and was made the next colonial governor. During his period of office, he reinvigorated the administration and began to solidify Portuguese control over Mozambique. In 1898, the capital was also moved from Mozambique Island in the north to Lourenço Marques, as the area was directly under state control (Newitt 1995; Penvenne 1995).

However, the effects of the Gaza wars went beyond a revitalised colonial administration. Although Frelimo was later to portray Gungunhana as a proto-nationalist hero, at the time his influence was deeply divisive. As previously stated, other ethnic groups, tired of Gaza depredations, had joined the Portuguese war effort. When Gungunhana was captured, his own men began to chant: 'Away with you, vulture, slaughterer of our chickens' (quoted in Honwana 1988: 43). Despite Gungunhana's ignominious departure from the political scene, his resistance later became a nationalist myth. Samora Machel stated that he began to develop his political consciousness as a young man through hearing the stories of his grandfather who was a commander in Gungunhana's armies (Christie 1989). Machel's successor, Joaquim Chissano, also had ancestors who fought with Gungunhana. Like many nationalist myths, the reality was far more contradictory. This can be seen in the ancestry of other members of the Frelimo leadership. For example, Eduardo Mondlane, the founder of Frelimo, came from the Chope, a coastal group living further to the north whose people had been victimised by the Gaza Empire and had on occasion sided with the Portuguese. Members of other southern groups, such as the Ronga, also aided the Portuguese in the conquest of Gaza. One such example is the father of Raúl Honwana, the patriarch of a prominent Frelimo family. He had fought with the Portuguese during the Gaza wars and later served as a translator.

The destruction of the Gaza Empire was to have wider implications for the future structure of the colony, and eventually for the formation of the Frelimo leadership. When the Portuguese went to war with the Gaza Empire, they made no attempt to preserve its structures or to utilise them for the purposes of indirect rule after the conflict, leaving a power vacuum concerning so-called traditional authorities. This was another blow to the power structures of the south, which had already been battered by the slave trade and by the chaos unleashed by the Gaza Empire's incursions and Portuguese colonial expansion. The power vacuum accelerated the penetration of international capital and the importance of migrant labour. In Gaza, Portuguese allies were being promoted to positions of power and the remainder of the population had to find sources of income that could pay the ever-increasing government taxes. The future for ambitious young Africans in the south, especially in the areas near Maputo, no longer lay in rising in the ranks of traditional power structures, as these positions were being filled by outsiders, but with finding employment in the mines of South Africa or in the capital.

The formation of the colonial elite

After the destruction of the Gaza Empire, the future African elite became more tightly bound to Mozambique's urban centres. In the last years of the Portuguese monarchy, from 1877 to 1910, Lourenço Marques had an open economic policy (in contrast to other Mozambican ports); in combination with the growth of the mining industry in the Transvaal, this transformed the capital from a backwater fort to a centre of commerce, although the lion's share of trade was controlled by British capital. By the first decade of the twentieth century, the city had a modern port with a hydraulic crane, 40 or so miles of macadam roadway, hotels, and handsome villas with mosquito-proofed verandas (Penvenne 1995: 33). As the colonial capital developed modern amenities for the white population, this was the beginning of the steady disenfranchisement of the African population.

While the colonial state's reach and effective administration were severely limited throughout much of its rule, the systems of categorising the population, the enduring links between status and access to state power, and the way in which this shaped the legacy of the resulting forms of boundary drawing continue to resonate in the present (see also Wedeen 2008 for a similar discussion about Yemen). Throughout much of the empire's history, many of the predominantly male colonialists married into African families, often recognising and giving their nationality to the children of these unions, who were then able to find relatively high-ranking positions in trade or in the colonial administration (Hedges 1999; Mateus 1999; Penvenne 1989; 1995). Although the phenomenon of local elites obtaining high positions was not unknown in other parts of Africa, it tended to characterise only the early periods of colonialism; barriers became stronger during the nineteenth and twentieth centuries with the growth of so-called scientific racism (Dubow 1995; Mann 1985; Stoler 1997). The fact that the Portuguese men often recognised their children by

Figure 2.1 A scene of colonial Lourenço Marques: the Gil Vicente
Theatre.
Source: Zoonar GmbH / Alamy Stock Photo.

local wives or mistresses led to charges of miscegenation and degeneracy
from other European powers. The Portuguese responded by stating that
they were bringing European civilisation to those who were deemed
natives and that this demonstrated the Portuguese's ability to understand
and interact with their subject population. During the New State
(1932–74), this became a full-blown ideological justification of Portuguese
colonial domination. This ideology, known as *lusotropicalismo*, stated that,
unlike the racist rule of other colonial powers, Portugal was uniquely
endowed with the ability to reign over Africans in harmony and advance
their level of civilisation (Hedges 1999; Newitt 1981; Roberts 1986).

Although the ideology of *lusotropicalismo* was a hypocritical lie at best,
this form of colonialism did give the Mozambican elite a distinctive
character. Many members of this group found the grand claims of
Portuguese colonialism laughable and only participated in order to gain
its benefits for themselves and their families, but it did begin to create an
identification with a form of largely urban, metropolitan culture, if not
the specific metropolitan power (Honwana 1988; Sithole and Ingwane
1977). It also created an indigenous elite, as was often the case under
colonialism, which was complicit to some degree with the colonial
system.

The Portuguese may have made some concessions to African elites,
but for the majority of the population their rule was marked by poverty

and brutality. The government soon realised that its major resource, apart from a deep-water port, was the local population (Hanlon 1990). By 1897, Portugal had signed treaties with the *Zuid-Afrikaanse Republiek* over the amount of migrant labour that would be exported to South Africa; this form of labour had huge social ramifications as young men were no longer directly dependent on their elders in order to gain the resources necessary for *lobolo*. These treaties survived the Anglo-Boer war. It was also decided that the South Africans would send workers' salaries directly to the Portuguese colonial administration, where they would take a portion and then deliver the rest to the worker (Harries 1994; Norman 2004). In addition, the south saw the widespread use of *chibalo* (forced labour). It was declared that it was an African's duty to work, and if someone did not have a job they were sent to do *chibalo*, with minimal, if any, payment, either for public works or for private companies (Hedges 1999; Newitt; 1995; Penvenne 1995). Conditions of *chibalo* were little better than slavery. Although the workers were often referred to as 'volunteers', the name was a fiction. The early nationalist icon Raúl Honwana recalled a Portuguese official presenting 12 *chibalo* labourers to his boss and saying, 'I hereby present 12 volunteers, all duly manacled' (Honwana 1988: 87).

While members of the emergent elite were spared this indignity, and many, especially members of prestigious associations of *Gremio* (a Roman Catholic, *mulato*-dominated network of powerful old families) and *Instituto Negrofilo* (a black- and Protestant-dominated elite association with fewer ties to the Portuguese state) raised their voices against colonial abuses, some of these same people also directly profited from them (Casimiro 1979; Penvenne 1989; 1995). In addition, although the emerging elite also suffered discrimination, discriminatory measures such as *chibalo* could also serve the class interests of some members. Although many were critical of the colonial state, their attitude concerning the majority of the population was often characterised by class-based perspectives and patronising condescension towards what they viewed as backward or 'bush blacks' (Penvenne 1989). The claims of the Mozambican elite to be more culturally advanced than 'the masses' have a long history. Emerging elites occupied an uneasy place between the Portuguese and almost everyone else, and were regarded with suspicion by both.

The high point for the local elite in southern Mozambique was the period between the late nineteenth century and the beginning of republican rule (1910–26); this was especially the case for *mulatos*, who were known as *brancas da terra* (whites of the land, or local whites). As the colonial state consolidated its hold on Mozambique, the status of and opportunities for the local elites dwindled. The political and economic weakness of the mother country, which had originally been a source of empowerment, now began to work against them. The Portuguese government increasingly imported administrators and settlers whose undivided loyalty it commanded. During the monarchy, the Portuguese also imported Indians from their possessions in Goa. Goans were well established in both the lower and middle ranges of the administration, and Indians connected with British colonies and the long-standing trade diaspora had filled a mercantile niche in Mozambique. At the same time, white immigration, which had begun to increase after the republican revolution, became a flood during the New State, especially after World War Two. The competition for suitable positions became a tripartite racial struggle (Birmingham 1992: 15–16).

White supremacy was ensured in a variety of ways, both directly through the colonial state and through associated institutions. Portugal had outsourced much of the education provision for the African population to the Catholic Church, whose policies had the overall effect of drastically limiting the possibility of black Mozambicans gaining access to higher education. Roberto was born in the early 1960s to a reasonably well-off family. Despite their relatively privileged status, he described his early education as a 'joke'. Roberto attended a Catholic mission school, the most common educational option for the black population, in the province of Inhambane. This was not his parents' first choice as they were Protestant, but it was all that was available. The school itself was in one huge hall, where all the various grades were crammed together reciting the alphabet. After lunch, they would then have to work on the fields. Roberto felt that the school was a scam to extort labour from the students rather than an educational institution. The limited and substandard educational prospects available to the black population heightened the drastic shortage of skills in the colony.

Migrants from Portugal typically came from the mother country's rural poor and frequently had low levels of education and literacy. The state systematically starved Africans of resources to provide amenities for whites and to ensure a relatively high standard of living for Portuguese migrants, but despite their continuing efforts, the skills of many whites were sufficient only for menial positions (Hedges 1999; Penvenne 1995). White settlers in Mozambique worked as taxi drivers, waiters, and barbers. By the 1950s, '[b]lack cobblers, street vendors, bakers, housemaids, bus-conductors, bar tenders and prostitutes all found their jobs threatened by poor whites' (Birmingham 1992: 21). The social divisions between whites in Mozambique were also extensive. Whites who were born in Mozambique were known as *segundos* (literally 'second') and were largely barred from holding the highest administrative positions, although social class could cut across such boundaries, with a locally born industrialist easily outranking a recently arrived illiterate peasant.

Although the colonies were a key justification for the empire, the social horizons of the settlers were often far removed from Mozambique. Flora, whom I introduced Chapter 1, is a white Mozambican who was born shortly after World War Two and later joined Frelimo. According to her, the bourgeois of Maputo were turned towards Europe and that was their main point of reference. 'They would have their holidays in Portugal and read Portuguese newspapers. South Africa was considered fit for shopping, but if you had any money whatsoever then you went off to Europe for the summer.' Many viewed Mozambique as decidedly second-rate. Everyone who was anyone in Portugal wanted to go to Brazil. They had every imaginable natural resource, they had huge cities, and it was 'civilised'. For the Portuguese, it was like the old stories of America, a place where the streets were paved with gold. If Brazil was the first choice, Angola with its amazing mineral wealth was the obvious second choice, and Mozambique was rather far down the list. As Flora said: 'The only thing we have here is malaria.' Although the New State appeared to wield unchallenged power, by the late 1960s the social situation in Mozambique was characterised by simmering tensions, both between broad social categories such as black or white and within these overarching groups. The path for upward social mobility for non-whites was increasing blocked and the black population – and to some extent the *mulato* elite – found its old position as *civilizados* (civilised) coming under attack, largely by those who would have preferred to be somewhere else.

The *assimilados* (the assimilated) and the *indígenas* (natives)

The result of the state's discriminatory policies was the hardening of the indigenous class structure through the implementation of specific legislation to divide the population into categories with corresponding privileges and rights. Between 1913 and 1927, the Portuguese state began to tighten and regulate the definition of urban African elites. As white immigration increased, the government set about disenfranchising the small existing African elite and controlling its numbers and privileges by introducing the *álvara de assimilação* (certificate of assimilation), which gave its bearers honorary white status and made them subject to the Portuguese legal code as opposed to most of the population who were deemed *indígenas* (Penvenne 1979: 18). The *álvara de assimilação* was vigorously resisted by members of the more established indigenous elite, who were insulted by having to apply for what had previously been their birthright. During the republican period, legislation dealing with *assimilação* was being continually and repeatedly drawn up, but political weakness, irregular implementation, local resistance, and a bewildering succession of governments that rapidly gained power in Portugal – and just as quickly lost it – limited its effects. This changed after the over-throw of the republic and local resistance to *assimilação* faded as the consequences became more severe (Hedges 1999; Penvenne 1989).

The overall result of the new legislation was that the previous measures of independence and power available to local elites were drastically curtailed. While *assimilados* still enjoyed many privileges in comparison to the majority of the population, their role had been transformed from a self-confident indigenous elite to low-level functionaries of the colonial administration. Their very existence was now dependent on their access to the state and governed by the colonial bureaucracy, as one can see by the requirements necessary to gain the status of *assimilado*. To become an *assimilado*, a man (the position was unapologetically gendered) had to apply to the colonial government and satisfy a set of criteria:

1. He must read, write, and speak Portuguese fluently.
2. He must have sufficient means to support his family.
3. He must be of good conduct.
4. He must have the necessary education and individual and social habits to make it possible to apply the public and private law of Portugal to him.
5. He must make a request to the administrative authority of the area, which will pass it on to the governor of the district for approval (Mondlane 1969: 48).

Once approval was granted, the individual was then theoretically given the same rights and privileges as a settler. This, however, was not the case in practice. *Assimilados* received lower wages, had to live in specific parts of town, and suffered routine discrimination. Despite the blatant double standards connected to *assimilação* (for instance, whites did not have to be literate to enjoy civil rights), people continued to seek this status and to subject themselves to the humiliation of certification. *Assimilados* were exempt from forced labour and military service, they could travel freely within Mozambique, they were allowed urban residence, they had increased access to education for themselves and their families, and they enjoyed relatively more opportunities for advancement, especially in the civil service (in many cases *assimilado* status was a requirement for such a position).

While the legal category existed (it was abolished in the 1960s), *assimilados* were never more than a tiny minority of the population. In 1950, they numbered 4,439, or less than 1 per cent of the population (Sheldon 2002: 59). As the requirements show, it was assumed that an *assimilado* would be a man, although wives and children of *assimilados* were normally granted the status as well. Out of the 4,439 *assimilados* in 1950, 2,651 were men and 1,788 were women (ibid.). Even after the status of *assimilado* was obtained, one had to be careful in one's actions, as the status could be rescinded for backsliding into former, so-called heathen habits such as polygamy or the practice of traditional religions.

Although the actual numbers of assimilated Africans in Mozambique were miniscule, the colonial state used the existence of *assimilados* to justify its claims of developing a uniquely harmonious and non-racialist form of colonialism. As noted by Hall and Young (1997), while Portuguese colonial territories avoided some of the crudest aspects of the colour bar, at least for the privileged, the sense of racial humiliation and grievance among *assimilados* was as profound as what was found in other colonies. The memoirs of many former *assimilados* reflect this sense of humiliation. After independence, Raúl Honwana bitterly explained to an interviewer the process one had to go through to become an *assimilado*:

Africans who wanted to be considered "civilized" had to pass an examination by answering certain questions and by allowing a committee to go to their homes to see how they lived and if they knew how to eat at a table the way whites did, if they wore shoes, and if they had only one wife. When Africans passed these examinations, they were given a document called the "certificate of assimilation" for which they paid half a pound sterling or its equivalent. (Honwana 1988: 52)

Another former *assimilado* described the humiliation in an interview shortly after independence:

R. You see, comrade, an *assimilado* was one who was taught to despise his own mother. To despise his own father. To have nothing to do with his relatives.
Q. But the Portuguese did treat *assimilados* as they did themselves?
R. Nothing of the sort. They taught us to despise our own people and to praise them.
Q. Them who?
R. The Portuguese ... They taught us to be ashamed of ourselves ... We were ashamed to be found together with our friends and relatives who were not *assimilados* ... Then you were in danger of becoming a *non-assimilado*.

(Sithole and Ingwane 1977: 5–6)

The institution of *assimilação* was envisioned as an act of boundary making, drawing a firm distinction between a colonially aligned, privileged class and the wider population. The boundary was enforced through a particular set of legal rights and expressed through cultural behaviours, such as the use of Portuguese at home, the renunciation of so-called traditional customs, and the need to conform to a monogamous, nuclear family. Those who did not obey these strictures could always have their status rescinded. In reality, though, even these boundaries were porous. Claudia was the daughter of an *assimilado* and his so-called African wife, a woman he secretly married in addition to his legally recognised first wife. Claudia's father used his connections and relatively substantial salary for the time to ensure that the children of both his wives received an education that very few black Mozambicans could aspire to during the colonial period. The privilege enjoyed by Claudia and her siblings came to an abrupt end after her father's untimely death. They were plunged into poverty, as they had no legal claim to either his pension or his estate. Social boundaries were not absolute, but privilege was intertwined with vulnerability. Claudia had access to the best education available, but only through her father and with no wider legal or familial protection. Claudia's father had sufficient resources to support two families; however, if he had been caught, he stood to lose everything.

Assimilados in the late colonial period were in many ways betwixt and between, trying to occupy an inherently precarious middle position between the colonisers and the wider population.

Assimilados were always vulnerable to white tolerance, due in part to their own aspirations for equal treatment, and their historical role as a comprador group. Thus, they often found themselves the first to be sacrificed to white ambition. They were harassed and humiliated by whites and tolerated, distrusted, or despised by other blacks. They were called "pocket whites" or "paper whites", black men who, due to the legal papers they carried in their pockets, were encouraged to identify with whites, as distinct from "natives", but only when it suited white needs. They enjoyed token material benefits as favored sons, but the fragility of their position became increasingly obvious as the century progressed and the white population grew. (Penvenne 1979: 18)

The more embittered and alienated sections of the African elite began to see a common cause between themselves and the wider population as victims of colonial oppression and humiliation. Newitt demonstrates this with wry understatement: 'It is difficult not to conclude that the New State made a fundamental error in allowing a small *assimilado* class to emerge and then systematically subjecting it to personal humiliation and depressed status' (1995: 477).

This 'fundamental error' can be seen in the writings of a former *assimilado*, Luís Honwana. The Honwana family were *assimilados*, and Raúl Honwana, Luís' father, worked for the colonial civil service. His family, while not wealthy, was relatively privileged by African standards. In addition to Raúl's position with the state, the family also owned a small freehold farm and livestock, and employed the services of a young African *empregada*. Luís Honwana wrote a book of short stories in which he describes his upbringing in colonial Mozambique. Many of his stories depict the racism, brutality, and humiliation that even Mozambicans from the higher social strata had to endure. In one of his most famous stories, 'Papa, the snake and I', Luís recalls the ways in which the racial

domination at the heart of the colonial system could poison the relationships between people in even the most mundane situations. In this case, a
snake killed a white neighbour's hunting dog.

At that point Senhor Castro's [the white neighbour] car drew up in front of our
house. Papa walked up to him, and Mama went to talk to Sartina. I followed
after Papa.
"Good afternoon, Senhor Castro ..."
"Listen, I have just found that my pointer is dead, and his chest is all
swollen. My natives tell me that he came howling back from your house before
he died. I don't want any back chat, and I am telling you – either you pay
compensation or I'll make a complaint at the Administration. He was the best
pointer I ever had."
"I've just come back from work – I don't know anything ..."
"I don't care a damn about that. Don't argue. Are you going to pay or aren't
you?"
"But Senhor Castro ..."
"Senhor Castro nothing. Its 700 paus. And it's better if the matter rests here."
"As you like, Senhor Castro, but I don't have the money now ..."
"We'll see about that later. I'll wait until the end of the month, and if you don't
pay then there will be a row."
"Senhor Castro, we've known each other such a long time, and there's
never ..."
"Don't try that with me. I know what you all need – a bloody good hiding is the
only thing ..."
Senhor Castro climbed into his car and pulled away. Papa stayed watching
while the car drove off.
"Son of a bitch ..."
"Papa, why didn't you say that to his face?"
He didn't answer. (Honwana 1969: 45)

By the standards of the time, Raúl Honwana was quite well off for an
African man. Yet in comparison to white colonialists he would always be
poor, and not just in the material sense. Despite everything he achieved
in his life under colonialism, he would always be of subordinate status to
whites, no matter what the papers in his pocket said. This story expresses
the lie at the centre of *assimilação*; although he was legally the equal of a
Portuguese colonialist he could always be reduced to powerless humiliation by a white man's whim. As I was once warned by a friend who was
arranging an interview for me with her uncle, a man who was once an
assimilado: 'Watch it, he hates the word *assimilado*. If you mention that he
will throw you out of his house.'
As the colonial period progressed and *assimilados* realised that their
social mobility would be permanently blocked under this humiliating
system, many became progressively more alienated from the colonial
state. This was especially the case for Protestant-educated *assimilados*,
who historically had an insecure relationship with the state, as Protestant

missions were suspected of 'de-nationalising' Portuguese subjects and were treated with suspicion (Cruz e Silva 2001). *Assimilados* were not alone in perceiving that social mobility under colonialism would remain limited at best. Although poverty in Mozambique was shocking, widespread, and deep, some of the post–World War Two economic boom eventually began to trickle down. Roberto, introduced earlier in this chapter, came from a reasonably well-off family. His father and many uncles had worked in the mines in South Africa and were able to send money home. His family was not officially recognised by the state as *assimilados*, but they were affluent by local standards and had access to education, a well, and a sewing machine – far more than many of their neighbours. They were a respected family, so they were thought of, locally at least, as *assimilados*. When his family moved to Maputo, they prevailed on a white family friend to use his connections to have Roberto enrolled in an elite white school. Roberto was one of ten black students and recalls being subjected to much abuse. This was compounded by the fact that his school was next to a military base where the elite Portuguese commandos were stationed. When Roberto walked by, the soldiers would hang out at the fence, pelting him with fruit while shouting racist insults. As Roberto's experience demonstrates, even the most privileged blacks were dependent on the whims of whites and subject to cruel and humiliating treatment. Their ability to ascend past primary and secondary education was also restricted. When Flora studied at university in Maputo in the 1960s, she remembers that there was only one black student in the entire student body. Others I have spoken to claimed that there were higher numbers, but never more than ten out of a student body of around 3,000.

As African nationalist movements elsewhere began to score successes and liberate their respective countries, many among the more privileged Mozambican groups began to feel that a far better future was possible in an independent nation. In contrast to the case with other colonial powers, such as Britain and France, Portugal was ruled by an authoritarian government that had firmly invested its legitimacy on the continuance of the empire. Thus, there was no question of a peaceful or negotiated settlement that would lead to independence. In the bloody conflict that followed, the revolutionary movement was led by those who were often drawn from *assimilado* or prospective *assimilado* origins but were ashamed of its servile and collaborationist connotations. The Frelimo leadership was a group that became progressively more radical as they envisioned the entire recreation of a society based on a modernist vision and disciplinary project (Hall and Young 1997; Mateus 1999; Newitt 1995). This vision – the ideology of the blank slate where social change is predicated on abolishing the old and transforming the populace – has appealed to embittered intellectuals throughout the world and has been an underlying theme of the great revolutions of the twentieth century (see Cheng 2009).

A luta armada (the armed struggle or liberation struggle)

A luta armada has become the foundational myth of the postcolonial political order. The binary rhetoric, what Coelho has insightfully termed the liberation script (2013), is the mythico-history that serves as a charter for Frelimo's legitimacy, justifying its right to rule from independence to the present day. Frelimo drew on various pre-existing elements, such as the cultural underpinnings of parts of Christianity and *assimilação*, for its transformative project, but these elements took on new meaning when combined with the trials and experiments of the liberation struggle. The legacies of the heroism, atrocities, friendships, hopes, failures, betrayals, and purges of this period continue to weigh heavily on the nation.

The path to independence in Mozambique was long and tortuous, with numerous internal conflicts that would come to shape the post-independence order. As previously stated, until the very end, Portugal refused to countenance any thought of independence for its African colonies. The colonial secret police (International and State Defence Police or PIDE) was very efficient in discovering and suppressing political activity among the African population. Due to the repressive climate, the movement that grew into Frelimo had fragmentary beginnings. It was based on disaffected southern intellectuals and central and northern embryonic political movements that had grown among migrant workers residing in Tanzania, Malawi, and Rhodesia.

Frelimo was formed on 25 June 1962 in Tanzania. It was an amalgamation of the National Democratic Union of Mozambique (Udenamo), which had been formed in Rhodesia; the Mozambican African National Union (MANU), which was formed in Tanzania and grew out of the ethnic-based Makonde African National Union; and finally, the National African Union of Independent Mozambique (UNAMI), which was based in Malawi and also drew heavily on ethnic and regional support from Tete Province (Munslow 1983: 79–80). Leaders of the three movements, under pressure from the Organisation of African Unity (OAU), decided to broaden their appeal by forming a united front to work for the liberation of Mozambique. Dr Eduardo Mondlane, a foreign-educated prominent southern intellectual, nationalist figure, and the first black Mozambican to obtain a PhD, was elected as the overall president. Dr Mondlane was able to utilise international contacts he made through his previous post at the UN to bring the movement to international attention. He was also able to recruit educated southerners through the Nucleus of Mozambican Secondary Students (NESAM), a movement founded by him and later banned by the Portuguese, whose membership included future top-ranking Frelimo officials such as Joaquim Chissano and Armando Guebuza, both of whom later became president of the republic (Casimiro 1979). After the bloody suppression of the abortive Angolan rebellion of 1961, Frelimo decided that armed struggle was the only way to achieve independence.

Almost immediately after Frelimo was formed, the party was beset by factionalism and internal disputes (Finnegan 1992; Mondlane 1966; 1969; Opello 1975). The original leaders of MANU, Udenamo, and UNAMI were soon displaced and leadership positions were often filled by an influx of better-educated southerners who had come with Mondlane (Cabrita 2000). Many of the displaced responded with accusations of growing southern domination. While Frelimo absorbed most of the rank-and-file members of the former parties, especially MANU, these displaced former leaders attempted to reconstitute their organisations with small numbers of followers or formed splinter groups (Opello 1975). They appeared and disappeared with a bewildering succession of acronyms, ideologies, and overall goals. The majority were still-born paper organisations based on the personality of the leader and had little overall influence. In 1964, four of these groups – MANU, Moreco, Udenamo-Moçambique, and Undenamo-Monomotapa – joined to form the Mozambican Revolutionary Committee (Coremo) and were later joined by further dissidents from Frelimo (Opello 1975). Coremo was the closest thing Frelimo faced to a nationalist rival, but for the most part was politically and militarily insignificant (Finnegan 1992; Opello 1975).

Despite the internal turmoil within Frelimo, the party was able to launch the armed struggle on 25 September 1964 after two years of preparation. Frelimo had its primary headquarters in Tanzania and devoted its initial efforts to infiltrating the northern provinces of Cabo Delgado and the sparsely populated Niassa. Their greatest early successes were in Cabo Delgado, on the Mueda Plateau among the Makonde. Makonde immigrants who were originally trying to escape the slave trade in Mozambique had settled the Mueda Plateau; it was relatively inaccessible and ideal for guerrilla tactics. The Makonde also had a history of hostility to the Portuguese, based on, among other things, a recent massacre when a demonstration primarily by Makonde protestors had been fired upon by the Portuguese military. Building from the former MANU's strong base among the Makonde, Frelimo was well established on the Mueda Plateau and the Makonde served as Frelimo foot soldiers. In the early period of the struggle, Frelimo put relatively little thought into administering the areas where it was dominant. Initially, *regulos* (so-called traditional chiefs, often originally appointed by the Portuguese) who were thought to side with the colonial state were assassinated, while Frelimo tried to develop a working relationship with *regulos* who were more sympathetic to their cause (Munslow 1983; Opello 1975).

Although Frelimo had early successes in parts of Cabo Delgado, by 1966 it had suffered a series of military setbacks. The campaign in Niassa stalled shortly after its launch and suffered reverses. Frelimo cells in the capital were infiltrated by PIDE and members were rounded up. Finally, efforts failed to open new fronts in provinces in the centre and Frelimo was driven back. This series of setbacks, combined with the fact that Frelimo was organised as a broad front of Mozambican nationalists and incorporated people of various ethnicities, class positions, and overall political opinions, led to still more internal conflict. Different groups within the party had drastically divergent ideas on how to win independence and what form the country would take afterwards. There were two principal groupings in the second round of power struggles that racked the party. The first coalesced around Mondlane and the relatively well-educated, cosmopolitan southerners who formed a powerful multiracial contingent. Many members of this group had studied in foreign universities and were influenced by the socialist ideas they encountered abroad. Southerners with less education, such as Samora Machel and some of the younger generation of northern guerrilla commanders, were also leading members (Finnegan 1992). The southerners and the younger generation generally tended to follow a radical line that became more pronounced through the struggle. They defined social class as the central point of oppression and felt that, in addition to ending colonial rule, it was also necessary to fight a protracted people's war that would lead to an egalitarian social revolution to re-make Mozambique (Hall and Young 1997; Newitt 1995; Opello 1975). The principal opposition to the radical younger generation came primarily from older, more conservative members of the leadership from the centre and north of Mozambique. They defined race as the central cause of oppression and opposed allowing non-blacks to hold leadership positions. They had a stronger social base among the relatively well-off sections of the peasantry (Bowen 2000) and leaned towards various forms of capitalism; some supposedly had substantial business interests. In general, they distrusted many elements of the social revolution championed by the more radical faction (Bowen 2000; Cabrita 2000; Hall and Young 1997; Newitt 1995; Opello 1975).

As the internal conflict continued throughout the 1960s, Frelimo's leadership was deeply divided. The ages of the members of the central committee ranged from barely 30 for the youngest member, Jorge Rebelo, to close to twice that for the oldest, Lazaro Nkavandame. Besides the generation gap, the ideological differences between the factions became more pronounced. These differences soon spilled over to strategy. The younger radicals wanted to politicise the army and prepare for a long, drawn-out struggle to make the population politically aware, while older conservatives wished to concentrate on the war rather than social revolution (Isaacman and Isaacman 1983; Munslow 1983; Newitt 1995). More conservative members of the central committee became alarmed at the strength of southern *assimilados* within the leadership and made frequent accusations of discrimination against northerners (Mateus 1999; Minter 1994). In 1966, Felipe Magaia, the head of the military and a northerner, was killed and replaced by a southerner, Samora Machel. This infuriated some Makonde leaders who claimed that their people were doing all the fighting while southerners monopolised the leadership positions. Some claimed that Magaia had been assassinated and that this was part of a southern/Shangaan coup. In 1968, conflict broke out in bases in Tanzania as a priest and instructor at the Frelimo school, Father Mateus Gwenjere, helped instigate a revolt among students who claimed that they were being denied foreign scholarships that had been promised them, and refused to fight in the struggle. The revolt had to be put down by the Tanzanian police. The internal conflict reached a fever pitch between what became known in Frelimo mythology as the 'two lines', which represented the principal groupings in the power struggle. One was composed of the more conservative party members from the central and northern parts of Mozambique. This group included Gwenjere, Uria Simango, vice-president of Frelimo, and Lazaro Nkavandame, head of the Department of Commerce. Their position, though, was considerably weakened, especially as the radicals now controlled the army, and Nkavandame began to advocate a federal state with autonomy for the Makonde (Isaacman and Isaacman 1983; Newitt 1995). The other line was the radical bloc, which contained many prominent southerners such as Eduardo Mondlane, Samora Machel, Marcelino Dos Santos (Secretary of Foreign Affairs), and Joaquim Chissano, the chairman of the Department of Security. This group also included younger northerners such as Chipande, a military commander who led the first attack in the struggle.

The conflict between these two lines demonstrated some of the underlying weaknesses of Frelimo's original formation in 1962 as a broad front united by its desire to end colonialism. While all the groups within Frelimo agreed that the current system of colonial rule had to end, the question of what was to follow was far more vexing. The conservatives, with their attempts at creating an ethnic power base and with their more prosperous peasant and mercantile backgrounds, leaned towards a federal state, as the removal of the Portuguese would open up opportunities for Mozambicans (Bowen 2000). For the radicals, a group that contained many urban southerners, this was exactly what they wanted to avoid. Their aversion to the proposals of the conservatives grew from both ideology and political realism. The radicals believed that the only way to bring prosperity to the people was to eradicate the colonial influence and create a strong, 'modern', unitary socialist nation (see Sumich 2012). For this goal to succeed, the radicals felt that what they viewed as obstacles, such as ethnic nationalism and many aspects of rural social and economic relations, had to be swept away. The radical faction also knew that, with their particular social background and their southern origins in a conflict largely restricted to the north of the country, they lacked an ethnic power base and could not compete with their rivals along these lines.

Conflict crystallised in 1968 over where the second party congress would be held. The conservative line wanted it in Tanzania, where they felt strongest, while the radicals wanted to hold the congress in liberated territory in Mozambique that was held by their military power base. The radicals won this conflict and the second congress was held in July 1968 in Niassa, a province in the north of Mozambique. As prominent members of the opposing line did not attend, the radical platform was accepted with minimal opposition (Cabrita 2000; Newitt 1995). Efforts were made by Mondlane to heal the breach with Nkavandame, but attempts at reconciliation failed. Nkavandame was attacked by the radicals as a corrupt exploiter. He ran a network of cooperatives that supplied commercial needs for the liberated areas, and he was accused of profiteering and of assassinating opponents within the movement (Cabrita 2000; Isaacman and Isaacman 1983; Munslow 1983; Newitt 1995). Nkavandame vigorously denied the charges, claimed that Frelimo was the victim of a southern/Shangaan coup, and called for Makonde soldiers to desert. His calls for ethnic solidarity went unheeded by the majority of Frelimo troops and his attempts to take over Frelimo-held areas in the liberated territories were beaten back by loyalists (Opello 1975). Some analysts claim that the ideological struggles between these groups simply masked elites jockeying for position, as the claims of the various factions of the leadership had relatively little effect on the rank and file of the party (Opello 1975). Although there is undoubtedly an element of truth to this, it is instructive to note that the majority of the primarily Makonde troops of Frelimo did not heed calls for ethnic solidarity but joined forces with the radicals, many of whom were southerners, which could indicate that the radical line held a degree of ideological appeal.

In 1969, after five years of revolutionary war and with a further five years of conflict in the future, Mondlane was assassinated with a parcel bomb, allegedly arranged by PIDE. Although Uria Simango was vice-president, his leadership bid did not have the support of the rest of the executive committee. Instead, Mondlane was succeeded by a 'Council of the Presidency' consisting of Simango of the conservative faction and Machel and Dos Santos of the radical faction. The struggle for power continued throughout 1969 with several defections from Frelimo, one causing the collapse of the military front in Tete Province. By 1970, with Machel's assumption of unitary leadership, the radical faction was firmly in power and the conservatives were defeated. Simango was accused of complicity in the death of Mondlane and was expelled from Frelimo. He eventually joined Coremo and was executed on the charge of counter-revolution after independence. Samora Machel was installed as the leader in 1970 and held the post – which he later combined with that of president – until his death in 1986. The party leadership remained remarkably cohesive after Machel's ascent to power; they were now united in their desire for radical social change.

The schisms during the struggle had a profound effect on the victorious radical faction. For them, schisms confirmed the popular desire for a social revolution, especially among a politicised army and party supporters who had been taught to recognise how such a revolution would serve their supposed true interests. Schisms also taught the radical faction that their movement was beset by treason, especially by those who appeared to support independence, but, according to the radicals, had been corrupted by colonialism and wanted to use the struggle to advance their self-interest. A siege-like mentality fuelled the radical leadership's suspicion and intolerance of ethnically or racially based social organisation, quasi-traditional power structures, and any form of dissent as representing the ever-present threat of disunity and discord.

With Machel's victory, the liberated zones became – as the leadership would claim after independence – the crucible of the new man and the party's transformative project. In this deeply idealised view, the masses, under the direction of the party, would supposedly free themselves of colonial segregation and so-called backward cultural practices that would no longer serve them, and would dedicate themselves selflessly to the cause of the revolution. The social revolution was a disciplinary project to mould a new kind of citizen, and, after the ascendance of the radical faction, life in the liberated zones became more controlled and puritanical. Unauthorised sexual liaisons were forbidden and perpetrators were punished and sometimes forced to marry. One former militant recalls that he was forced to marry his partner multiple times as cadres kept losing his paperwork. 'I thought marriage was an outmoded, patriarchal, bourgeois institution – imagine my surprise when communists made me get married to the same person twice.' The party leadership also arranged marriages for high-ranking cadres, officially to create a mix of ethnic, regional, and class backgrounds. The end result, though, made the phrase 'Frelimo family' more than just a metaphor.

While an idealised vision of a new society was taking hold in the liberated zones, the military stalemate was beginning to change. Throughout the period of internal strife in Frelimo, Portugal was refining its counter-insurgency tactics, studying the examples of the Americans in

Vietnam and the British in Malaysia. In addition to Portugal's massive military superiority (at the height of the war, it had around 60,000 troops active in Mozambique, compared with the 8,000 to 10,000 Frelimo guerrillas), they constructed *aldeamentos* (fortified villages) to sever contact between the population and the guerrillas, used defoliants to destroy tree cover used by the guerrillas, and increasingly employed African troops – both fresh recruits and guerrillas the military turned to their side – to infiltrate Frelimo areas. Using indigenous troops on the front lines allowed the state to keep Portuguese soldiers out of the line of fire as much as possible in an effort to reduce white casualties. The large numbers of African soldiers, who were considered traitors by Frelimo, proved to be a source of recruits for opposition forces in the later civil war (Minter 1994).

In 1970, the Portuguese launched Operation Gordian Knot, which was intended to destroy Frelimo and the areas it controlled. Although the Portuguese captured many bases, most had already been deserted as Frelimo pulled its troops back and then attacked in the centre of the country. The Portuguese were spending much of their effort in guarding the massive Cahora Bassa dam, the symbol of Portuguese permanence in Africa. Although Frelimo failed in its attempts to destroy the dam, it successfully concentrated Portuguese military strength on the dam's defence, leaving its own soldiers free to spread their attacks in the centre and further south. In Portugal itself, major changes were taking place. After the replacement of Salazar in 1968, Portuguese leaders began to question the necessity of the empire, especially as closer economic ties were being developed with Europe, and these were far more profitable than never-ending wars in far-off corners of the world (Newitt 1981; 1995).

By 1974 it had become obvious that, although the Portuguese were not defeated, they could not win. In addition, the strain of fighting three colonial wars at once was also becoming unbearable. In 1974, left-wing officers formed the MFA (Armed Forces Movement) and overthrew the government of Marcelo Caetano, Salazar's successor. Although more conservative members were opposed to this, the MFA formed a transitional government with Frelimo in 1974 and granted full power to the party as the only legitimate representative of the Mozambican people, without a general election, in 1975.

Conclusion

In this chapter, I have offered a brief and partial history of Mozambique until independence in 1975. The goal was to trace the origins of the themes that I shall examine in the following chapters. In particular, I wanted to focus on the social context that gave rise to a certain form of elite culture that would have such a profound effect on the nation after independence. It was through this culture that the elite, in Cohen's (1981) words, served their own sectional interests, by creating a powerful sense of exclusivity while also attempting to demonstrate that they legitimately represented the universal good by portraying themselves as a vanguard for the eventual transformation of the entire population, leading to prosperity and an end to humiliation. This grand project became deeply influential for an emerging post-independence middle class as it laid the foundations and parameters for the cultural politics of privilege.

The initial outline of the cultural politics of privilege was profoundly influenced by a particular experience with colonialism. The social formation of the Frelimo leadership was shaped by a history of growing disenfranchisement, by a progressive alienation from so-called traditional power structures and norms, and by the state becoming the primary source of social mobility. The privileges available to categories such as *assimilados* were combined with complicity and the humiliation of being conquered by a comparatively poor and weak nation that the other colonial powers often held in contempt. I have often been told by friends in Mozambique when speaking of their history: 'Our tragedy is that we were colonised by the Africa of Europe.' All of these factors were influential in the creation of 'blank slate' ideologies, where the past should be cast aside and the population would be formed into a new, national subject.

Chipkin (2007) argues that African nationalism should be seen not simply as resisting colonialism, but as trying to create something new. While the historical experience of colonialism is, to a degree, unique to Mozambique, this does not mean that the nation is then forever trapped in a form of logic that rigidly determines everything that follows. As we shall see in Chapter 3, the Frelimo leadership was influenced by its own history and struggles, but also by wider ideological currents and a vision for the future that has inspired millions the world over. Frelimo claimed legitimacy and exercised power through a one-party state in a manner that was found throughout the socialist world. However, the party did this while dealing with a particular set of social, economic, and geopolitical circumstances that set the stage for a brutal conflict.

3   Ascendance, 1974–83

At any one time, there are certain groups that are hegemonic, although it should be stressed that however hegemonic a particular power regime may appear, hegemony is never total; it is always, although to varying degrees, a struggle in process. Those groups that have power act, often in extremely subtle ways, to stifle the emergence of understandings of the world that challenge their accounts of reality.   (Crehan 2002: 146)

As argued by Crehan above, the establishment of hegemony is never total but always fraught and contingent. Nor is it a linear process. The basis for hegemony can be severely eroded, often by the actions undertaken in attempts to secure it. In the previous chapter, I discussed the social origins of a transformative project in Mozambique. In this chapter, I focus on the ascendency of Frelimo's social revolution from 1975 to 1983. For Angola, Schubert argues that the nationalist ideology of the ruling MPLA was based on a supra-ethnic, homogenising project, in part to deal with the contradiction of a national leadership dominated by a Creole elite who perceived themselves and were thought of as culturally different from the wider population over which they ruled (2014: 139). In a similar manner, Frelimo's leadership, dominated by southern, former *assimilados*, northern mission-educated military leaders, and multiracial embittered intellectuals, could also be perceived as culturally different to the vast majority of the population. Cultural and social distance, though, do not exist as a given fact outside of time, but are generated, reproduced, and transformed by the structures and power relations of a given society (Wedeen 2008). In the following, I will discuss how Frelimo's efforts to abolish the legacy of colonialism by moulding and disciplining the population in both subtle and overt ways generated new forms of difference. The quest for a homogeneous citizenry was ironically a fundamental factor in the drawing up of new social boundaries.

Frelimo's political project did not simply flow from the leadership to the various sections of the population, creating a new society that moved in perfect step with the vision of a completely united leadership. As with many postcolonial states, the regime's hegemonic ambitions were weakened by a lack of cadres, weak administrative control, and a tremendously socially diverse population spread over vast distances. The goals and practices of the social revolution were fiercely debated internally, and they were interpreted, creatively understood, resisted, and ignored by the wider population. In the following, I discuss Frelimo's often chaotic and contradictory attempts to transform the nation and the narratives and political structures that underlay this effort. I then explore the kind of state that Frelimo formed and the ways in which it attempted to set the parameters of what would be acceptable under the new order, how life should be led, what citizens should be, and the challenges and contradictions such efforts at social engineering created. By tracing the party's efforts to engineer the human soul, I also explore the formation of new social hierarchies and how the goal to build a united populace became the formation of privilege.

The inheritance

Liberation was the result not of an outright Frelimo victory, but rather of a Portuguese military coup caused by fighting three inconclusive wars simultaneously (in Angola, Guinea-Bissau, and Mozambique) and the internal political situation. The fall of the Portuguese new state took Frelimo by surprise. Paulo, a young militant during the liberation war, remembers hearing the news on the radio and rushing to tell Samora Machel that they had won. According to Paulo, Machel's response was surprising. Samora looked at him and said: 'Damn them, they fucked us yet again. We are not ready yet, we have not had time to bring the people with us. They [the Portuguese] have been here for centuries; I thought they could hold on awhile longer. We needed another ten years.' Although this response was unexpected, it provided a realistic summation for the country Samora would soon inherit. Frelimo theoretically controlled large sections of the country, but only a small percentage of the nation's population, and the party held no urban centres. Few people outside what Frelimo called the liberated zones were familiar with the details of the party's programme. How popular the party's social revolution was, and with whom, was an open question.

The first cracks in the fragile foundations of the new Mozambique erupted shortly after the coup. At that time, Frelimo's military forces were concentrated in the north and central parts of Mozambique. Some disaffected Portuguese settlers in the capital who were opposed to independence sensed the power vacuum and rebelled, trying to retain control of Mozambique or at least deny power to Frelimo. The settler movement was known as FICO, which means 'I stay' in Portuguese. On 7 September 1974, FICO took control of the radio station to broadcast its demands. The resulting incitements to rebellion influenced the most extreme elements of FICO, which started to attack the outlying black suburbs of Maputo. This soon degenerated into a killing spree. It seems that FICO hoped to convert elements of the Portuguese military to its cause and/or spark an intervention by neighbouring South Africa. FICO failed to achieve either of these goals and instead provoked a fierce reaction as anger over the killings combined with simmering resentments exploded.

Resistance against FICO was organised spontaneously, and people were soon engaged in bloody street battles (which took on racial dimensions) to put down the countercoup. In political terms, the countercoup was a disaster for the reactionary settlers. They were crushed, and black politicians opposed to Frelimo who were seen to support them were easily branded as traitors. The population came out to support Frelimo and even helped to force the hand of the military government in Portugal, increasing pressure on it to agree to Frelimo's demands to transfer power to the party as the sole legitimate political force in Mozambique (Hall and Young 1997). Yet it was a nervous victory for Frelimo as the chaos that followed the countercoup demonstrated both the party's tenuous control and the very different agendas that many erstwhile supporters may in fact have had and were capable of acting upon independently.

Roberto, whom I introduced in Chapter 2, was 12 years old in 1974. Like many other people in Maputo, he had little concrete knowledge of Frelimo, as the colonial government's information blackout about the party had been relatively effective. Other than snippets of the party's programme heard from occasional illicit gatherings that played Radio Frelimo, everything he knew came from his grandmother, who told him that Frelimo would come and help the blacks. On the day the countercoup erupted, Roberto was playing football with his friends in his *bairro*, Machava, on the outskirts of Maputo. During the game, Roberto noticed trucks full of whites with guns pulling up near where he and his friends were playing. Roberto was not worried because he knew some of the men and he thought they were shooting in the air to scare them. It was not until two of his friends were hit that Roberto began to realise what was happening; he then ran home. That evening, locals who had taken charge of the neighbourhood's defence demanded that every male above the age of ten must come and fight. I asked him if he was scared and he told me that, although he saw horrible things, he was excited. This was his chance to be with the men and do something important.

For Roberto, the fighting was terrifying, but also edifying. Residents of the capital lived far from the struggle and this was their chance to strike a blow for the cause. As Roberto told me: 'We won the battle for Maputo. When Frelimo arrived, victory was already waiting for them.' While Roberto and many others who largely spontaneously took part in fighting the coup considered themselves Frelimo supporters, their actions had little to do with party policy, whose details remained murky for much of the population. Spontaneous action challenged Frelimo's claim to be the sole directing force of resistance and added a racial element that recalled the party's earlier divisions. Furthermore, it highlighted Frelimo's lack of control over the nation, as it took help from Portuguese troops to control the disorder. The party's rhetoric was triumphant, but its hold was fragile.

The state

At the stroke of midnight on 25 June 1975 Samora Machel proclaimed Mozambican independence at the Machava Stadium on the outskirts of Maputo. Those who lived through this period describe the general mood as one of euphoria, and even the daunting task of the total transformation of Mozambique seemed to be within reach. As Naema, a teenager at the time, told me, after the difficulties of the previous decade, it seemed a better world was finally within reach.

> I am from the north, but we came to Maputo when I was very young. My father was Portuguese, but he was arrested during the struggle because he was smuggling weapons for Frelimo. My mother was left destitute and we came to Maputo to be with relatives. Some of them were quite prosperous; we managed to use their contacts to get my father transferred from a jail for political prisoners in the north to an easier one in Maputo. It was rough – we were very poor and dependent on relatives, sometimes I had to stay with them when my mother could not afford to take of care me. Life was very hard, but it seemed now everything would get better.
>
> I was 15 years old when we became independent and I was tremendously excited. Things had been bad during the provisional government, but I was very hopeful for the future. Frelimo had set up parties throughout the city. My mother had attended one of these parties in our neighbourhood. Others of my family, those who had done well under the old regime, stayed home. They were frightened about what would happen to them now and they did not want to be publicly humiliated. As for me, I wanted to go to Machava Stadium, where they were going to have the official ceremony. I went with my sister and my aunt and uncle. When we arrived, the stadium was completely packed with people. My aunt and uncle decided to stay in the car and listen to the ceremony on the radio, but my sister and I squeezed our way in. At midnight, Samora Machel gave his speech declaring independence and they raised our new flag. Everyone went crazy with joy. People were completely overcome with emotion – they were crying and cheering, they could not contain themselves. It was an incredible night.

Whatever lingering doubts remained about the transitional period, the rapturous reception of independence convinced the party leadership of the support for their transformative mission. Recent events had demonstrated that Frelimo faced a crisis of governmentality. The process of building a nation is dependent on the creation of national citizens, deciding who are to be included and who are not, and what kind of interventions are necessary to form the social order (Simone 2010).

Tentative guidelines were provided through what Coelho (2013) calls the 'Liberation Script', a didactic narrative that proclaimed the legitimacy of the new order and provided a roadmap to the society the party wished to build. According to Coelho, the message of the script was as follows:

The efficiency of the Liberation Script as an apparatus that granted the regime its legitimacy and unquestionable character depended on the clarity and straight-forwardness of the corpus, so that it could reach the masses and keep its vigour as a dictum; in other words, its efficiency depended on its simplicity. And simplicity was assured in particular by its linear unfolding on the basis of binary oppositions: fair versus unfair, nationalist versus colonial, revolutionary versus reactionary, modern versus traditional, military versus civil, rural versus urban and so on. Progress depended on the victory of the first element over the second inside each pair ... besides structuring the Script, this binary reasoning had spill-over effects that helped to strengthen the regime in symbolical terms, for example, as the triumph of the rural over the urban or of revolutionary modernity over traditional reactionary culture. (Coelho 2013: 22–3)

The liberation script turned the premises, assumptions, symbols, and goals of the party leadership's social revolution into a set of binary oppositions. It offered a simple guide for how Mozambicans were supposed to understand events, as unfolding in a linear progression of victories always under the guidance and direction of the party.

Although Frelimo may have publicly claimed victory, the challenges facing the new government were immense. The colonial economy was geared towards providing services to wealthier powers, and most transport links were focused on connecting neighbouring territories to Mozambican ports, leaving weak inter-regional networks. In the decades preceding independence, the economy had grown, especially in the 1960s, when the country was supposedly the eighth largest industrial economy in Africa. Much of this growth, however, was financed by speculative capital and achieved through debt. The new government was left with the bill. An estimated 100,000 black Mozambicans participated in organs that supported the Portuguese New State, including those who served in the military and as informers for the secret police (Machava 2011: 600). Despite the proclamation of a multiracial society, the relationship between the party and the majority of the Portuguese population deteriorated and the settler exodus grew. As they left, numerous acts of sabotage were committed. Infrastructure was rendered inoperable, livestock were killed, cement was poured down toilets and drains, and property that could not be moved back to Portugal was destroyed (Bowen 2000; Hall and Young 1997). Frelimo came to power with a strong belief in centralisation and state intervention, but the flight of the Portuguese forced the party to move in an interventionist direction far more quickly than had originally been anticipated (Pitcher 2002).

Additionally, Mozambique soon had a full-blown employment crisis. The abandonment of Portuguese farms and the dismantling of previous controls on mobility facilitated a massive movement to the cities, especially Maputo (Bowen 2000; Pinsky 1982). When Frelimo cut economic ties with the white minority regime of Rhodesia in accordance with international sanctions, and gave support to Zimbabwean liberation movements, the already struggling economy took a severe blow. This was combined with military retaliation by the Rhodesians, bringing Mozambique to a state of war in the central regions (Hall and Young 1997). Apartheid South Africa began to cut back on recruiting Mozambican miners, an economic mainstay for the south of the country, and the government lost an important form of revenue through salaries paid at favourable rates to them. Finally, the exodus of the Portuguese also decimated rural commercial networks, causing severe shortages throughout the countryside, which Frelimo's agricultural policies often exacerbated (Bowen 2000).

The cities in general and Maputo in particular could ill afford the influx of new residents. While there was a burgeoning rural economic crisis, conditions in the city were also difficult. Shortly after independence, a so-called 24/20 decree was imposed. Anyone in possession of foreign or dual citizenship was ordered to renounce immediately any other ties and apply for Mozambican citizenship, or they had 24 hours to leave the country, and they could take 20 kilograms of personal possessions with them. The vast majority of the remaining Portuguese population left. Frelimo was left to run a bankrupt country with virtually no trained people. The illiteracy rate was over 90 per cent. There were 6 economists, 2 agronomists, not a single geologist, and fewer than a 1,000 black high school graduates in all of Mozambique. Of the 350 railway engineers working in 1975, just 1 was black, and he had been an agent of the PIDE (Finnegan 1992: 30). By 1976, industrial enterprises came to a standstill due to a lack of materials, spare parts, and technical skills (Pinsky 1982: 6). In a bid to reform urban social relations, in 1976 Frelimo nationalised all rental housing, encompassing 25,000 housing units in Maputo alone (Pinsky 1982). The goal was to end the practice of speculative rent and to begin to transfer urban residents from the slums (which contained 80 per cent of the city's residents and could presumably be counted on to support Frelimo) to abandoned properties in the city centre (ibid.: 16). While this did change the social composition of the city, the housing construction industry ground to a halt. Frelimo was trying to create a new society, radically different from what preceded it, but this ambitious goal had to be carried out with a weak and bankrupt state apparatus, amidst economic crisis and falling living standards, while remaining at the mercy of powerful and hostile neighbours and international institutions.

The party initially tried to overcome the crises it faced by popular mobilisation. Frelimo had long preached *poder popular* (people's power), which promised a form of direct democracy. Through *poder popular* the party would be an expression of the popular will while radically transforming existing social relations and hierarchies from above. Frelimo was engaged in the cultural construction of the state (Bickford 2011): the ways in which power was to be understood and used to transform social relations. But grand transformative projects do not occur in a vacuum; they have to build on what actually exists. In urban areas, former mechanisms of social control from the colonial era had collapsed, Frelimo had few long-serving cadres, and the party leadership was not sure if they could trust the many claimants who presented themselves at the moment of victory. Starting in September 1974, when Frelimo first began to enter urban areas, it organised *Grupos Dinamizadores* (Dynamising Groups or GDs) in neighbourhoods, factories, institutions, and the bureaucracy (Andersen, Jenkins, and Nielsen 2015b). The goal of the GDs was to extend Frelimo's control into areas that it had not managed to mobilise during the struggle and to get the moribund machinery of the state apparatus and economy moving again. Whenever possible, the party nominated trusted militants, but their numbers were insufficient. Frelimo therefore turned to so-called natural leaders, those who were seen to be already active in their communities (Pinsky 1982: 12). Nominated candidates were confirmed in public meetings, although party officials had the ultimate say (Hall and Young 1997).

In addition to the so-called natural leaders, Frelimo was committed to overthrowing what the party saw as the gerontocratic, patriarchal hierarchy of the old regime. The party attempted to draw people who would have been previously marginalised – such as the young, women, the poor, and those who tended to enthusiastically support Frelimo – into positions of responsibility. Naema, who was introduced at the beginning of the chapter, became involved with her local GD while she was still a high school student.

In the beginning I was pretty idealistic, so were most of the young people. Independence was like a breath of fresh air. We could finally talk about things. During the struggle, I would occasionally see the word Frelimo written on a wall. When I asked what it meant, my family told me to be quiet and never say that word because it was dangerous and I could get into trouble. That just made me want to know more. Now Frelimo was everywhere and the party said that we, the young, were important and gave us responsibility. The party had to – not all of the old people were happy with the new government. My father fought for Frelimo, but my grandfather was high up in a bank and so was my uncle; many fled to Portugal after Frelimo took power. My mother had told me that when my father was released from prison everything would be better, but that is not how it turned out. The party gave him a house, a car and a job in gratitude for his services, but he started drinking a lot and he eventually left us and started a new family. Money was still very tight and it was hard to get books to study. Despite everything, though I was very active; I joined the GD and various school committees. We organised people to clean the streets and take care of the houses. There were some difficulties; I may have had some power outside the house, but my mother still ran things inside the house. We are Muslims, and she did not like me always being called to meetings, especially because some were at night and had both boys and girls. My mother also refused to do communal cleaning. She was not going to clean for strangers. She had grown up with a maid – also I think as an Indian, she did not want to clean for blacks. Although she would not go to any meetings, she let me have a few at the house. She would sit quietly, but she did not complain even though she thought they were a waste of time.

The early independence period was characterised by contradictions; as demonstrated by Naema, there was hope among the young and other groups who previously felt marginalised, even if their elders were more wary. While enthusiasm was high, living conditions were often grim, there was general economic chaos as the Portuguese fled the country, industrial know-how and capital were in short supply, and there was violent hostility from powerful neighbours. However, despite recurring crises, the early revolutionary period was characterised by an upsurge in social mobility. The party's determination to overturn the old order and entrust responsibility to new actors was combined with an exodus of the Portuguese. This meant that almost all of the professional and managerial positions in the country were left vacant and Mozambicans who had any type of qualification or basic education were promoted to the colonialists' former positions. Those who were close to the party and could access its structures, the young, women, and those who could claim a peasant or worker background (even if this was not entirely accurate) benefited from positive discrimination in education and jobs; such people became the *emergentes* (emergent) referred to in Chapter 1. Social mobility, though, was largely focused in party and state structures, meaning that the bureaucracy began to surpass Frelimo's commitments to workers and peasants as the party's theoretical social base (Bowen 2000).

The period from 1975 to 1977 was considered by many to be a liberal one when, despite official prohibitions, the lucky and the connected were able to accumulate wealth, possessions, and privilege with relative freedom, at least compared with what followed. However, the party leadership wanted far more dramatic and wide-reaching changes. The crises of the immediate post-independence period did not dampen their ambition; rather, it convinced them of the need to press on with their social revolution with redoubled vigour. In 1977, Frelimo held its third party congress and announced that it was transforming itself from a broad liberation front into a Marxist-Leninist vanguard party. The transformation of the party was done, in part, to gain access to support from the Soviet Bloc (Hall and Young 1997), but it was also to discipline party and state organs, which the regime felt were slipping from its grasp. The Frelimo party state was presented by its members as a monolith, whose goal was to reforge social relations with itself as the mediator. Despite structural transformations, the party's ability to command compliance with its stated vision was sporadic and its militants' understanding of what that vision meant varied widely.

In desperation, Samora Machel frequently attacked what he felt was the infiltration of reactionaries, former PIDE agents, opportunists, and self-seekers into party and state institutions to subvert Frelimo's goals (Buur 2010; Pinsky 1982). Officially, the revolution was to be guided by the people and their lived experience. With the advent of the vanguard party, this began to change. The new watchword was discipline. Rui was a teenager during the socialist period. Although he idolised Samora, he thought that there were serious problems. The security services were very strict; he said that there was a curfew that came into effect at 10 p.m., as supposedly there was no reason for anyone to be out later than that. According to Rui, the officials of the new state often abused their power. Members of the GD were often informers and they could denounce anyone. If there was a quarrel, or if someone aroused the jealously of a member of the GD or spurned their advances, they could simply denounce the person as an 'enemy of the people', who would then be dealt with officially.

Rui's concerns highlight another contradiction of the early independence period. While the fear of informers was almost universal, and, as we shall see in Chapter 4, people lived in fear of being denounced by their neighbour, many also claimed that the hardships of the time brought them closer together. Fatima moved to Maputo shortly after independence and remembers it as a difficult time:

It was very hard; the stores were closed and you could not get anything. I was new here [in Maputo] and did not know many people, there was no one to help me. I was working at a bank, but I had to quit when we had my first child. My husband had a professional job and he taught nights, but his salary was pathetic. We had to scrounge just to get bread. There were government rations, but it was never enough. You had to hustle to survive. My sister would occasionally send us food from the provinces and it was like a party when it arrived. Gradually things got better though. Life was so difficult that everyone had to depend on each other. We made friends and we were all very close; we were always together and we shared what we could. The weeks were so tough that you just dreamed of the weekends. We just went to each other's houses – there was not all that much else to do and the communists [Frelimo, but especially referring to the party leadership] were very strict. They even cancelled Christmas for a few years. But we would make dinners with whatever we could find. If I somehow got a piece of meat, I would not keep it for myself or my family, but immediately call my friends and have a party.

Many of those I know had fond recollections of house parties during the socialist period. In line with the overall atmosphere of austere puritanism that was typical of the early days of the revolution, many were tame affairs in comparison with the raucous nightclub scene of modern-day Maputo, with the festivities fuelled by whatever limited quantities of beer, soft drinks, and food people could get their hands on. What became clear from so many stories of people sleeping ten together at someone's house so as not to break curfew, and the complicated chains of affection, sharing, and mutual dependence necessary for survival, was the formation of an 'us' among an emerging group who, though not members of the top leadership, were privileged, but whose lives were characterised by privation. These relationships enabled people to survive the socialist period and the civil war, and they are still prevalent today. The tight networks of both real and elective kin created an immense sense of cohesion and tightly policed boundaries between 'us' and 'them'. However, while these relationships permeated the private domain, public life was marked by a quest for conformity, and control would supposedly encompass not only the party, the state, and the population, but even time, as the economy would be disciplined through the five-year plan (Coelho 2013). In the words of Coelho: 'If with independence the rural had invaded the urban, now the opposite was about to happen, with the new order radiating from the city capital Maputo to the provinces and the rural areas' (ibid.: 23–4). Maputo would now be the source of a grand disciplinary project, flowing into the countryside to forge a new citizenry, however haphazardly and imperfectly in practice.

Frelimo in the early independence period was similar to what Mbembe has termed the 'Theologian State': that is, 'a state which is preoccupied not only with practices concerning the distribution of power and influence, social relations, economical arrangements and political processes. It is also [a state] which aspires explicitly at defining for social agents the way they have to see themselves, interpret themselves and interpret the world' (cited in Machava 2011: 597). As society became based on a more rigid hierarchy, those who could adapt were able to secure positions of privilege. These included party cadres and both true believers and opportunists who developed the cultural capital to understand the citizen-building project and adapt themselves to it – or at least publicly appear to do so. Those who did not adapt were viewed by the party as potential enemies, an ever-present threat to Frelimo's hegemony.

As with other Marxist movements in Africa, socialism came with officially sponsored attacks on elements of traditional culture that were viewed by the party leadership as impediments to the building of new nations (see Davidson 1984). Samora Machel explained his party's motivation as follows:

When Frelimo took up arms to defeat the old order ... We felt the obscure need to create a new society, strong healthy and prosperous, in which people freed from all exploitation would co-operate for the progress of all. In the course of our struggle, in the tough fight we had to wage against reactionary elements, we came to understand our objectives more clearly. We felt especially that the struggle to create new structures would fall within the creation of a new mentality. (Davidson 1984: 800)

Samora Machel spoke in the terms of nationalist mobilisation for sweeping change, yet the underlying message was that the ideas for the new society would flow from the party to the population, and it was the people who would have to adapt to them. During the socialist period, the blending of the roles of party, state, and nation was official policy. The state was declared subordinate to the party, membership was often overlapping, and in a dispute one's position in the party hierarchy often trumped that of state office. The military and the security services were seen as the armed wing of Frelimo and their duty was to defend the revolution, as the nation was considered to be an extension of the revolutionary process. In classic Stalinist fashion, the new men were to lead the transformation and the peasantry would bear the brunt of it.

Economically, the peasantry was seen by the leadership as *tabula rasa*: they supposedly existed in a timeless state of subsistence agriculture. Therefore, all available resources could be focused on industrial projects and industrialised agriculture (O'Laughlin 2000). Between 1975 and 1983, around 97 per cent of rural investment was channelled to massive state farms (ibid.). This coincided with the collapse of rural shops and trading posts due to the Portuguese exodus, and there was soon a 'goods famine' in the countryside, where even necessary basic implements such as hoes were almost impossible to find. Many peasants soon stopped selling surpluses, as there was little for them to buy, creating food shortages. Furthermore, Frelimo's plans ignored the complicated economic strategies that existed for much of the peasantry, combining migrant labour with agriculture, and did not recognise the social differentiation that existed in the countryside (Bowen 2000). As an unintended consequence, Frelimo's strategies began to increase differentiation among the peasantry, as those with party connections or those who were better able to manipulate policies secured benefits that were denied to others.

If the peasantry were *tabula rasa* economically for the party leadership, socially they were the embodiment of everything that held the nation back, and they had to be recreated as modern citizens for a modern nation. In the leadership's view, society in general and the peasantry in particular had internalised oppression due to the brutality of colonialism and because of the 'backward' nature of the family, which supposedly made the patriarch all-powerful within his limited domain (Sheldon 2002: 131–5). The goal of the social revolution was to root out the political and cultural practices that made oppression possible and destroy them. Traditional leadership was abolished, as the party leadership viewed it as a corrupt colonial institution and a source of what was termed rural feudalism. Polygamous men were denied entry into the party, and *lobola* (bridewealth) was abolished so that women would be free of 'family feudalism' and, in Samora's words, 'no longer be traded like goods in a shop' (Sheldon 2002). Young people and women were appointed to positions of local importance so as to break the hold of the older, supposedly conservative and male gerontocracy that had traditionally held authority. Ceremonies were banned, religious organisations and institutions were viewed with suspicion, practitioners of sorcery could be sent to re-education camps, and efforts were made to move the peasantry from their former scattered hamlets to centralised communal villages, which would become cities in the bush. Intense effort was focused on combating what was termed superstition or obscurantism, and to replace this with rationality and scientific socialism. All the former structures of power were to be broken and dismantled, leaving only Frelimo.

The reaction to Frelimo's social revolution varied throughout the country. In some parts, its projects were relatively successful. Norman (2004) recounts how, following the destruction of homes in a flood and a pre-existing distrust of traditional authority, Frelimo's plans to move villagers to communal villages and abolish traditional authority were not unpopular in the southern province of Gaza, a Frelimo stronghold. In the Mueda Plateau of Cabo Delgado, which was termed the 'cradle of the revolution' as it had been a central base in the liberation struggle, the effects were contradictory. West (2001) describes how aspects of villagisation programmes were welcomed and the concentration of large groups of people created new avenues of sociability, yet they were also accompanied by accusations of witchcraft as previous sanctions against sorcery proved ineffective for a large population. Reactions to Frelimo's grand ambitions often depended on finely nuanced local conditions, and the different ways in which particular areas were incorporated into the economy and the nation were rarely taken into account by planners in Maputo.

Shortly after independence, Rhodesia began to train and provide support to Mozambican dissidents in retaliation for Frelimo's support of the ZANU-PF liberation movement and in hopes of destabilising a majority-ruled Marxist neighbour. Initially, Mozambican dissidents in Renamo[1] acted as auxiliaries to Rhodesian forces in military actions in Mozambique. By 1977, Renamo was conducting attacks on its own, although benefiting from Rhodesian logistical support. While Renamo

---

[1] Originally, Renamo was known by the English acronym MNR (Mozambique National Resistance), but this was soon changed to downplay Renamo's associations with Rhodesia.

was created as a military movement through its associations with Rhodesian intelligence and, after Zimbabwean independence, acting under apartheid South African patronage with devastating effect, it was able over time to build bases of support in some areas of Mozambique and fashion its own system of signification. Renamo explained that it was engaged in a 'war of the spirits' and intended to reclaim 'traditions' from the alien Marxism of Frelimo. Renamo supporters such as Hoile (1994) and Cabrita (2000) have argued that the civil war in Mozambique grew out of a peasant response to an alien, urban, Creole Frelimo elite that insulted and suppressed the population's traditions and destroyed their supposedly timeless way of life. In a less propagandistic vein, scholars such as Geffray (1991) have also pointed out the deep discontent caused by Frelimo's policies of abolishing traditional authority, moving rural populations into communal villages, and starving peasants of investment in certain areas of the country. The social contract that was the foundation of Frelimo's rule promised a glorious future dependent on the transformation of Mozambicans into new national subjects. The past and the present were to be sacrificed to achieve this goal. Such rhetoric was tied to a specific narrative view of reality and a promise of what was to come. This was an ideological vision that appealed to some sections of the population, although interpretations of what this meant in practice varied widely as the present became ever more arduous as the promised radiant future continued to recede.

Citizenship and nation building

If, as argued by Bickford (2011), the state is a statement of its own cultural construction, then the concept of citizenship is the core of such a statement. While every state is composed of varied – and, at times, competing – assemblages, the symbol of a good citizen demonstrates a unity of purpose. The officially promoted practices that define a good citizen embody the message the state is trying to send as to how social relationships are to be maintained or transformed under its direction, what behaviours make certain citizens exemplars to be emulated and what puts one beyond the moral boundaries of the community. Citizenship defines 'the people', who are the source of the state's power and in whose name the state speaks, and is a central component of Frelimo's system of signification. For Agamben (2000: 31), the concept of the people is an attempt to create a 'pure source of identity [which has yet] to be redefined and [which purifies] itself continuously according to exclusion, language, blood, and territory'. While Frelimo was also concerned with continuous purification, the endless process of refining the pure and good citizen from the enemy, the common denominators of blood and language were of less use. Mozambique at independence was a mosaic of different languages, social structures, myths of origin, and moral imaginaries that had been cobbled together by colonial administrative control, however thin and incomplete that control had been in much of Mozambique's territory. For the incoming Frelimo government, the official view of citizenship was not imagined as the binding of some sort of primordial essence, but instead as a process still unfolding, with the party acting as midwife.

According to one of Frelimo's leading theorists, Sergio Vieira, the true citizenship of the authentic national subject would be based on science, 'rationality', and collective labour, but this subject was still in the process of being born (1977: 25). True citizenship was a process whereby, through an individual act of will, one joined the wider collective under Frelimo's leadership. According to the party, the previous social order as expressed by both colonialism and tradition was illegitimate (Coelho 2004). If the past, writ large, was a cause of degradation, then only Frelimo, with its experience of building a new society through the liberation struggle, was a source of legitimate authority (ibid.). Participation in the social revolution and the adoption of this world view led to a lack of exteriority to the party's system of signification, even if such a person was a critic of Frelimo's actions. All other sources of knowledge and social organisation were illegitimate and they were bound tightly to the party and its modernist political projects. Those who challenged Frelimo or upheld alternative sources of legitimacy ran the risk of being labelled enemies of the people (Machava 2011). This, in the words of Mouffe (2005) and Schmitt (1985), defined the political limit of citizenship in early post-independence Mozambique – the line that separated those who were to be included as good or true citizens from those who would be excluded as the other or an enemy.

One of the defining characteristics of the official definition of full Mozambican citizenship after liberation in 1975 was loyalty to Frelimo and commitment to its social revolution (Buur 2010; Dinerman 2006). At independence, some groups, including party members, Frelimo soldiers, and 'the masses' (not what members of this ill-defined group actually were, but what they were supposed to become) were, in Chipkin's terms, 'authentic national subjects' (2007). Other social groups, including those who had worked in the Portuguese administration, such as the military or the security services, or anyone who could be branded a collaborator, were inherently suspect and often treated quite brutally. An inability or unwillingness to adapt to the new society and join the collective was seen as a failure of individual will. Such failure was symbolised by the figure of Xiconhoca. Xico is the diminutive of Francisco and *nhoca* means snake, so 'Frankie the snake' became a signifier that combined familiarity with treachery (Coelho 2004: 7) and appeared in national newspapers as a pedagogical cartoon strip. Xiconhoca was variously depicted as a drunkard, a corrupt bureaucrat, a lazy worker always angling for more pay, an agitator, an abuser of women, a traitor, a drug user, and more. He was the embodiment of everything that Frelimo deemed necessary to be eradicated for the new society to take shape (Buur 2010; Coelho 2004). The wide, ever-increasing range of attributes he symbolised raised the possibility that no one could actually be the pure social subject needed for the new society. If being a reactionary was based on individual behaviour and insufficient will, this opened up the possibility that anyone was a potential traitor, no matter what their background or history. Stark social binaries characterised the early socialist period, as the party's primary emphasis was on ideology, morality, violence, and punishment (Machava 2011: 594). The newly established re-education camps would police the political limit by reforming those who continued to be 'wicked', acted against the party, or 'flaunted' their attachment to the old ways. Theoretically, the re-education camps would instil Frelimo's narrative and values into dissidents. Such efforts appear to have been counterproductive in practice. Conditions were harsh (the slang term for inmates was 'crocodile food'), creating pools of opposition. Renamo took full advantage of this, targeting camps and recruiting inmates in the early period of the civil war.

With enemies constantly being discovered, it was necessary to clearly demonstrate what a good citizen should be. In rural areas, this often consisted of those who joined *aldeias comunais* (communal villages),[2] which were the cornerstone of the party's rural development policy. Here, the state would theoretically be able to reform social relations, provide services, and create the new man who broke with the past and diligently laboured under the direction of the party, not for personal gain but to build the nation (Buur 2010). A vast transformation would have to occur in urban areas as well in order to overturn the legacy of colonial degradation. As with rural areas, to become a new man one had to purge oneself of the past to create something new. While the origins of Frelimo's transformative project drew on the particular social experience of the party elite, it was also shaped by intellectual currents that were coursing through the postcolonial world. A prime example is Frantz Fanon. Fanon, one of the prophets of anti-imperialism and a psychologist by training, described how indigenous cultures, in his view, inevitably began to crumble under foreign onslaught as colonised populations

---

[2] The communal villages were very similar to the *aldeamentos* (protected villages) built by the Portuguese during the liberation struggle to break contact between rural populations and Frelimo. They were often constructed on the same sites (Buur 2010; Hall and Young 1997). During the liberation struggle, Frelimo denounced protected villages as concentration camps, an irony not lost on many people herded into them.

internalised racist ideologies and identified with the dominant culture of the colonial state (1967).

Fanon was particularly dubious about the role of African elites. Having been educated under the colonial system, he felt that they would equate civilisation with the metropolitan culture and view the mass of their own populations as backward (1963; 1967). Yet there was no easy answer to the question of how to counter this kind of slavish imitation. Fanon argued that a cultural revival of precolonial forms would be pointless. These forms had been corrupted beyond repair and were simply another form of mystification to lull the masses with past glories, while leaving them trapped in colonial or neo-colonial relations (1967). Fanon theorised that the only way to create a new and viable form for colonised countries was through the purifying violence of a liberation struggle. Only then would a new and free national culture be born (Wolf 1973). The dividing line between the past and the present is always porous, though, even for the promised new national culture created by the protracted violence of a liberation struggle.

Fry (2000) argues that socialism in Mozambique followed an *assimilado* logic:

In spite of the anti-colonial discourse of the center and FRELIMO in general, it is impossible not to observe that the socialist project for Mozambique was if anything more 'assimilationist' than the Portuguese ever dared to imagine and it is tempting to suggest that this is one of the reasons why the Mozambican elite found the socialist program so attractive. Structurally speaking there was little difference between an authoritarian capitalist state run by a small body of 'illuminated' Portuguese and *assimilados* and an authoritarian socialist state run by an equally diminutive and equally enlightened vanguard party. (Fry 2000: 129)

Fry makes an important point by recognising some of the ideological continuities between *assimilação* and the post-independence socialist project. In its quest to build a new society, the Frelimo leadership built from pre-existing assumptions and beliefs. The necessity of personal transformation as a way to end 'backwardness', the championing of particular kinds of family and marriage, the denigration of the peasantry, the insecurity of status and dependence on access to the state in the new society, and the public performance of a rigid moral code all had similarities to *assimilação*. These beliefs and cultural practices, as noted by Fry, made Frelimo's social revolution attractive to certain segments of the population – those whose social background meant that they were already familiar with elements of the party's symbolic vocabulary and systems of signification. Frelimo's socialism, however, was more than just Portuguese colonialism on steroids. Previous structures were imbued with new, far more totalising meaning. The transformative project of the social revolution was not restricted solely to a few favoured

sons of colonialism but would theoretically encompass the entire population, willingly or otherwise. Frelimo tried to establish what Yurchak has
called 'the hegemony of representation', as 'a symbolic order of tightly
interconnected signifiers that were exclusively state controlled and permeated most aspects of everyday life in the official sphere' (1997: 166).
The meaning and utility of these signifiers to the population at large were
in doubt. The combination of trying to reform a potentially hostile
peasantry, attempting to abolish traditional leadership structures, and
guarding the party from the infiltration of opportunists also shaped the
practices of the social revolution, accentuating a reliance on coercion and
the militarisation of the party hierarchy. Being outside the party's orbit
meant one was an enemy, but even those who wholeheartedly supported
Frelimo faced the danger of being denounced as opportunists or internal
enemies.

Insecurity of status was a constant factor, even for many relatively
privileged citizens, as the party leadership viewed themselves as under
siege from both within and without (Hall and Young 1997: 52). This was
due to the party's overall weakness, but also to the specific type of
Marxist class analysis. Class, as it expressed itself in public speeches or
rallies, was more than just a relationship to the means of production. It
was also a type of moral relationship to the nation (Hall and Young 1997:
65–6). As stated by Henriksen, 'Frelimo castigates capitalism more as a
wicked instinct than as a mode of production' (quoted in Hall and Young
1997: 66). Class enemies and agents of imperialism were not defined
solely by class status, but also by personal behaviour. Those who used
drugs, went about badly dressed or had long hair, criminals, prostitutes,
or those who wanted higher wages and went on strike were all seen as
imperialist agents and enemies of the people and had to be swept away
for the growth of a new society (Hall and Young 1997: 66). While this
effort was often deeply repressive in practice, it was a system of
signification that held out the appeal of future prosperity through selfless
dedication and personal transformation. As a former high-ranking
Frelimo official told me: 'To be called a new man by Samora Machel
was truly thrilling, we were going to build a new nation, part of a new
world, everything was urgent ... we lived in a permanent state of exult-
ation.' Furthermore, even the moral stain of having a family member who
was an 'enemy of the people' need not be a permanent black mark. Nuno
grew up in a Frelimo family; his grandfather had studied in Kenya during
the colonial period and joined Frelimo in the early days of the independence struggle as a high-ranking cadre. While his grandfather was passion-
ately pro-independence, he opposed Samora Machel and socialism.
After the radical faction consolidated power, Nuno's grandfather was
declared an enemy of the people and executed. His family stopped using
their last name due to its associations, and his father and uncle were

mercilessly taunted in school as the sons of an infamous traitor. Nuno's father was something of a rebel; he refused to join the party and wanted to study, but was instead conscripted, and later became a member of the security services in a provincial capital where Nuno's mother was a low-level civil servant. Nuno's uncle, in contrast, dedicated himself to the party, becoming in Nuno's terms '110 per cent Frelimo'. Frelimo ensured his uncle's education, and provided him with employment and the opportunity for advancement. He became a high-ranking official based in Maputo, serving the party that killed his father. The insecurity of status and the sense that anyone could be a traitor also spurred people to greater loyalty.

The making of the new man

The adoption of a Marxist-Leninist vanguard model in 1977 led to a more technocratic and hierarchical political order with privileges focused in certain social strata. James Ferguson argues that, for South Africa, in a situation where personhood is often seen as a relational concept instead of the autonomous individual of liberal ideology, dependence can create larger relationships and mutual obligations in hierarchical social orders (2013). While such systems can be paternalistic, brutal, and exploitative, they are people-hungry; the goal is to increase the membership of the polity, and, while this is based on subordination, there is the promise of security and even upward mobility. In Mozambique, one had a paradoxical situation: there was a constant search for enemies and the need to purge the body politic was always present in the early period (Buur 2010), yet the new political system needed workers, administrators, farmers, cadres, and soldiers and was committed to transforming the entire population to bring them within its orbit. The grand result was frequent purges accompanied by dramatic upward mobility for those who were considered loyal.

An example of this new social mobility is Chuabo. Chuabo was born in 1964 in one of the poorest and most remote provinces in northern Mozambique. His village was near an Anglican mission that also had the best school in the area. Most of the students, including Chuabo, came from rural backgrounds, but due to the education they received and the opportunities created after the revolution, many subsequently became high-level cadres. In 1977, the best students, often those from disadvantaged backgrounds, were selected to study in Cuba, and Chuabo was picked to go. First, they were sent to Maputo for orientation. The trip had quite an effect on him: 'It was the first time I ever took a plane and Maputo was the biggest city I had ever seen. I met people from all over the country, from different provinces, backgrounds and cultures. It was an amazing time.'

Upon his return from Cuba, Chuabo gained a government post and was gradually promoted from provincial capitals until he obtained a high-ranking position in Maputo, a long way from the village in which he was born. A primary factor of the new social mobility was education. Investing in education served a variety of needs for the party: it increased the desperately low level of technical skills held by the population, it gained the party popularity, and in Frelimo's role as a theologian state, it provided the party a pulpit from which to spread its transformative message to shape and discipline 'the masses'. As seen with Chuabo, education and the opportunities and social mobility that went with it helped create a wider sense of belonging and identification with the nation-building project.

Education served as a potent political symbol in almost all postcolonial nations, and this was probably especially acute for Lusophone Africa. The Portuguese had made few provisions for African education during their rule and the rate of illiteracy at independence was staggering (Hanlon 1990; Newitt 1995). Those who already had some education were poised for a dramatic social rise. In symbolic terms, the lack of educational provision during the colonial period was a bitter reminder of the exclusion of the vast majority of the population from positions of status. Education was to be the foundation of all of the wider goals of the struggle (Mondlane 1969). The educational sector was to be a crucial enactment of governmentality, in Simone's (2010) terms. Through education, ideology could be made flesh, and it was education that would allow the emergence of the new man, free from the chains of the past. Frelimo defined its system's educational goals as follows:

The New System of Education has as its central objective the formation of the New Man, a man free from obscurantism, superstition, and the colonial-bourgeois mentality, a man who will assume the values of a socialist society. (People's Republic of Mozambique 1985, quoted in Gómez 1999: 356)[3]

Education during the socialist period was a prime expression of Frelimo's social revolution, based on the idea that Mozambique was unformed clay (after the eradication of inappropriate cultural behaviours) waiting to be shaped. Frelimo's educational policies would ideally bind the populace more tightly to the party and serve as a means of transmitting the values of the social revolution to the people. In practice, education's role as the midwife of a new society was both emancipatory and repressive. While Frelimo promised that it would educate the masses to create opportunities, modernise the population, and free it from gerontocracy and patriarchy, this could only happen within the narrow confines of the leadership's transformative project – and deviation from

---

[3] Translation by the author.

this project was not tolerated. Social mobility was combined with repressive puritanism, as can be seen in the example of one woman who became pregnant as an unmarried secondary school student. As she was from a high-ranking family, she was allowed to continue her studies, but first she was sent to schools across the country to be paraded as a warning of the moral dangers of 'promiscuity'. Echoes of *assimilação* were evident as Portuguese was the only medium of instruction and students were punished for speaking African languages (in Mozambican Portuguese, African languages are often referred to as 'dialects', while the various tongues of Europe qualify as languages). The educational system in independent Mozambique remained authoritarian and hierarchical despite the egalitarian rhetoric of the new government, and was later thought to be a source of many of the revolutionary period's failures. A former high-ranking official explained to me that:

Those were very exciting days. We were sure that we could do a better job than the Portuguese had. They were foreigners and they wanted to exploit the country for their own purposes. We were Mozambican and we were going to make things better for our people. We were very ambitious and very young; we had immense responsibilities for people our age. That was part of the problem I guess. We wanted to educate the nation, but we were barely educated ourselves.

If education was the hallmark of the social revolution, it soon also became rife with contradiction between Frelimo's utopian aspects of the social revolution and the boundary making of a consolidating elite. The party state did make dramatic gains in education. Schools were opened throughout the country and in urban areas adult education was available for all (and in some cases obligatory). Those who could read and write were enlisted as 'barefoot' teachers in emulation of revolutionary Cuba and China's literacy campaigns (Hanlon 1990). The new teaching conditions were not always ideal; experience in the revolution was initially considered to be an important qualification for the struggle to create national citizens, especially as qualified teachers were a rarity. As a Mozambican friend, who attended school shortly after liberation before she left for Portugal, explained to me:

It was a strange time. Former guerrilla soldiers would just come to schools and start classes. Many of them did not have any education, but they had just freed the nation from the Portuguese and they thought that was enough. They would sit in front of the students and just talk about their lives. They thought that was teaching. Even the other teachers had almost no experience. Many of them were very young and they just had a few years of school themselves. My teachers and I learned how to read together.

Others, while not commenting on the academic quality of the educational system, strongly appreciated its nationalist character. According to Naema, who was a secondary student at the time:

When Frelimo came and got rid of the Portuguese we were all rejoicing, especially the young. We were going to build a new Mozambique. They would come to schools and teach us about our new country. They [Frelimo] would often have demonstrations, everyone would hold a placard and together it would form the flag, you know like the North Koreans do. I was always picked for the demonstrations; I was very small and cute. They would also give those who took part in the demonstrations lunch and it could be hard to get food then. We would do voluntary cleaning in the city on Sundays; they wanted us to be good citizens.

The efforts to form a new kind of citizen, one dedicated to the struggle and the common good, gave Frelimo's social revolution moral legitimacy with many people. The lofty goals of the revolution were frequently undermined by its authoritarian practices. In the early period, however, such contradictions could be conceptualised as the faults of the party state, which could appear as separate from the figure of the leader, Samora Machel. He was the charismatic face and embodiment of the revolution whose dictates and meaning were communicated to the urban population through mass rallies, events that were crucial for creating party-dominated forms of urban belonging (Coelho 2004). Machel and the transformative project could even be seen as a balance to the ambitions of an overweening state and its tyrannical agents.

Osvaldo was born in 1969 in Maputo. He comes from an old southern *assimilado* family that was well off during the colonial period. His elder brother had been a member of the Portuguese scouts, despite the fact that it was almost unheard of to be able to enter this organisation if one were black. His father worked with the Portuguese army and also owned several houses. He derived a good portion of his income from the rents from his properties. Independence was a traumatic event for the family; they stayed in their house listening to the sounds of the riots outside and worried about their father, who was with the Portuguese military. Many of his relatives fled the country, although his father stayed because he was happy about some aspects of independence. Despite Osvaldo's father's guarded welcome of Frelimo, he was declared an enemy of the people and most of his properties were nationalised. The family's fortunes declined and his father ended up working at the state-owned brewery. Osvaldo had conflicting emotions about the socialist period in Mozambique. On the one hand, he said it was 'too communist', government officials were everywhere, you were not allowed to publicly voice disagreement, and the right to private property was severely limited. On the other, as a child he had worshipped Samora Machel. He fondly remembered an occasion when Samora gave an impromptu speech at his school. During this visit, Samora brought the headmaster on stage and proceeded to give him a brutal dressing down in front of the students for the fact that the school was in such a state of disrepair. The students considered the headmaster a terror and his humiliation contributed to a

Figure 3.1 Samora Machel greeting supporters.
Source: TiConUno s.r.l. / Alamy Stock Photo.

day of joy that demonstrated that there was someone who could offer protection from arbitrary, dictatorial authority. Samora's speeches were famously marathon affairs, sometimes running up to six hours or more, but, according to Osvaldo, they were not boring and it was obvious that Machel really cared about the people.

Frelimo, as with most Marxist-Leninist movements, struggled with what Yurchak has defined as the central paradox of Leninism: absolute freedom and total equality are the result of utter subordination to the party (2006). The centralisation of power and claim to specialist knowledge necessary to direct a social revolution whose goal was total transformation also began to create new hierarchies and forms of domination, despite Frelimo's egalitarian pretension. Education, which was central to the formation of a new kind of citizen, also became a major boundary between the elite and privileged. The revolutionary government made concerted efforts to bring its ideal of education to the nation as a whole, although, as previously stated, this was done in a rather chaotic manner. As with other socialist nations in Africa, such as Angola and Tanzania, education was rapidly expanded, but the infrastructure to absorb increasing numbers of students was inadequate (Hodges 2001; Samoff 1979). In the attempt to provide teachers, many were not properly trained. Furthermore, even in the capital, according to many informants, schools were overcrowded and classes huge. The demand was so great that many schools had to run throughout the day and evening in shifts, a practice that continues today.

The difficulties in creating a new educational system were even more pronounced at the tertiary level. Ignacio, a university professor, explained to me the goals of higher education during the early socialist period. According to him:

> The goal of education in the socialist period was to bring it to the masses, by expanding the system and through campaigns, like the literacy campaign where we sent people to the villages to teach people how to read. Education was also seen by the leadership as an important vehicle through which to spread our ideology. Education was viewed as a central front in the struggle and a cornerstone of the revolution. We even tried to bring higher education and university to the masses, although it proved very difficult to 'massify' education. Our curriculum did not really work and we did not have the necessary resources. It became very top down – the leadership decided what the revolution needed, so it was like, you be a doctor, you over there be an engineer, and you will be a technician. The 'massifying' of the university never really came off.

In the university itself, renamed Universidade Eduardo Mondlane (UEM) after independence, there was a severe shortage of personnel. Some of the final year students who remained after independence recall receiving their BA diplomas and then being promoted to professors on the spot. However, even this was not enough to cover the shortfall, and the party wanted to ensure that education was 'ideologically sound'. Jose, who was a professor at the time, explained to me that the solution was to bring in lecturers from the eastern bloc and create a specialised faculty to form the 'new man'. Such efforts met with limited success, though, as the following example demonstrates. According to Jose:

> The university created a faculty of Marxist-Leninism. Originally East Germans staffed it; they were imported to bring their 'wisdom' to the Mozambicans. There were some problems with them though; they were arrogant and perhaps a bit racist. What they taught was very abstract and theoretical, it had nothing to do with the conditions that we faced. Some of us thought that maybe Mozambican teachers could bring in a bit more historic specificity and talk more about the party and the history of Frelimo. So, the university brought in three Mozambicans and a Canadian. From the beginning, there was a lot of friction between us and the Germans. The head of the East German contingent was a real fanatic, he would say that he teaches Marxist-Leninism and so will his son after him and his grandson. He would often storm into my office before a lecture and rather insolently toss me a book and say here, maybe you should read this. He was implying that I was not ready to be lecturing on too much of anything. I thought his arrogance was a bit misplaced, because I heard that he had been a Luftwaffe pilot in World War Two. One day, I had enough and when the German came in and threw a book at me, I yelled sarcastically, 'So did you enjoy flying Hitler's plane and shooting the Jewish pigs?' The German went livid and stormed out; he immediately went to the head of the party cell in the university and complained. We [the Mozambican teachers] were called into a meeting and it was pretty

stormy; I was immediately fired. I went home and told my wife what had happened. I did not know what to do, I did not know if the police were going to come for me. Later that day I was given a call by the Dean and told to report to the university. I was nervous, I did not know what awaited me. I was told to start teaching again. There had been a power struggle between the Dean and the head of the party cell – both people wanted places on the central committee. The Dean won and he was not so enamoured with the Germans. One of the Mozambican lecturers [the most senior] though was sent to Niassa for a year to a re-education camp.

The goal of the revolutionary education system was to inculcate Frelimo's ideology in the people and create the conditions for the great transformation of the population into the new man, the basis of the party's system of signification. However, how that was to be accomplished was not entirely clear. Was the new man a product of a universal ideology and could therefore be taught by foreigners with longer experience of socialism? From the power struggle described above it seems that there were various, contradictory answers to these questions within Frelimo, and the results of early battles were often inconclusive. The central underlying tension, though – Is education best entrusted to a specially trained elite who carefully guard access to knowledge, or does it arise from the lives and experiences of the people? – gradually became resolved in favour of the elite.

To complicate the inadequacies of the educational system, Frelimo itself was instrumental in creating an educational class structure. The Frelimo leadership was an elite and its elitist tendencies became more pronounced after Frelimo redefined itself as a vanguard party in 1977. Joseph Hanlon was present at a meeting at the Ministry of Education that described this trend:

In 1980, I attended a seminar on mathematics teaching. At one session led by Education Minister Graça Machel, several educators spoke in flowery Portuguese about didactic methods and teaching aids. Finally, a primary school teacher from Niassa stood up. In basic but clear Portuguese, he pointed out that this elevated discussion was meaningless when he did not have a blackboard or textbooks, taught classes of 60 pupils or more, and he and his fellow teachers only had four years of primary schooling themselves. The audience broke into laughter. It was a time when an astute political intervention could have reversed the meeting. The Minister could have said it was important to consider the problems of the bulk of the teachers. Instead, she joined in the laughter. The embarrassed teacher sat down and the colonial-trained educators continued their discourse. (Hanlon 1990: 199)

Although the social revolution was predicated on mass mobilisation, it required an enlightened vanguard to lead the way. Soon after independence, the party created the Frelimo School, which was to exclusively serve the children of high-ranking party members. As the following example demonstrates, despite the school's underlying socialist ideology, it created the foundations of new forms of inequality.

Catarina was born in 1975 and came from a Frelimo family. Her father had been a minister in the socialist government. Catarina was educated at the Frelimo School until the ninth grade. There were 30 people in her class, all of whom were the children of high-ranking Frelimo members. Discipline was extremely strict; when the teacher entered the room all the students had to stand to attention and wait for permission to sit. The curriculum was rigorous and students were also required to work in the fields as part of the party's efforts to keep the elite close to the people during the early socialist period. The teachers were mostly expats from other socialist countries; many were East German and well trained. The students were provided with better food than in other schools. In addition, students were provided with a bus to transport them to and from school. The normal students walking to school would often mock them and make comparisons with the school bus and cattle transport trucks. Another friend of mine remembered resenting the Frelimo School and its privileges, and recalls her friends throwing rocks at the bus as they walked to school.

As Catrina's example demonstrates, the elitism inherent in the idea of a social vanguard began to harden into a firm social boundary, one expression of which was differing access to education. The ruling elite soon began to commandeer the necessary physical and social resources to ensure their social reproduction. Below them, the privileged and politically connected – whether they assumed such a position through their social background, talent, luck, party membership, or a combination of factors – also secured some necessary symbolic resources for social advancement that were widely noted and resented. Although conditions were difficult after independence and difficulties increased from 1977, social mobility and the sense that previous wrongs were being redressed helped secure the loyalty of many who became members of the middle class. However, the same processes also set the stage for increasing social polarisation, a factor that remained long after, for many people, enthusiasm and belief had faded.

Conclusion

At independence, Frelimo inherited a country beset with divisions, while surrounded by powerful and hostile neighbours. Despite the delicacy of the situation, the leadership pressed on with ambitious plans for social transformation. While the first two years of independence were relatively liberal by the standards of what was to come, the state that was being constructed and the view of citizenship that underlay it became ever more exclusionary. The political limit of the new regime divided the world into starkly antagonistic blocs: either wholehearted acceptance of Frelimo's social revolution and all it entailed, or the risk of being labelled an enemy. While the early nation-building project depended on mass mobilisation, as is the case with many revolutionary movements, this was accompanied by periodic purges and an elastic definition of what made one an enemy of the people.

Growing authoritarianism was initially offset by previously unimaginable social mobility if one was deemed loyal (a label that could always be rescinded). This set the foundations for the cultural construction of privilege, one that allowed rapid mobility but was tempered by a watchful state whose suspicions encompassed the very core of its support base. The rhetoric of the early independence state was one of radical egalitarianism, with the present as a mere stepping stone to a radiant future. However, this future was available only to those who had sufficiently adapted themselves to the new order.

In the early independence period, Frelimo enjoyed broad legitimacy among the population for overthrowing the generally detested colonial rule and promising a prosperous, more egalitarian future. The symbolic universe and systems of signification that underlay Frelimo's social revolution, however, tended to appeal to certain segments of the population, especially those who had been relatively privileged during the colonial period. Such groups, those who had some access to education, and officially valued social categories such as veterans of the liberation struggle were well placed to take advantage of the social mobility unleashed by liberation. Despite Frelimo's seemingly secure hold on power, the party leadership was uneasy amid a population they did not necessarily trust while facing powerful external enemies. Consequently, a tendency towards elitism became increasingly manifest, especially after 1977. As the leadership became more insulated, there was a widening gap between its ideas about what was necessary to transform the country and the expectations many held for the fruits of independence, especially as the party state's efforts to transform and discipline the population were often implemented in a haphazard and contradictory manner. The rift between the leadership and the majority of the population grew as latent weaknesses in the party's control came to the fore, and, as we shall see in Chapter 4, Frelimo's hold over the country became more tenuous.

4   Collapse, 1983–92

> Revolution, in short, is a time when everything seems at stake
> and, consequently, when everything can – and sometimes does –
> go wrong.   (Scott 2014: 34)

In previous chapters, I have discussed the ways in which Frelimo came to
power and the social revolution the party attempted to unleash. The goal
was not simply to hold power, but to create totally new political subjectivities, to transform social relations, forms of identification, and concep-
tualisations of citizenship through an adherence to a rigid, modernist
moral code. Frelimo tried to achieve what Yurchak calls 'hegemony of
representation'. This does not necessarily mean that the ruling pronouncements are believed, but that they are ubiquitous; no competing
or dissident statements are allowed in the official sphere, and the over-
representation of specific messages creates a sort of imagined community
as it is an experience shared by all (Yurchak 1997: 167). This was largely
true for many of the relatively privileged urbanites I have spoken with,
who intimately understood the message and, being closer to the centre of
power, were more tightly policed by the party state. In the rural areas,
however, the hegemony of representation rested on brittle foundations
and members of the wider population and party cadres themselves interpreted Frelimo's message in very different ways. This became especially
apparent throughout the 1980s as the promise of a better future receded
in the face of the devastation wrought by the civil war (1977–92).

As the euphoria of the initial post-independence period began to wane,
the limits of what could be accomplished by mass mobilisation were
reached. Frelimo originally claimed that power belonged to the 'people',
with the party as the embodiment of the people's will. With the transition
to a Marxist-Leninist vanguard party, the political structure became
increasingly hierarchical and rigid, with directives concerning the transformation flowing from the leadership to be obeyed without question by
those at the bottom. Coelho argues that, after Frelimo took power, its
rhetoric and world view – the liberation script – became increasingly
rigid. Instead of celebrating all those who contributed to the struggle, it
became an apparatus that could be interpreted and understood only by

party leaders whose dictates had to be obeyed without question (Coelho 2013). What was once a discursive roadmap to a better future, in opposition to the present, was now the legitimising discourse of power. As the 1980s wore on, Frelimo's ideological exclusivity became increasingly obvious, while its promises were delayed ever further.

In this chapter, I explore the ways in which Frelimo's social revolution devolved into a brutal civil war. I provide a brief overview of the basic outlines and trajectory of the war for the country as a whole. I then discuss the ways in which the challenges of the civil war completely reshaped Frelimo's transformative project. In the final section of this chapter, I discuss how the conflict, borderline economic collapse, and political transformations contributed to the later formation of the middle class in Maputo.

The civil war

As the 1980s began, Samora Machel could survey Mozambique with a growing sense of relief as five years of crises seemed to be drawing to an end. The party was consolidating its hold over the nation, the economy was beginning to recover in certain areas, and, most importantly of all, the war with Rhodesia had finally come to an end (Hall and Young 1997). After years of military support for the ZANU-PF and an unlikely diplomatic alliance between Machel and Margaret Thatcher, the white

Figure 4.1 Mural depicting the civil war.
Source: Ariadne Van Zandbergen / Alamy Stock Photo.

minority regime of Rhodesia had surrendered power through protracted negotiations and a friendly government took control. Mozambique could now focus on the Herculean task of building socialism internally, and of supporting efforts to end white supremacy in the region externally. Although there were rumbles of discontent, the party state appeared largely secure and the leadership pressed on with its social revolution.

After the first heady days of independence, the Frelimo leadership reacted to growing social problems and a mounting insurgency by falling back on previous military models of organisation. Hierarchy became more pronounced and official rhetoric was militarised. There were 'campaigns' for increased production on the labour 'front' (Hall and Young 1997). Tomas, a long-time resident of Maputo, told me that during the socialist period, when he was a young man, there was a flag-raising ceremony. When the flag was raised, everyone who could see it was supposed to stop and salute the flag, no matter what they were doing at the time, or they could be beaten by the security services. If one was driving, one was supposed to park the car, exit the vehicle, stand to attention, and salute. Soon, people would stop and salute when they saw someone in the distance stopping. Tomas would ask people why they stopped to salute at nothing and they would reply, 'I don't know, but I do not want to get into trouble.' Thus, *poder popular* (people's power) degenerated into a set of ritualised practices. The leadership had initially distrusted the more privileged urbanites as they were more exposed to supposed colonial decadence and few had been involved in the struggle. Yet they soon came to depend on them, for they shared similar social backgrounds and the privileged urbanites were one of the few groups who had the skills to staff the growing bureaucracy.

As Frelimo's dependence on these groups increased, its distance from the peasantry grew. It was the peasants, some of whom had worked closely with the party during the struggle, who found themselves marginalised. If the liberation struggle had been the victory of the countryside over the town, power now radiated out from Maputo into the rural areas (Coelho 2013). While this book is primarily concerned with the middle class of Maputo, the crucible of the civil war (even if its origins were due to foreign aggression) was in the rural areas, especially in the north and centre of the country. The increasingly exclusionary political limit, where meaningful citizenship was a function of loyalty to Frelimo, and where vague social categories comprising large numbers of people could instantly be declared enemies, was both a cause and an effect of the civil war. This is the legacy that still haunts the nation today.

After taking power, the leadership was convinced of the superiority of collective production and realised that agriculture would be the basis of the economy for some time to come. Party cadres tried to create massive collective farms where they could both increase and rationalise production and extend their control over the scattered peasantry (Coelho 1998; Harrison 1996). The move towards communal villages was supposed to be an organic evolution from the types of production practised in the liberated zones during the *luta armada*. Yet only a small proportion of the population had any experience with this, and in practice the nuclei of many communal villages were the widely detested *aldeamentos* (strategic villages) used by the Portuguese to try to wean the population away from contact with Frelimo during the struggle (Coelho 1998). While Frelimo promised that communal villages would facilitate services such as health clinics, education, and water, the benefits rarely arrived, and those that did were rarely maintained. Theoretically, villagers were allowed to choose whether they wanted to join communal villages. In practice, though, when persuasion failed, peasants were forcibly relocated (ibid.). Even for those who managed to stay on their own land, almost the entire agricultural budget was swallowed by communal villages and state farms, meaning that little was available for independent farmers. The 'tightly interconnected signifiers' that were the basis of the transformative project – the grand goal of reshaping the population from 'backward', rural feudalists to rational, collectively minded, socially advanced modernists – offered little for many people in the rural areas (Dinerman 2006). Nor were these signifiers necessarily understood by the cadres who were tasked with enforcing Frelimo's hegemony of representation (ibid.). As the decade continued, the party state utopian promise of social revolution often meant coercion in practice.

In the international arena, Mozambique suffered greatly from the decision to comply with sanctions against Rhodesia. In contrast was Frelimo's relationship with South Africa, its far more powerful neighbour. While Frelimo was outspoken in its support for the ANC, it did not wish to overly antagonise South Africa, a country with which it had numerous economic links, and so it maintained a cautious stance until the beginning of the 1980s. With the election of Ronald Reagan in the United States, the previous practice of Cold War détente was jettisoned in favour of 'rolling back' international communism, and the Reagan government funded numerous proxy wars throughout the world to aid in this effort. At the same time, a more hard-line and militarist government, under P. W. Botha, had come to power in South Africa and once again détente was discarded for a new strategy of 'total onslaught'. Yet, despite the Frelimo state's limited capabilities and a hostile international environment, or perhaps in desperation because of its weak position, the government decided to attempt a massive restructuring of Mozambican society by trying to industrialise the nation, create communal villages, establish large-scale state farms, and abolish traditional leadership. These grandly ambitious plans soon fell into difficulties. After the fall of Rhodesia, South Africa, angry at Frelimo's support of the ANC and nervous about the example that a 'black Marxist state' could set, became the paymasters of the Rhodesian-trained Mozambican dissidents (Hanlon 1990; Minter 1994). Instead of Zimbabwe's independence bringing an end to internal conflict in Mozambique, the war between Frelimo and Renamo soon reached previously unimaginable levels of brutality (Hanlon 1990; Minter 1994; Newitt 1995).

Many analysts have questioned whether one could actually character-ise the post-independence war in Mozambique as a 'civil war', since the rebels were trained, supported, and financed by Rhodesia and then South Africa (Hanlon 1990; Minter 1994). Although the war did feed on internal discontent, it is extremely unlikely that it could have ever reached the levels it did, or last for as long, without the direct involve-ment of South Africa. Chabal (2002) argues that the leaders of Renamo knew (at least initially) that the Frelimo government was widely regarded as legitimate, and Renamo tended to build support through the war rather than going to war for a specific constituency (ibid.). The overall strategy of the apartheid government of South Africa was not to over-throw Frelimo and install Renamo, but rather to weaken the Mozambi-can state (Minter 1994).

Yet, it is also true that the direction of the social revolution undertaken by the Frelimo leadership alienated sections of the population and made them more receptive to anti-government rebels. Foreigners funded the civil war, but it also grew out of the cultural gap between Frelimo, the party's social base, and large segments of the population. Scholars such as K. B. Wilson have argued that Renamo's ritualised destruction of property, infrastructure, schools, and clinics – and anything associated with Frelimo's vision of the future – may have initially been viewed as an act of revenge against an arrogant and alien elite that had oppressed them through the colonial period and into independence in certain areas of the country (Wilson 1992: 538).

The unpopularity of aspects of the party's social revolution was com-pounded by the fact that the grand designs of Frelimo often lacked sufficient resources and were chaotically implemented. While the leadership may have had brutal modernist ambitions to transform social relations and render the country legible, to 'see like a state' in James Scott's (1998) terms, the results of this grand effort were ad hoc, hap-hazard, badly coordinated, understaffed, under-resourced, and often contradictory. This became more evident as the war dragged on. By the mid- to late 1980s, pragmatism often trumped ideology, and Frelimo began to steal Renamo's tactics by courting those previously slated for destruction, such as by using traditional leaders and enlisting its own sorcerers for the war of the spirits (Dinerman 2006; Wilson 1992). Such practices may have been militarily effective, yet they demonstrate the brittleness of Frelimo's hegemony of representation in many parts of the country. The regime claimed its legitimacy on enacting a revolution that would wipe out practices that ironically were bolstering its military effectiveness, and the goal of transformation gave way to clinging to power.

Paradoxically, as the country slipped ever further into bloody chaos, Frelimo began to score notable diplomatic victories and managed its external relations with growing sophistication. Frelimo's diplomatic prowess was surprising, considering that the 1980s had begun poorly: Mozambique had twice been rejected for membership of the Council for Mutual Economic Assistance (Comecon), which put a cap on the level of aid it could realistically expect from the Soviet bloc. As the war gained in intensity, the party was finally forced to negotiate with South Africa to win some breathing space. This resulted in the 1984 Nkomati Accord, in which Mozambique and South Africa signed a treaty that pledged that neither would support the internal enemies of the other (Minter 1994). The Nkomati Accord gravely weakened the party state's legitimacy. No longer valid was the claim that everything was foreseen and presided over by an enlightened vanguard with unique access to credible specialist knowledge. As Coelho argued:

developments like the 1984 Nkomati Non-Aggression Pact seriously affected the mechanics of functioning of the Liberation Script. In a few words, the Pact stated that South Africa would end the support to Renamo in exchange for the withdrawal of Mozambican support to the ANC. Certainly there is a strong argument that the Pact was an act of survival in the face of the difficult military, economic and humanitarian situation. However, it is also undeniable that it represented a blow to the contents and mechanics of the Liberation Script. For the first time, the teleological principle of the fair always winning did not manifest; the binary conflict was not settled by the victory of the revolutionary forces but by a pact – in fact, by a stall. The Pact proved that a formerly infallible itinerary was now doomed to include setbacks. Victory was not a given. Or, put in a different way, for the first time reality could not be explained by the logics of the Script. (Coelho 2013: 26)

In addition to the damage suffered to the image of Frelimo as an enlightened vanguard leading the masses to an inevitable series of victories, the accord proved impossible for the regime to enforce. Frelimo followed the accord and banned all ANC operations beyond some token representation. South Africa, or at least elements of the South African military, did not reciprocate. Renamo received massive shipments of arms and supplies before the signing of the accord, and regular shipments of armaments and supplies continued afterwards (Hall and Young 1997; Hanlon 1990; Vines 1996). Instead of reducing the pressure on Frelimo, the war intensified, spreading throughout the nation. By the mid-1980s, Frelimo had lost effective control of around 85 per cent of the nation's territory. South African-sponsored peace talks between Frelimo and Renamo quickly broke down. Yet, Frelimo's acceptance of internal market-based economic reforms and diplomatic openness began to win support and desperately needed aid from the West. It could also rely on assistance from members of the Southern African Development Coordination Conference (SADCC), an organisation consisting of nations that banded together to try to resist South Africa's economic dominance of the region. While this was ineffectual overall, other front-line states (those that politically opposed South Africa while being geographically close to it) sent military aid. At the height of the war, Zimbabwe had around 10,000 troops operating in Mozambique, both in repayment for Frelimo's assistance during their own liberation struggle and to protect transport corridors so that they could export their goods through the central Mozambican port of Beira. Tanzania also lent military assistance in northern Mozambique (Minter 1994).

Renamo was in the opposite position, but its hold on Mozambique was getting stronger. From a few hundred men, its ranks had grown to around 20,000 by the mid-1980s. Renamo could move through large areas of the country at will and had de facto control over many rural areas (Hall 1990; Nilsson 1993a; 1993b; Morgan 1990). South Africa had supplied it with sophisticated communications equipment, which allowed Renamo greater coordination and a high degree of centralisation. Its external relations, on the other hand, were shambolic. Many of Renamo's external representatives were picked simply because they had residency in the country in question (Vines 1996). The lack of a coherent political programme and the communications failures between the internal and external wings, in addition to widely publicised atrocities committed by Renamo, damaged its public image (ibid.). Renamo's external support drew on connections with the governments of South Africa, Malawi, and Kenya, a few reactionary American senators such as Jesse Helms, private extreme right-wing funding, and favourable coverage from magazines such as *Soldier of Fortune* (ibid.). Frelimo's skilful diplomacy and Renamo's lack of capability in public relations, coupled with the latter's frequent demonstrations of brutality, allowed the government to create an external lifeline. Even nations such as the United States that were firmly opposed to the party's ideological project recognised Frelimo as the legitimate government and provided much-needed aid. While Frelimo's writ did not extend very far outside the major cities, there was little chance that Renamo could dislodge it. At the same time, Frelimo could not destroy Renamo's presence in the countryside.

Citizenship and the fading social revolution in Maputo

In *Everything Was Forever Until It Was No More: the last Soviet generation*, Yurchak discusses how Stalin occupied a structural role of external editor that was both constituted by the guiding ideology and simultaneously outside it (2006). In this case, Stalin stood above ideological discourse, and, through his unique access to the external canon (Marxist-Leninism), was able to independently evaluate whether something was correct or a deviation, while simultaneously concealing internal paradoxes (ibid.: 13). After Stalin's death, there was no longer an external voice to conceal the paradoxes within Soviet ideology, a development that contributed to its later collapse. Although Frelimo was far less brutal than Stalin's USSR and lacked both the administrative control and the personality cult that characterised Stalinism, Samora occupied a somewhat similar position. In many ways, Samora was the living embodiment of Frelimo's social revolution. He was the public face of the party, communicating its message through public rallies and broadcast speeches, and he occupied a position above society. His pronouncements were programmatic, spelling out the ways in which Mozambique would be transformed, what a loyal citizen would be, and, conversely, what behaviours and ideas made one an internal enemy. Unlike the traditionalist posturing of some African rulers, leading cadres portrayed themselves as culturally advanced, the only ones who could arbitrate between the supposedly less advanced conflictual social groups (Dinerman 2006: 273). This was the underlying legitimation of the self-assigned right of Samora in particular, and of the party leadership in general, to determine who was a citizen.

While Frelimo's self-assigned right to determine what constituted an 'authentic' citizen of the new order was based on an elitist project to transform the nation, attempts to legitimise that vision rested on the claim that such a transformation was necessary to bring about progress and development. In the 1980s, the gap between the promised benefits of the social revolution and reality became glaring. Instead of the victorious march of progress, there was chaos and devastation. Despite harsh measures, the growing destruction caused by the civil war and the chaos unleashed by Frelimo's own policies made urban areas increasingly difficult to order and control. The party reacted with desperation, turning on elements of its remaining social base, a prominent example of this being the now infamous Operation Production in 1983 that exiled all who could not prove their residence or employment in the city to the far north, to 'build cities in the forest' (Newitt 1995).

This pronouncement was almost universally greeted with dread by those I knew, even if they felt that migration to Maputo had become a severe social problem. According to Naema, the situation in the capital was becoming increasingly authoritarian and grim.

It started with independence. When Samora made the speech on 24 July announcing the nationalisation of everything, people simply poured into the towns and tried to live new urban lives. The problem was, though, there was nothing for them to do here, they were not trained or educated and there was no one left to grow food. So soon everyone was hungry and the government went bankrupt importing food from foreign countries. The factories did not work because everyone who had technical skills was Portuguese and they ran away; sometimes they sabotaged the factory before they left, nothing was getting done. Things started to get tense. The police were everywhere and you had to watch what you said or you might get into trouble. You needed a pass just to go to Matola [a neighbouring city]. I could not even visit my sister without permission. It got even worse with Operation Production – it was a disaster. The police would just walk around and ask you for your papers. Sometimes people had left them at home; if you did not have residence papers on you, you were loaded into a truck and off you went to the rural areas. One was not even allowed to contact one's family or pack their stuff. The police had so much power back then; the police were Frelimo and Frelimo was the police. They were not corrupt in a monetary sense, but they abused the power that they had.

Marta, another early supporter of Frelimo, had a similar assessment:

Operation Production was the symbol of many of the things going wrong. It highlighted the totalitarian aspects of the government. It was getting worse because Frelimo was losing and becoming coercive. In such a situation, Operation Production fit the logic of our rulers. No one producing much of anything and the factories were not really working. It seems they actually thought this project might work and clear up the disorder. It was also a show of power. I remember the army doing sweeps [unlike Naema, Marta did not mention the police specifically], where they would bring in trucks and block off both sides of the street and then go through everyone's house with weapons and check documents and make sure that anyone illegal was not there. I was hiding a few people in my house. It was pretty big, so it was not that hard to hide people, but the soldiers did come brandishing weapons, pulling my children out of bed and terrifying them.

An estimated 30,000 to 50,000 people were forcibly removed (Buur 2010: 25). Operation Production undermined Frelimo's urban support and created a climate of fear throughout all sectors of the population. The social contract became, in Nugent's (2010) terms, ever more coercive.

As the situation deteriorated, Frelimo established severe punishments for many forms of what was labelled economic sabotage. Contrary to the party's professed anti-racialism and universal vision of citizenship, certain social groups, such as Indian merchants, were often singled out under these laws, undermining the universalist pretensions of the social revolution. An infamous example concerned an Indian who was convicted of black marketeering in 1983. His punishment was intended as a public warning and his execution by firing squad was broadcast live on the radio. Punishments such as public floggings were not uncommon, although the supposed enemies of the people punished in this way were 'guilty' of a wide range of what the state deemed to be crimes. As the party's control over large parts of the country veered between tenuous and non-existent, the categories of friend, enemy, citizen, and other oscillated continuously.

Disillusionment became widespread, even among party cadres. Chuabo, who was introduced in the previous chapter, had become a true believer as the revolution opened up opportunities he had never imagined and took him from one of Mozambique's most remote provinces for secondary and university study in Cuba. When he returned home from Cuba in 1986, during the height of the civil war, he was assigned to a government department. He found the country completely transformed; the euphoria he remembered had given way to despondency, and working for the government was disheartening. Everything was conducted in a top-down manner. It was impossible to do something without the consent of someone higher up; therefore, little was actually done. Official representations of the party working for the people were continually contradicted by the myriad privileges accorded to cadres.[1]

While it became obvious that Frelimo's goal of completely transforming the population and ushering in a golden age of prosperity was no longer viable, the party maintained its hold on Maputo. Even if the promise of unity, progress, and prosperity seemed laughable as the 1980s wore on, Renamo's neo-traditional message had little appeal for many in the capital. This was compounded by Renamo's habit of summary execution for anyone connected to Frelimo and of spectacular acts of brutality, especially in the south of the nation where the rebels had little support and where many residents of Maputo had family. As one man told me:

I am from Gaza [a southern province that is a Frelimo stronghold]. I could never support Renamo. Renamo did terrible barbaric things during the war there that cannot be imagined. They made children rape their parents and parents kill their children. Afonso Dhlakama [Renamo's leader] said he will deport the people from Gaza to South Africa, because, according to him, we are not real Mozambicans.

Another woman told me she was shocked when she saw pictures of Dhlakama and other high-ranking Renamo members because it never occurred to her that they were human. From all the official

---

[1] At this time, popular jokes in Maputo became increasingly bitter about the deteriorating situation. One example is as follows. Two men caught a large fish. One fisherman said to the other, 'Oh, this will be great. We will cook it with rice.' The other fisherman said, 'We can't. There is no rice at the *loja do povo* [people's shop where the state made goods available to the population].' The first said, 'Oh well, we will cook it with some potatoes.' The other said, 'It is impossible because there are no potatoes.' The first said, 'Oh well, we will cook it with porridge.' And the other said, 'We can't, there is no porridge.' The first fisherman said, 'Fuck it,' and decided to throw the fish back. As the fish hit the water he came up and said: 'Viva Frelimo.'

pronouncements and media representations, she had been expecting some sort of twisted goblin-like creatures. It is doubtful that Dhlakama ever threatened to deport the population of an entire province, and not only were Renamo's leaders human, some, like Dhlakama, had been Frelimo soldiers during the liberation struggle, much like many of the family members of those I know in Maputo.

The Frelimo leadership argued that the first step in dragging Mozambique from poverty was the transformation of its people into the 'new man'. The victorious conclusion of the liberation struggle, Samora's charisma, and the popular desire for change all made such ambitious goals seem possible to many – for a time, at least. The form the new man was to take drew from a specific symbolic repertoire, and its attractions were far more limited than initially thought, a weakness that became increasingly evident during the course of the war. Such revelations did not destroy the project; rather, they gradually transformed it. If Frelimo could not universalise its view of citizenship, the party successfully appropriated the symbolic meaning of modernity, a concept that became central in drawing boundaries between the privileged and the wider population.[2] This transformation was central to the formation of a middle class based on its access to the state, even as the social revolution collapsed.

In practice, Samora Machel was a skilful politician who adapted his position to changing circumstances. In his role as external editor, however, he was the embodiment of the revolution and the incarnation of Frelimo's message and goals. Samora Machel bears a striking similarity to David Scott's description of Maurice Bishop in Grenada:

> revolutions are not only an extraordinary time of social and political upheaval. They are also a time of exceptional human beings who stand – momentarily – at the animating center of political affairs, whose actions are of unusual intensity and urgency; and who therefore inspire, by turns and sometimes together, awe and sympathy, admiration and terror; and whose errors, misjudgements, or conceits can bring ruin not only on themselves but also upon the whole of which they are a leading part. (Scott 2014: 34)

Beginning in 1983, and especially after Samora's death in 1986, Frelimo moved towards a mixed economy in an effort to boost production and find urgently needed friends and resources in the West (Hall and Young 1997). The Frelimo leadership came to an agreement with the

---

[2] In a similar manner, Soares de Oliveira argues that the MPLA, despite its incompetence in actually administering the country, has seized a 'virtual monopoly' over what it means to be modern in Angola. This symbolic resource and the fact that the MPLA has long been the party of the educated and the urban have been central in creating forms of inclusion and exclusion, especially with regard to their UNITA rivals, who are unceasingly portrayed as a primitive throwback, incapable of managing a modern state (Soares de Oliveira 2015: 116).

International Monetary Fund (IMF) and the World Bank, agreeing to implement pro-market reforms (Harrison 1996). The reforms did have some effect, and as a result the economy that had been declining 8 per cent per year from 1982 showed a growth rate of 3.6 per cent in 1986 (Marshall 1990). However, this did little to offset the incredible destruction of the war. Samora was the iconic image of a victorious revolution, but now he presided over a devastated nation and commanded a regime teetering on the edge of collapse. After his suspicious death in a plane crash,[3] his successor, Joaquim Chissano (president from 1986 to 2005), found it difficult to assume Samora's role. Chissano was a talented, pragmatic politician who managed eventually to negotiate the peace, but he was less convincing as the embodiment of revolutionary will, standing above society.

While Chissano managed to gain the state some desperately needed economic aid, the clarity of the party's initial message had faltered. The goals and practices of the new man striving for the collective became increasingly impossible in times of economic crisis (Buur 2010). The grand proclamations of previous years – concerning the abolition of the patriarchy, new forms of gender relations, and the transcendence of ethnicity, region, and class in the face of a selfless citizenry striving for the collective good – seemed utterly fantastical. Xiconhoca had begun as a pedagogical exercise to point out social ills, but by the mid-1980s it seemed more an ironic primer on the practices necessary for survival, a trope that continues to this day (Nielsen 2014). The result of selfless striving for the collective would almost guarantee starvation, and the black market was soon supplying many basic necessities. Frelimo championed new forms of kin relationships in its attempt to abolish patriarchal and gerontocratic forms of oppression. Increasing authoritarianism and the war strengthened some family bonds, with kin serving as safe havens from informers. I have been told by many how they survived on food sent from rural kin and were able to send their children to areas where food was more readily available. This was counterbalanced by the vast influx of people streaming into the comparative safety of cities, putting both state- and kinship-based forms of redistribution under incredible strain. Daily life served as a constant rebuttal to the promises of the social revolution. The party's efforts to act as a theologian state and create a new kind of national citizen was replaced by empty formalism. Naema, a former Frelimo supporter, speaking of the mid-1980s, recalls that:

---

[3] It is widely believed that Samora Machel was assassinated by elements of the South African apartheid state, who tampered with a radio beacon causing his plane to crash. It has also long been rumoured that dissatisfied factions within Frelimo aided the South Africans in the assassination.

Everyone had to trade on the black market. My husband was sent to prison for having foreign currency, but my daughter was sick and needed milk. It was the only way we could get it. We still spoke the socialist slogans in public, but it did not really mean anything. Anyone who spoke like that privately would be considered bizarre.

In a similar vein, the vast distance between official rhetoric and observable reality in the former Soviet Union did not engender resistance, according to Yurchak, but instead was conceptualised by people in a manner similar to what he describes as the 'cynical reason of late socialism' (1997). 'Cynical reason' is the strategy of simulating belief while repressing recognition of the act of stimulation (ibid.: 162–3): people are aware of the falsity of official representation, but pretend that it is real. The sacrifices that were supposed to ensure future prosperity had brought devastation, and instead of relative privilege being the first step in a grand transformation of the entire nation, it became the mark of an increasingly besieged elite. As noted by Naema, very few took official discourse seriously, and the promise of being the first link in the chain of transformation was stillborn, but she and many like her remained bound to Frelimo both to secure their social positions and to protect them from the existential threat of Renamo. In many ways, the social revolution and its associated rhetoric and practices began to fulfil a similar role to Wedeen's (1999) description of President Hafez al-Assad's personality cult in Syria. It was not dependent so much on genuine belief, even if facets of the rhetoric did resonate with the population. Instead, its rituals and pronouncements acted as a disciplinary device that policed what was permissible. Citizens such as Naema may have no longer believed the slogans they were forced to parrot publicly, or knew why they were blindly saluting an invisible presence in the distance, but they demonstrated their compliance by doing so regardless of what they may have thought privately.

O tempo de fome (the time of hunger)

For members of the middle class in Maputo, tales of the privations of the war period are common. Once, when attending a dinner given by a middle-class Mozambican family, the mother pulled out a photograph album filled with pictures of her and her husband marrying and establishing a family shortly after the revolution. Her children and some other relatives were present during the dinner and they all began to laugh while looking through the pictures. As with teenagers everywhere, the children were amused by the photographs of the outmoded fashions of their parents – in this case bell-bottom trousers and large Afro hairstyles. They were also shocked at how thin everyone was and the shabby quality of the clothes and home furnishings. The eldest daughter was particularly offended by the sandals everyone wore, while her mother tried to explain that nothing else was available. The mother mentioned many times that it was *o tempo de fome* (the time of hunger). During much of the socialist period and the civil war, urban residents were on a strict system of rationing. The old socialists in Maputo pointed out that, while food was not plentiful, at least the state tried to make sure that everyone was fed. Yet others referred to the system of rationing as *quilo-quilo* (kilo-kilo), a derogatory reference to the pitiful monthly amounts that were allowed. As was explained to me, the monthly rations comprised one kilo of rice per person, one kilo of beans, and *carapau*, small bony fishes of dubious flavour that are still viewed with distaste today, although they remain a staple of the poor.[4] Many people recalled sleeping in front of the shops so as to secure a good position in the line and get even these paltry rations before they ran out. One woman, who used to date the son of Samora Machel, was once invited to dinner at the *Presidencia*. She was later devastated to find that they ate the same rations there as everyone else (or at least, they did in front of company), and the dream of a good dinner evaporated. Others told me that one of their favourite games was to sneak into the foreign exchange shops, shops that sold rare and hard-to-find goods for foreign currency, the possession of which was illegal for Mozambicans. While the shops would not be all that impressive now, they were a cornucopia of goods in this era. Children would gaze longingly at ice cream displays before being chased out by guards.

Even the existence of a display of ice cream, as unavailable as it was to the average urbanite, was something from the realm of utter fantasy for most Mozambicans outside Maputo. While residence in Maputo was a privilege that those in the war-ravaged rural areas could only dream of, life for the city's citizens was becoming increasingly arduous. Throughout the 1980s, the pressure on Maputo steadily increased. The city was in an economic doldrums. Even the port, one of the largest employers, was struggling due to difficulties in management and a reduction in South African cargo goods (O'Laughlin 2000). Access to rare consumer goods became a mark of distinction and privilege in the hardening socialist hierarchy, as few had the ability or the social connections to obtain them; even then, the supply was limited. I was told that the Maputo airport would take on the appearance of a street market when those who had been visiting relatives in Portugal returned laden with consumer goods. For the young, anyone returning from a trip abroad made sure to bring many copies of cassettes of popular music, with which one enjoyed great esteem among one's friends. However, access to scarce consumer goods,

---

[4] The *carapau* was a symbol of the socialist period, and a staple butt of jokes. For example: 'What is a *carapau*? A whale that has gone through the process of socialist transformation.'

while bringing esteem, could also be dangerous and inspire jealousy, as the following example illustrates.

Cristina comes from a Frelimo family. Her mother went to school with many top members of the party leadership and held a high state position after independence. Shortages became endemic, and Cristina's mother began using her contacts to smuggle goods in from Swaziland in 1982. This was a dangerous, if relatively common, option; it could be considered economic sabotage, which attracted severe penalties. Cristina remembers that they would have to cover the windows with towels when they were cooking, as the neighbouring children would stare through the windows and they could not explain how they obtained food that was not officially available. Eventually, her mother was reported by Cristina's teacher, who noticed that Cristina and her sister had shoes that could not be purchased in Mozambique. That night, members of the security services came to their home and ordered her mother to accompany them. Cristina's sister faked an asthma attack and the police took pity on them and said they would return the next day. Cristina's mother used the reprieve to mobilise her contacts and avoided punishment. Due to their place in the social order, Cristina's family was able to manipulate the system in a way that many others could not. While this brought benefits, it did not necessarily bring security. Despite their status and background, they remained vulnerable to the envy of their neighbours and dependent on a party that was unpredictable.

By 1983, key figures in the party leadership came to realise that their economic system simply was not working. Prices were set seemingly at random, such as a car tyre costing the same as 15 kilograms of lettuce, and heavy investment in communal villages and state farms was not having the desired effect. The new thinking was summarised in a speech given by Samora when he declared the job of the state was to concentrate on heavy industry, natural resources, health, and social services, not to sell matches and tomatoes on street corners. After Samora's death in 1986, Chissano increased the pace of reform. The *Programa de Restruturação Economica* (Programme of Economic Reconstruction or PRE) was instituted as Mozambique embarked on the path of structural adjustment.[5] According to Senhor Cortês, who was a minister during the socialist period, the process of reform was torturous:

Previous attempts at liberalisation were piecemeal and ineffective. Our major breakthrough was to sell vegetables and agricultural products at market price. However, this was tremendously unpopular, both with the wider population and the party leadership, who thought the reforms only benefited a narrow segment of

---

[5] The effects of structural adjustment in Africa are widely discussed in the available scholarship and are beyond the scope of this chapter. For a further discussion of the Mozambican case, see Castel-Branco (1994) and Hanlon (1990; 1996).

the population. We did not really have a choice, though. By 1986 the economy was not working at all. Factories were at a standstill. When the factories had input A, they did not have B; when they had B, they were waiting for C – nothing was being done at all. Furthermore, our major donors took the IMF/World Bank line and told us there would be no more support unless we started implementing more market-based reforms. Internally we had debates; some thought this would mean a loss of sovereignty, but the reformers had the upper hand – things were a wreck.

The deregulation of the economy hit urbanites hard as the currency was massively devalued, salaries were frozen, and subsidies were removed (Marshall 1990). For many of the residents of Maputo, life became even more difficult and corruption began to flourish, as civil servants could no longer live on their salaries. At the same time, restrictions against personal accumulation among the Frelimo elite lessened (Marshall 1990; Pitcher 2002). Salaries were inadequate but necessary, as one had to be officially employed to maintain the right of residence in the city. In many cases, people supplemented their incomes with second jobs, or one family member worked for the state while another engaged in petty trade. The effects of this could be seen in major cities, as the previously barren shelves of shops began filling with goods. Yet, as the aphorism goes, during socialism, everyone has money but the shops are empty; under capitalism, the shops are full but no one has any money.

While civic life was characterised by growing social polarisation, the military situation was also worsening. Renamo was able to mount attacks on the outskirts of the nearby city of Matola, and it was difficult to drive more than 15 kilometres outside the town without risking ambush. Residence controls had largely broken down as refugees streamed in from the countryside. I was often told that in the early independence period there was little crime, although cynics claimed that this was because there was nothing to steal. Whether or not this was the case, the ability to leave household goods outside overnight and expect them to still be there the following morning had become legend. Even some of the bitterest critics of the socialist period told me that they appreciated how ordered everything was. I am not sure if such descriptions were basically accurate or whether they were the rose-tinted result of nostalgic reminiscences, but the situation had changed for the worse by the mid- to late 1980s, and violent crime was on the rise. Morale in the security services was low, and they became a source of danger themselves, sometimes using their weapons to supplement meagre to non-existent salaries.

While the ideal of the new man was severely undermined and life was becoming increasingly arduous, many of the privileged were still tied to Frelimo through their jobs in state-controlled agencies, through the rations they received, the apartments they inhabited, and because the party claimed that it could protect them from Renamo. Additionally, although many of the socialist slogans had degenerated into meaninglessness, privileged urbanites shared the party leadership's symbolic vocabulary and systems of signification. All these factors deepened relationships of dependence, but dependence was supposed to lead to a new age of security. As the 1980s progressed, it was possible with the right connections to make a fortune in the more open economic climate, using a variety of practices often glossed over by the meta-label of corruption. In the overall climate of insecurity, dependence and privilege were based on changing government policy, massive economic instability, growing authoritarianism, and the misfortunes of the civil war. Many previous supporters began to despair and stories of Frelimo's incompetence became legion. A friend of mine recalled her father, a high-ranking official, listing to his family some of the most egregious examples. She remembers the stories as follows:

When the army got tanks, they took them out for an attack. The tanks were battery-powered and the soldiers wanted to listen to the radio. They used up all the power and when they arrived at the battle they could not move and had to sit in their tanks. Another tank battalion was moving in to attack Renamo. The commander looked at the map and plotted a straight line to where they thought Renamo was. The commander did not know how to read the contours of a map and the tanks drove straight into a mountain and could not go any further. Things were incredibly lax even in Maputo. During a national holiday the soldiers and officers manning a missile battery somehow managed to have a drinking party. Something happened, someone got drunk and dropped a cigarette somewhere and the missiles shot off. The battery was right outside of Maputo and it caused a massive panic as the missiles went off towards Katemba [a neighbouring peninsula]. People thought there was an invasion coming and a government meeting was hurriedly called but no one showed up; they were getting ready to flee. My dad realised that no one cared about the people, they just cared about themselves.

Even supporters were beginning to ask themselves why the party seemed so incredibly incompetent, if it had won the right to rule and transform the population through its unique access to superior knowledge. There were few satisfying answers. The underlying promise of Frelimo's social revolution, the thing that made it so attractive to a privileged social stratum, was the homogenisation of a set of cultural patterns and a world view that would lead to prosperity for all. Instead, it appeared as though it was leading to quasi-universal destitution.

Conclusion

By the late 1980s, the war had reached a brutal stalemate. Both sides' patrons were tiring of the conflict and had more pressing concerns at home. Mozambique also lacked the resources for either side to continue the war independently. For Frelimo, the economy was still in deep recession with growing discontent in the urban areas. Renamo, on the other hand, had supplanted decreasing South African aid with an economy of plunder (Dinerman 1994; Vines 1996; Wilson 1992). Renamo would systematically strip the villages they attacked and sell their loot in South Africa or Malawi, and was heavily involved in smuggling elephant ivory out of Mozambique. During the years of war, the countryside had been repeatedly ravaged. Renamo was facing the law of diminishing returns and it was becoming more difficult for the rebels to continue to reproduce themselves. While estimates vary, by the end of the conflict up to a million people had died through violence, disease, and starvation; around 25 per cent of the population were internal or external refuges; and 85 per cent of the nation's infrastructure had been destroyed (Hall and Young 1997). With a military stalemate, potential economic collapse, a changing international environment, and a profoundly war-weary population, both Renamo and Frelimo began to seriously consider negotiations.

On 15 October 1992, Frelimo and Renamo finally signed a peace agreement that brought the civil war to an end. Although peace was greeted with guarded optimism, the country was devastated. Many of the impressive gains of the revolution, such as widely available healthcare services and education provisions, were now returned to a state that was worse than pre-independence levels. Rural areas had suffered the worst during the civil war, and the nation's infrastructure was in ruins. The Frelimo leadership's dream of presiding over the creation of a specific national subject, based on the new man, also appeared by the end of the war to have been relegated to the realm of fantasy. Mozambique's structural adjustment programme resulted in the slashing of government subsidies and services for the poor, while simultaneously devaluing the currency and making thousands of workers redundant (Hanlon 1996). Capitalism was also a disciplinary project that was more than capable of unleashing its own share of brutalities. Although conditions for many urbanites were precarious, corruption was becoming entrenched and state officials were now, in contradiction to previous egalitarian norms, openly displaying their new wealth (ibid.). Economically, Mozambique appeared to mirror its pre-independence role, serving as a transport hub for South Africa and Zimbabwe and as a producer of primarily agricultural products. The country was also the centre of a growing illegal economy. Both drugs from Asia and cars stolen in South Africa found their way to Europe through Mozambique's ports (Ellis 1999; Hanlon 1996; Hibou 1999). While Frelimo still ruled Mozambique, the country bore only the slightest resemblance to the vision it had proclaimed at independence.

African nationalism is not simply resistance to colonialism, but an attempt to create something new (Chipkin 2007). However, as demonstrated in Mozambique, the relationship between the attempt to build something new and the actual outlines of the society that was created was complicated and often deeply contradictory. The promises of the social revolution were relegated to nostalgic despair or ironic mockery amid the ruins and rapidly escalating inequalities of the initial post-war period. When engaging in a post-mortem of the social revolution, some cadres felt that the failure to transform the population was due to the wider population itself. For example, Paulo, a former high-ranking official, told me:

The British and the French created an elite who could work with the neo-colonial system. The Portuguese did not try until the final six years of colonialism. Frelimo was progressive; the goal was not simply to free the nation, but also to transform it. For this the party wanted to create a modern socialist state but we simply did not have the conditions. We did not have the social preparation to make a revolution. At independence most people were peasants; even those who lived in the urban areas were psychologically peasants. The cities did not fulfil their historic role by making them workers; most people were servants and now they wanted to be masters. We tried to turn peasants into workers, but we failed. We lived in an imaginary nation, the dream of the nation we wanted to create, not the flesh and blood nation we actually had. We thought everyone was pure as angels and they could be easily reformed. This meant we let in thieves, the lumpen proletariat, informers, former agents of the Portuguese secret police, opportunists who subverted the party's goals.

Others, such as Senhor Cortês, argued that the collapse and failure of the social revolution were, in many ways, inevitable (see Sumich 2010):

We, especially in the leadership, have a long history together. We lived together, fought for an ideal, argued with each other, gotten sick of each other and became friends and loved each other. Also, we won, we succeeded in our main goal [national liberation as opposed to social transformation] and we still have responsibility. There was a time when we only spoke to each other and did not allow criticism. We felt the criticism was unfair considering everything we had achieved. The people cannot be made to continually suffer, even if we are sure what we are doing is the right thing. Eventually we realised this and opened ourselves to criticism and to change. Really, just about everyone knew that the system was not working. One of our major problems was that our form of socialism was extremely distributive, but it penalised accumulation. We were trying to distribute ever dwindling resources to ever more people. Also, there was a group that had already progressed through socialism – they had enjoyed all the benefits, the free housing, free medical care and free education, and now they wanted more. They watched Zimbabwe, where the cadres got farms and they wondered why can't we liberate the nation and be rich. I remember telling a friend in the late 1970s that all of the great statists will remain so as long as the state serves their interests. When it no longer does they will take a different line. This is basically human nature; it's not a great surprise.

While debates rage over the specific reasons why the social revolution failed, whether it was a noble but doomed crusade or a vicious and brutal programme of social engineering, very few seem to doubt that it did fail. In the revolutionary period, Frelimo took on many of the characteristics that Mbembe (2001) classifies as the theologian state. Despite the totalitarian aspects of such a goal, it often resembles methods of governance inculcated through schooling, media, and sanctioned representations of what makes a good citizen, in regimes spanning the spectrum from despotism to liberal democracy. It is not necessarily the goal that stands out, but the methods employed to achieve it.

Like the USSR described by Yurchak (1997), shortly after independence Frelimo attempted to achieve the hegemony of representation, where a tightly interconnected set of symbolic signifiers is completely under state control, permeating the official sphere to such a degree that even if the symbolic tropes are manifestly false, no others are allowed. Unlike the USSR, however, Frelimo lacked the power, the cadres, and the overall stability to enforce this hegemony throughout the nation. While Frelimo's message and depiction of reality became increasingly irrelevant for citizens in vast tracts of Mozambique, its hegemony of representation did take hold for the relatively privileged urbanites who became the middle class of Maputo. It is people such as these who became what Yurchak referred to as a sort of imagined community (ibid.: 167) based on a shared understanding of what the state was trying to achieve through radical transformation. In contrast to the USSR, the party state managed to abandon the great transformative social revolution on which it once based its legitimacy while surviving the transition to multiparty elections and maintaining and enhancing its overall structure and reach. With the end of the war, privilege started to become separated from rank in the party hierarchy as new avenues of prosperity, legal and otherwise, were opened up. As we shall see in Chapter 5, these transformations were part of a wider process as Frelimo's citizen-building project morphed into an elitist fragment of the previous social revolution. Privilege was no longer the symbol of what was to come for everyone; in fact, in the post-war period, privilege was increasingly based on a negation of everything the social revolution once stood for.

> contemporary political life does not seem to manifest a structure of constituted classes, but rather acts as an instrument of class formation.
>
> (Georges Balandier cited in Bayart 1993: 176)

Introduction

In previous chapters I explored the rise and fall of Frelimo's social revolution and how this set the stage for the emergence of a particular form of middle class in Maputo. During the fifth Frelimo party congress, held in 1989, the last remaining vestiges of socialism were quietly abandoned while the party embraced a new vision of multiparty elections and the so-called neoliberal turn as a prelude to peace (Dinerman 2006; Pitcher 2006). By the end of the war in 1992, Frelimo's vision of the revolutionary transformation of the nation from an agricultural backwater into a prosperous, industrial power populated by the new man seemed, at best, stillborn and, at worst, a contributing factor to the events that devastated the nation. Peace was accompanied by a wrenching structural adjustment programme and large-scale privatisations. Mass mobilisation as part of a larger modernising project faded as the former champions of socialism now spoke in almost messianic terms about the benefits of free enterprise, the need to form a national bourgeoisie, and the redemptive qualities of foreign investment (Pitcher 2002; 2006).[1] The burning ambition and political vision of the early socialist period had given way to new goals, which were more concerned with managing inequality than with building a brave new world. The loss of thousands of jobs, though, was combined with elements of liberalism, the relaxation of

---

[1] Southall argues that the ideological 'hollowing out' of liberation movements once they assume power is a common occurrence in Southern Africa. As the party transforms from a vehicle to ensure social transformation to a party machine, a bitterly contested instrument of accumulation battled over by factional elites, its core constituency tends to become a politically connected bourgeoisie (Southall 2013: 248). Similar processes are under way in Mozambique, although Frelimo has relatively more room to manoeuvre as opposed to the other liberation movements in South Africa, Namibia, and Zimbabwe discussed by Southall, as the nation's economy is not dominated by white former settlers.

political scrutiny and, especially for the privileged, a growth of opportunities resulting in a cautious optimism for the future. The austere puritanism of the early socialist period and the wartime deprivation of the 1980s
were slowly replaced by hedonistic, conspicuous consumption. If life was
even more unequal, for the privileged at least it could be a lot more fun.
As one man told me in 2002:

> With the end of the war things felt different. There was a new constitution, the
> media was reporting things differently, and people were speaking about the
> government in a way they would have never dared before. Of course, the most
> dramatic thing was the end of the war. One could actually feel it in their veins
> things were finally getting better. It was surreal; after all those years of war and
> destruction there was going to be peace. Many of the changes were generally
> good, although some things stayed the same, the same people are still on top and
> they still have all the power.

In this chapter, I shall trace the ways in which post-war political life
shaped the process of middle-class formation. While the transformations
brought about by the Mozambican version of capitalism are central to
this story, I do not reduce these processes to the result of a universalising
neoliberal logic that has supposedly colonised Africa, the Global South,
and the world in the last few decades. Instead, I discuss the often
contradictory ways in which contemporary political visions and the legacies of previous projects contribute to the ongoing processes of stratification. As argued by Coelho, the emergence of multiparty politics should
have transformed the ways in which power in Mozambique was conceptualised and legitimated, but this was not the case.

> according to the new democratic rule, at least in theoretical terms, the source for
> political legitimacy was to be transferred from the history of liberation to the
> electoral process. From then on, it seemed, the most important arguments for
> democratic scrutiny would be based on concrete aspects of current life included
> in party programmes, much more than on historical roles performed according to
> disputable accounts. Such a context would probably dictate the end of the
> Liberation Script as an apparatus, or at least entail its profound transformation.
> Surprisingly, or maybe not, developments took a different course since the
> political forces were not prepared to give up relying on the old apparatus to
> legitimise and strengthen their power. The Liberation Script became therefore
> a central matter of political dispute. As a consequence, not only did it not lose its
> centrality; it was also recuperated by Frelimo as an asset in the democratic contest
> to the extent that the organisation claimed to be its one and only heir. (Coelho
> 2013: 28–9)

The 1980s and 1990s in Mozambique, as in much of Africa, brought
about a political sea change. The Soviet Union collapsed, the ability of
states to play off Cold War rivalries ended, and the economics of structural adjustment became more deeply entrenched, increasing inequality
at the same time as what was known as the democratic wave spread

through the continent. In a manner that was to become familiar throughout Africa, Frelimo's grip on power survived while its symbolic
vocabulary and systems of signification were in flux, as were the structures that underwrote positions of status and privilege. For those
who had climbed the ladder as former exemplars of the political and
economic order, an order that was now crumbling, questions raged over
the contours of the future. Who would now be the ideal national subject
and who would now become the enemy? In the following, I address these
questions through a discussion of how Mozambique's political transformation affected conceptions of citizenship, the material basis of the
middle class, and, finally, attempts to create new forms of legitimation
for privilege and how they were received by my interlocutors.

Citizenship after the social revolution

As Mozambique slowly rebuilt itself, the late Chissano period
(1992–2004) became known as *deixa andar* (let it go, or let it roll),
referring to a new, more relaxed attitude concerning personal accumulation and/or corruption. In order to court the favour of various international agencies, such as the IMF and the World Bank, for desperately
needed resources, Frelimo enacted political and economic reforms.
These reforms entrenched capitalism and opened the party to previously
excluded social categories, such as merchants and religious organisations
(Morier-Genoud 2009). The process of reform also, perhaps uninten-
tionally, allowed the party and the ruling elite access to the resources
necessary to cement their status and power.[2] Exploding corruption
coincided with an expansion of personal freedoms, but this did not come
without cost (ibid.). Economic reforms bolstered growing inequality
amidst national economic growth, yet the vast majority continued to
eke out a living through whatever opportunities they could find on the
lower rungs of the formal economy, or, far more commonly, they were
abandoned to a precarious existence in the so-called informal sector.[3]

---

[2] In her insightful analysis of the political economy of obedience in Tunisia during the
dictatorship of Ben Ali, Hibou argues that political reforms are in fact an instrument of
domination (2011). Whether or not reforms achieved their stated objectives was often
beside the point; instead, Ben Ali exercised power through a continuous process of
reform. 'By perpetuating themselves endlessly, the reforms succeed because the
domains to be reformed are always more numerous, since the instrument, procedures
and mechanisms of discipline are forever extending themselves' (ibid.: 264). The result
was that citizens were confronted by a seemingly all-pervasive power in a social context
characterised by radical unpredictability and uncertainty.
[3] Groes-Green argues that young marginalised men in Maputo purposely engage in risky
and dangerous behaviours as this is the only way in which they can display sovereignty,
fearlessness, and masculinity in the post-socialist vacuum of legitimacy and in a neoliberal
economy where they have few, if any, possible roles to play (2010: 387).

The privileged few took advantage of opportunities with the often inter-connected government, business, aid, and service sectors. They often comprised those who were able to study at special party schools and/or private institutions, later attending universities at home or abroad.

A major goal of the Frelimo leadership after the abandonment of socialism was the formation and consolidation of a national bourgeoisie. High-ranking former officials explained to me that this national bour-geoisie must also be black, so as to better represent the vast majority of the population and provide a counterpoint to the continuation of privil-ege for non-blacks in the postcolonial era. Much of the mercantile sector, though, was dominated by Mozambican Indians, often in close alliance with high-ranking members of Frelimo, while positions in the state bureaucracy had been the traditional route of social mobility for black Mozambicans. While the official conception of a member of the national bourgeoisie was meant to signify a capitalist who was locally rooted and acted in the national interest, by far the best represented in this class were party insiders who occupied positions that were out of reach of even the privileged and who had the connections and political clout to amass wealth. Democracy was touted as government by and for the majority, but the growing social polarisation of post-socialist Mozambique made it difficult for many formerly protected groups, such as industrial workers, to see just what benefits being a member of the majority was meant to bring, as they found their few remaining jobs increasingly under threat. During the scramble for the spoils of the new era, the conceptual gap between the promises of democracy and the reality played out in a variety of discursive registers. This was especially apparent in the post-war lack of consensus on the meaning of citizenship. During socialism, internal cleavages based on race, ethnicity, or region were taboo in official discourse; this is best demonstrated by Samora Machel's famous statement: 'To unite all Mozambicans, transcending traditions and different languages, requires that the tribe must die in our consciousness so that the nation may be born' (Machel 1974: 39). Citizenship was not based so much on what one was, but on what one was supposed to become, guided by Samora as the external editor who stood above society directing the social revolution. Beginning with the death of Samora, Frelimo gradually abandoned many of its exclusivist positions in a desperate effort to survive, gradually sap-ping its self-proclaimed authority to define what a good Mozambican was.

The uncertainty concerning the definition of 'Mozambicanness' became more pronounced following the official abandonment of socialism. Previous conceptions of citizenship and belonging were now challenged, both from the emerging opposition and from within the party itself. Whether the new democratic authentic citizen would continue to be based on a modernist new man, a form of revitalised tradition, or something else entirely was now an open question. During this period,

Hama Thay, a Frelimo veteran, fought to have the meaning of 'Mozambican' changed in the constitution. He argued:

If I were to define who is of Mozambican origin, I would put it this way: the original Mozambican is anyone who in the colonial period was known as a native [*indígena*]. Of Mozambican origin is anyone who in the colonial period paid the hut tax. Of Mozambican origin is anyone whose ancestors or descendants were deported to São Tomé and Príncipe, to Angola and to other unknown places. And I would say more, of Mozambican origin are all those who did forced labor [*chibalo*], all those who after Gungunhana's defeat in 1895 were deported with him to Fourth Island or Third Island or whatever it was exactly, to die there far away, separated from their wives, never more to father children of Mozambican origin. (quoted in O'Laughlin 2000: 6)

Thay's definition of a Mozambican is tangentially connected to place of birth, but it reserves full citizenship for those (especially men) who suffered the most under colonialism. Such a definition casts doubts on the citizenship of those Mozambicans who held a privileged position under the colonial regime, including whites, Indians, *mulatos*, and *assimilados* (who were explicitly defined as not native). Ironically, it is members of those groups who occupied much of the Frelimo leadership (Mateus 1999), and Thay's argument did not prevail. The original 1975 constitution bestowed citizenship on all those born in Mozambique who did not opt for another nationality, and it was amended in 2004 to allow Mozambican women who married foreigners the same rights as Mozambican men to pass their nationality to their spouses. Citizens were officially defined in the liberal conception as individuals who were entitled to political and human rights by virtue of birth. The fact that Thay's argument could be made by a leading member of the ruling party demonstrated just how unclear the concept of true citizenship was in the new order. In Mozambique, the concept of a good citizen had been central to the transformative project, but with the fall of socialism, citizenship increasingly became a floating signifier (Lévi-Strauss 1950), a powerful symbol, but one with no fixed meaning. The gradual erosion of the former meaning of citizenship meant that the concept served equally as a populist rallying call and a critique of the inequalities of the new regime.

The evolution of citizenship from a keystone of the transformative project to a floating signifier stemmed from Mozambique's particular experiences in the colonial and independence periods. It was also due to the adoption of at least a nominally liberal democratic political order. Liberal democracy makes universalistic claims of an all-embracing set of human rights through legal equality. In practice, these are rooted in national belonging and are dependent on a strict division between insider and outsider. Mouffe argues that:

The democratic conception, however, requires the possibility of distinguishing who belongs to the demos and who is exterior to it; for that reason, it cannot exist without the necessary correlate of inequality. Despite liberal claims, a democracy of mankind, if it was ever likely, would be a pure abstraction, because equality can only exist through its specific meaning in particular spheres – as political equality, economic equality and so forth. But those specific equalities always entail, as their very condition of possibility, some form of inequality. (Mouffe 2005: 39; see also Schmitt 1985)

The point above has been employed to understand the persistence of structural inequality and exclusion under a regime based on full political equality for groups such as marginalised minorities, or the passions raised by seemingly trivial marks of difference, such as the widespread public support in France for the ban of head scarves or Switzerland's banning of the construction of minarets on mosques. Democracy is always based on relationships of inclusion and exclusion (Mouffe 2005). However, democratic theory seems unable to conceptualise its internal political limit (ibid.; see also Chipkin 2007). During the socialist period, the definition of the political limit was explicitly connected to the party: those who dedicated themselves to Frelimo's transformative project, or at least those who appeared to do so, were true citizens, while those who did not were enemies of the people. Following the war, it was extremely difficult to say who was a true or authentic national citizen.

If, as Bickford argues, politics is primarily an act of symbolism (2011: 29), then ideologies are signs saturated with meaning; they attempt to define and structure narratives and projects about the way life should be and what are the legitimate bases for power. The construction of an official discourse of citizenship is a programme of social engineering – the selection of traits and attributes, real and imagined, that should exemplify what Chipkin (2007) termed the authentic bearers of the nation. In the socialist period, the authentic bearer of the nation was the new man, and the privileges bestowed upon those who reached these lofty heights were supposedly a preview of what was to follow for the masses. In reality, this idea was contested and probably dismissed by large segments of the population, but it still could be meaningful for the party faithful who aspired to such status. After the official adoption of capitalism, the issue was far more confused. Why did behaviours that were formerly denounced as unjust and exploitative now result in the acquisition of wealth and power? Were former national heroes and prominent examples of the new man under socialism now suspect citizens because they had non-black or *assimilado* backgrounds? If the new authentic citizen was to be based on the majority, why were the majority so poor and why were potentially suspect citizens so rich? Would there be a unitary national culture, and, if so, what would be its foundations? While all these questions spoke to the very heart of the political order, few answers were provided.

New opportunities for the privileged few to amass wealth and influence appeared at the same time as official justifications for privilege crumbled, replaced by increasingly vocal claims of social distance between the leadership and the privileged as well as between the privileged and the wider population, spanning the spectrum from politics to kinship.

Isabel, a former Frelimo militant who now has a high-ranking position in the aid sector, provides an example of this process. She and her husband, also a former state official and now a prosperous businessman, exemplified the benefits of the new order. In addition to the numerous properties they have amassed, they have a large house in one of the most desirable sections of town and were able to send their children to study abroad from secondary school through university and postgraduate degrees. Isabel is in conflict with the less prosperous members of her extended family. She feels that her nuclear family should not be responsible for supporting poorer members of the extended family, as their resources should be concentrated on assuring the security and future prosperity of their own children. In her view, she and her husband have risen to where they are through their own effort and she does not see why other members of her family cannot take responsibility and try to help themselves. Isabel also barred her husband from supporting the poorer members of his side of the family, as, in her opinion, they have not made good use of any previous support. Her attempts to cut off her poorer kin have been contentious. After a series of family tragedies, her sister accused her, among others, of using sorcery to kill various family members in return for their wealth. This caused an open schism in the family between those who felt that both the accusations and witchcraft itself were completely unfounded and beyond the realm of believability, and those who backed Isabel's sister. There is almost no contact between the two sides and Isabel is deeply embarrassed by the scandal. After dedicating herself to a transformative project that was supposed to abolish supposed superstition, Isabel was accused of being a witch by her own sister.

From high politics to domestic disputes, grand projects of progress and transformation gave way to rueful admissions that little could actually be done. According to a woman from a party-connected family, 'We made a terrible mistake during socialism; we broke the tribal system most people lived in, but we did not really have anything to replace it. Now it is chaos.' Power remained with those who liberated the nation, but more questions were being raised about what had been built in the postcolonial period. The growth of a fabulously wealthy elite and the consolidation of an emerging middle class were accompanied by a political limit that became ever more opaque. Frelimo's claim that it was the champion of national unity appeared to be contradicted by the nurturing of party-connected privilege. If, during the revolution, the party state tried to

Figure 5.1 A building with a Frelimo election poster saying
'Vote Frelimo'.
Source: Joerg Boethling / Alamy Stock Photo.

destroy all competing forms of identification and claims of loyalty, the
liberal period undermined the rights and claims of the socialist period. If
there was still a transformative project, it had narrowed to a small,
privileged stratum and it appeared that the vast majority would largely
be left to their own devices.

Housing, politics, and the basis of the middle class

In his discussion of the socialist period in Dar es Salaam, James Brennan
remarked on the difficult status of urban areas in nationalist discourse:
'National citizenship ideals in postcolonial Tanzania concerned public
performance at least as much as they did legal status. Because cities were
primarily sites of consumption that generated unwholesome divisions of
labour, the ideal urban citizen was someone who held urban life in
contempt' (2013: 48). While Frelimo held a dim view of the romanti-
cised conception of precolonial village communism that formed the
intellectual foundation of Tanzania's African socialism, Mozambican
cities also held an ideologically difficult position during the socialist
period. While the party leadership despaired over the 'backward' peasantry, urbanites were in danger of being contaminated by their exposure
to the supposedly decadent colonial culture. Maputo and other cities

were privileged sites for the party's experiments in the transformation of what the leadership viewed as the backward or contaminated population into a new national subject. This can be seen with the nationalisation of the abandoned housing stock in the formerly colonial centre of town and the distribution of flats to those who previously resided in under-served *bairros*. The goals of this decree were based in efforts to abolish the injustices of the colonial period and, in a pedagogical sense, to modernise the capital's inhabitants and bring them under closer surveillance by party organs. Throughout the socialist period, cities, especially Maputo, were simultaneously the centres of privilege, where residents were entitled to rations and other scarce resources, and the sites of periodic crackdowns, such as Operation Production.

The end of socialism did little to dampen the contradictions inherent in cities, which now focused on new wealth amid poverty, or to lessen its role in the construction of new kinds of citizens. In the post-socialist period, another great reform began to transform the city. This time, the government was divesting itself of the housing stock for nominal prices, creating a new class of homeowners and, increasingly, landlords. Senhor Marques, a former minister explained the process as follows:

> We had to get the government out of the housing market – the stock was rapidly deteriorating and the state simply could not take care of it. We thought that we had to help the people and so we did it; it was an ad hoc move without long-term planning. Although, in some respects, we have been more successful than South Africa: if one goes to a nice restaurant here it is full of black people, while in South Africa this is far more rare. Initially, with housing privatisation the idea was one was only able to buy the house that they were renting – the trading came later. However, there were many ways around this as people started registering houses in the names of their wives or children. They would buy houses, still cheap from a person whose salary was so small that they could not pay for it, or through trading.

The creation of a thriving property market was the unanticipated outcome of post-socialist reform. The property market introduced an important capitalist commodity, but in a fashion cloaked in ambiguity that allowed powerful actors significant leverage. To this day, the state does not have a reliable register of property rights, nor does it show much interest in creating one (Andersen, Jenkins, and Nielsen 2015a). In some areas, housing privatisation was carried out in an ad hoc manner, such as simply taking an abandoned house in an area that had been badly damaged by the war. In Maputo, an informal but highly organised market was created. This was part of a wider trend in which, in Lentz's (2015) terms, a distinct middle class took form, one whose social status and material resources were separate from those obtained directly from party or political rank, while still being largely dependent on access to Frelimo to maintain their privilege. As such, urban housing has created a material base for a party-connected middle class, but one whose practices nevertheless tend to reproduce the existing social order as well as the group's own dependence on the political elite. As example is Cristina, introduced in Chapter 4, who comes from a Frelimo family and grew up in Maputo during the socialist period. According to her, the property market quickly became an obsession of an emerging middle class – only those who had the resources and connections could truly take advantage of it:

> It was called selling the keys [*vender a chave*]. This is when you find a person who is renting a government house but does not have the money to buy, although they are very cheap; one trades the house they have for the rented one and then buys it from the government. When privatisation first started, my mother got a four-storey house for something like US$80. People were snapping up houses right and left. We should have gotten more, but we thought the process would go on for longer than it did. The boom in property prices was amazing. You could buy a house for under US$100 and then rent it to the Swiss or the UN and all the peacekeeping missions for thousands. People made fortunes.

If the new man was to be the master symbol of socialism, with the creation of this social subject as the fundamental precondition for the social revolution, then the national bourgeoisie became the master symbol of capitalism. The new man, while elitist in conception and practice, was what James Ferguson termed a 'people hungry' method of domination (2013). It was part of a wider strategy of mass mobilisations whose eventual goal was to encompass and transform as much of the population as possible, willingly or unwillingly. The formation of a national bourgeoisie was in many ways the exact opposite – a progressive narrowing as much of the wider population were no longer needed, not even as subordinates. Under successive structural adjustment programmes, industries were closing and salaries in the nation's largest employer, the state bureaucracy, were frozen. Entrance to the national bourgeoisie was largely restricted to high-ranking party members, their families, and associates who tended to be among the major beneficiaries of privatisation and who used their political base to accrue economic power (Castel-Branco, Cramer, and Hailu 2001; Pitcher 2002). Frelimo itself also became a major economic actor, both through partnerships with multinationals and in its own right, keeping important segments of the economy within the 'Frelimo family' by allowing trusted party members to take control of newly privatised economic concerns (Pitcher 2002). Few others had sufficient power to take advantage of the privatisations of state industries; in fact, most were far more likely to lose their jobs. Salaries, even for white-collar workers in state ministries, were low compared with the cost of living, often around the equivalent of US$300 per month with some added benefits, such as free lunches at specified restaurants. In such a situation, the effects of the housing giveaway were widely felt and the rents from such houses comprised a considerable part of many people's incomes. While this was still primarily restricted to relatively privileged urbanites and those with the political connections to gain and control property rights in a murky legal context, it was probably among the most economically inclusive aspects of capitalism in Maputo. These newly formed entrepreneurs, enterprising but not alienated from the state, and the national bourgeoisie who resided at the pinnacle of society created the nucleus of a post-socialist middle class, the social bedrock of the liberal project. As with housing privatisation in Angola, state-directed strategies of accumulation were largely able to keep middle-class formation within state structures, in an effort to keep the middle class loyal and dependent on access to the party state (Soares de Oliveira 2015).

Housing became one of the prime economic bases of a new capitalistic middle class, although this did not create the autonomy that the backers of liberal reforms had supposedly envisioned, or at least to which they paid lip service.[4] According to Senhor Marques:

The base of the middle class is the state. Frelimo is basically the party of the state and the state is what created the middle class to a large degree. It comprises various levels, but one of the first was state corruption, which has created new opportunities for accumulation. Another was the privatisation of housing; this is one of the things that does not depend directly on corruption. In the early 1990s when the state privatised houses, many made a good deal of money renting houses to the UN and the aid agencies that were flooding in. This began to change the character of the city. Before, during the socialist period, rents were controlled so the social mixture of the city was much greater than it is now. Now that is changing and the city is becoming quite a bit more stratified. However, this created a huge opportunity for many people throughout the city. Quite a few fortunes have been based on acquiring property.

Instead of creating the autonomous agent of the liberal dream, housing, as with so many other aspects of post-socialist Mozambique, created new forms of hierarchy and dependence. Some forms of dependence were specifically gender-based, in stark contrast to the party's revolutionary rhetoric of liberating women so that they could no longer be traded like goods in a shop. One way in which women could get a new house was through relationships with foreign men. As Claudia, a middle-class Mozambican woman who grew up in the socialist period, told me:

When the first non-communist foreigners came, the aid agencies, they caused a lot of interest. They had a lot of money and they were rather naïve. They were

---

[4] Privatised housing often becomes a basis for middle-class formation in post-socialist countries. See Fehérváry (2013) for a discussion of the ways in which the privatisation process and its resulting insecurities encouraged people to become property owners in Hungary.

spending, not just buying clothes and dinner; they were buying people houses and cars. Many of them also had children here with their mistresses; the house was kind of payment for leaving the children and going back to their wives and families in Europe.

The most common method of securing housing, however, was through a relationship with state officials. The emerging middle classes of Mozambique and Africa generally are largely an outgrowth of the state that created them. In a similar manner, the economic basis of members of the emerging middle class rarely tend to focus on productive enterprises, spreading money more widely through the economy, but instead cluster around economic sectors that depend on political access, such as property. Thus, the overall effect of liberal reforms was to transform and refine forms of dependence instead of creating autonomous individuals. Land in Mozambique is still owned by the state, although citizens can own surface rights (Andersen, Jenkins, and Nielsen 2015a). The lack of an overall clear legal framework concerning land rights and the seeming disinterest in creating one granted state officials significant leeway and bolstered the need for political connections.

Tara is a long-time member of Frelimo; both she and her husband have held high-ranking party and government positions. After leaving government services they went into real estate. By 2002, it was easy to rent out higher end houses for around US$5,000 a month or more. Business was doing so well that they managed to pay off a ten-year bank loan in just three and a half years. Tara was also able to pay to have her children educated in South Africa and Europe. They had a palatial home with a large yard and pool, carefully guarded by high windowless walls topped with broken glass, and the family embodied prosperity. Tara felt that her home was her most important investment: 'I do not want gold rings or jewellery or parties at the Polana [the most famous luxury hotel in Maputo]; my home is the most important thing for me and for my family.' This emerging 'cult of domesticity' was both a moral and a material means of drawing boundaries between members of the middle class and other social groups. It signifies that members of the middle class do not spend resources on transient, gaudy displays, but instead invest in the domestic sphere and in the family. It also means that they have the resources and political connections to do so. In 1987, Tara was able to buy for US$2 the surface rights to the plot where her family lives in one of the most exclusive parts of town.

Tara, in many ways, illustrates the ways in which the grand goals of the social revolution were not necessarily abandoned after the fall of socialism, but rather were increasingly narrowed: progress for all becomes progress for the deserving, and the stress on sovereignty is replaced with the trope of autonomy. In reality, though, the practices necessary to secure rewards and autonomy were frequently arbitrary and contradictory. An apt illustration occurred on a visit with a friend, Marco, to his *quinta* (country house or estate). Marco's family was well established during the colonial period and had been active with Frelimo since the liberation struggle. The house in question was acquired by Marco's father during the privatisation period. As we strolled across the spacious, well-tended grounds, Marco absently issued orders to deferential groundskeepers and outlined his plan to leave his government post and start businesses on his various properties. While Marco's property is part of a material strategy to consolidate himself, as discussed above, it is also a symbolic expression of an ideal of autonomy that is deeply interlinked with his position of status and moral worth, the cultural markers of privilege in Maputo. However, it is also symbolic of the contradictions of autonomy. When Marco's father took over the property, he failed to give the party its cut and the family fell into disgrace. Marco took a low-ranking position at a ministry to try to make amends. The reason we had driven to the *quinta* that day had been so that Marco could collect the monthly tribute for his boss from the 'fees' extracted by the traffic police who lined the route. Marco's *quinta*, like other houses of the privileged, symbolises autonomy, even while it bolsters dependence on the powerful.

Fehérváry argues that, in Hungary, the focus on the home was a way of escaping the gaze of an oppressive state while cultivating different, middle-class forms of identity (2013). In Mozambique, new forms of domesticity were less a means to escape the state (many of those featured in this book can be considered active parts of that state) than to escape the nation. As the transformative project failed for the nation as a whole, it turned inward, with new forms of domesticity as a way of cultivating a modern, middle-class identity for oneself and one's family, in opposition to the wider population. While the palace of Tara or even the *quinta* of Marco may have been beyond the reach of many, the immaculate and carefully furnished apartments of the city centre were direct rebukes to the decaying buildings in which they resided. Here, one could create a carefully cultivated middle-class ideal safely guarded by steel doors from the disorder of the outside world. For many in Maputo, the immediate post-war period was a time of hardship, as the rations once guaranteed to urbanites were discontinued and state-owned firms enacted huge layoffs or were closed down. For the lucky few, though – those who lived in the concrete city centre instead of the sprawling *bairros* on the outskirts, and those whose positions gave them sufficient access to take advantage of new opportunities – it was a time of promise. The economic base of privilege was becoming consolidated and new forms of domesticity were gaining ground, but the effort to reform the underlying narratives that legitimated the new inequalities was a more contested process.

Youth, tensions, and class consolidation

If the home is both the financial basis of the middle class and a fortress for the well-established family, class consolidation, especially among younger people, tended to play out through socialising and romantic relationships. The middle class living in Maputo often focuses on locating secure spaces, found in hubs spread throughout the city, for working, shopping, dining, drinking, and other entertainment. The costs of these venues was usually prohibitive for the average urbanite, and their very existence was, to some degree, a material manifestation of boundary drawing. For the younger members of the middle class, weekends often followed a predictable pattern in Maputo. On Fridays people would meet after work for drinks and perhaps dinner, then they would go home to rest and get ready for a night out. People would then meet again at around 11 in the evening for drinks at a bar, leaving for a disco at around midnight or one in the morning. They did not usually go home until around five in the morning. The popularity of any given disco was often fleeting, and they opened and closed with great regularity. Although there were frequently changing venues, the discos themselves tended to be rather uniform. They were dark with flashing lights and played similar combinations of popular Western dance music with Latin hits and occasional Afro-pop or Afro-jazz songs. The dance floors were usually full and surrounded by large groups of people who carefully watched and commented on the proceedings. Women were normally dressed in their best and most revealing Brazilian clothes, while hip-hop and faux-gangster styles were the height of fashion for young men, although some of the older men wore suits. At the most fashionable club at any given moment, the president's sons and their entourage were usually lounging in the corner wearing white panama suits and white fedoras while smoking Cuban cigars and drinking Johnnie Walker. Discos were sites where people of varying degrees of privilege could informally meet and interact with one another.

In a successful club, the balconies were teeming with people coming off the dance floor for more generalised flirting and to greet people. Most of the participants were well known to each other and often connected through webs of work, school, and familial and social relationships. The goals of these occasions were to relax and enjoy oneself, but there were also frequent conflicts. Due to the perceived prevalence of adultery, couples often watched each other with a jealous eye and relationships were frequently regarded with a degree of mild paranoia. Occasionally, violence would break out, usually as men accused one another of trying to steal their girlfriends. More rarely, violence would escalate and sometimes panic would ensue as one of the people involved in the fight would go to his car for his gun or knife. Less frequently, women would be involved in violence – once again, usually prompted by accusations that someone had tried to steal someone else's boyfriend.

During the socialist period, power, status, and privilege were tightly bound to the public performance of a rigid moral code. Of course, this was not always obeyed: I heard numerous stories from older male informants about heavy drinking, having multiple sexual partners, and, on occasion, multiple families. However, one had to keep such practices secret, or at least be discreet, or one could be branded a reactionary. In the capitalist period, the party hegemony of representation and the tightly bound signifiers of the 'new man' that bound the notion of being socially advanced to the display of certain cultural behaviours began to unravel. Now men at least could publicly celebrate behaviour that previously would have been condemned. According to Manuel (2014), men tend to justify engaging in adultery by an appeal to so-called African culture, which appears to be a direct rebuttal to the official modernist puritanism of the revolutionary period. However, as a rebuttal, it is selective. I have met members of the middle class who will excuse their sexual behaviour by citing 'African culture' but who have little but contempt for what they view as the 'peasant traditions of the bush' in almost every other aspect of life. Middle-class women, on the other hand, often made an appeal to a Samora-style discourse of the 'modern' relationship predicated on respect and equality, even though the puritanism of the revolutionary period and the strict performance of a moral code had been long abandoned (ibid.). This situation was compounded by the fact that many women felt at a disadvantage, as there was a common belief that women dramatically outnumbered men in Maputo. I was frequently told that the ratio was seven to one. Although this statement does not withstand statistical analysis, it was widely believed. Many women I knew felt that the availability of multiple sex partners for men meant that they had to make compromises or their partner could easily leave them and find someone else. It was widely recognised that relationships with privileged men were often one of the prime opportunities for material advancement for women of lower-ranking backgrounds.

The epitome of the new latitude allowed to Mozambican men was *o dia do homem* (the day of the man or man's day). This is not so much an official date as a running joke. It occurs on Fridays and is widely celebrated throughout the city. The most enthusiastic participants I encountered were men in their late twenties and their thirties who were involved in serious relationships or married, although it was observed by younger, more loosely attached men as well. As with other urban social activities, the day of the man also tended to follow a standard pattern. Men would meet each other at a bar on Friday night and have drinks. Conversation focused on issues such as work, politics, drinking, and, of course, sex. Whenever I asked a man where his partner was, I would usually be given a look of contempt, often accompanied by the reply: '*Ela esta na casa. Sexta-feira é o dia do homem*' (She is at home. Friday is the day of the man). This would normally draw exclamations of approval from the others present. As the night progressed, men would often complain that there were no women present and suggest that the party be relocated to a disco that would have mixed company. The day of the man did not have to be spent entirely with men; in fact, meeting new women was often one of its goals. The day of the man was about stereotypically male conversations with friends, but it was also about openly asserting the independence that came with the new era, something that women were usually aware of but often unable to stop.

The norms covering the behaviour of young women were also subject to considerable cultural tension. According to many younger middle-class women I know, there has been a gradual and often contested relaxation of the rules covering female conduct. In the circles with which I am familiar, women were able to talk openly about sex in mixed-gender situations and could take the initiative in forming romantic relationships without incurring much in the way of social sanctions. These changes began with reconceptualisations of gender in the socialist period and increased due to the continued 'liberalisation' of capitalism, even if they remained the cause of considerable generational conflict. While younger people looked to forms of cosmopolitan sophistication, this behaviour often drew harsh comments from the older generation. One middle-class woman I knew, who was in her early forties, went so far as to claim that the crime of rape was impossible because young women dress and act in such a provocative manner that any man could be excused for misreading a woman's intentions. She had recently been at a disco with her husband and was furious that a younger woman had approached her husband and openly flirted with him, requesting drinks, right in front of her. As she told me: 'I was standing right next to him, he had a ring on his finger, and she did not even care.'

There was and continues to be a strong discourse of endogamy among the middle class, although actions on the ground do not always reflect stated intentions. As mentioned earlier, there were frequent complaints among young privileged women that there was a lack of men in Maputo. After further observation, it often seemed that it was not an absolute lack of men that was the problem, but a lack of 'suitable' men. Class standing is a key factor in determining who is a suitable sexual partner, although it is not always acted upon. Generally, men are allowed more leeway, with relationships with poorer women being a major factor in social mobility. However, men are also often under considerable familial pressure to marry someone suitable. While some men defy convention and marry a poorer woman anyway, many other such women become 'outside' wives. These are women who may share their life with their partner and have children with them, but are often denied legal recognition. Families often view such latitude among women with more concern. There is the ever-present danger of a woman becoming pregnant, leading to the possibility of far more public long-term ties between a privileged family and a poorer one.

An example of these contradictory processes of exclusion and integration is provided by Varyna, a young middle-class woman who was in her mid-twenties at the time I knew her. Towards the end of my PhD fieldwork she formed a romantic relationship with a man from a lower-status background. He worked as a barman and had aspirations to become an artist. One day, over coffee, she mentioned to me that she was very nervous about introducing him to her parents, although she usually described her parents as very 'modern' and liberal. When I asked why her parents might disapprove of her new relationship, Varyna said that it was quite obvious. Her boyfriend cultivated an unconventional appearance; he worked as a barman, and he had never finished high school. She was worried about what her parents would think and felt that they would be deeply disappointed in her:

They [my parents] had to fight to get where they are today. They have worked really hard to make sure that their children have a nice life and a good education. They will not sit still and watch me take a step backwards for some guy with crazy-ass hair and no education, and worse still, no real plans to fix the situation. They would think he is not serious. I mean, what kind of life would I have?

Despite her actions, Varyna had seemingly internalised many class-based ideals concerning the nature of a 'suitable' partner. She did finally introduce him to her parents, who, if uncomfortable about him, did their best not to show it. Varyna, on the other hand, continually pressured him to improve his life, cut his hair, and return to school. She wanted him to 'make something' of himself and improve his social standing. In many ways, Varyna was employing a dual strategy of trying to maintain the relationship she wanted while transforming her partner into someone more 'suitable' at the same time. This strategy was not entirely successful and the relationship eventually ended badly.

As with Varyna, many others expressed concerns about jobs and the future prospects of their respective partners. Young women would often voice reservations about a possible relationship if they felt that they would have to bear a disproportionate share of the economic burden. As I heard some friends explain to a woman who was involved with a poorer man and was expecting a baby: 'Listen you have to understand that you will end up supporting him and the baby. That is not going to change no matter what you think. Are you really willing to do that?' Despite their advice to others, it always seemed different when they themselves were involved. Many would try to employ a similar dual strategy to that of

Varyna and form relationships outside a restricted social circle while trying to transform their partner into someone they felt would be suitable for membership within that circle. As in Varyna's case, these strategies often bore mixed results. As one woman told me after a failed relationship: 'The differences in background were just too much.' She was deeply disappointed by her boyfriend's suspected infidelities and because their plans to secure for him foreign schooling and start various money-making ventures had come to naught. Yet these differences do not form an airtight barrier, and the woman later resumed her relationship with the same man, although his overall circumstances had not changed, before finally leaving him and marrying what would be considered a far more suitable partner.

Modernity, prosperity, and discontent

Drawing on the work of Mbembe, Primorac describes a postcolonial master narrative as that which: 'seeks to govern the production of all other socially contested meanings' (2007: 434). In the immediate post-independence period, Frelimo's master narrative centred on the social revolution and its grand transformative project. While many agreed that the social revolution failed to achieve its ambitious goals, aspects of the revolutionary period continued into the new order. Forms of governmentality and the techniques of domination are successive rather than simultaneous; and the past, even if discredited, seeps into the present (Gupta 2012: 242). While mass mobilisation and the performance of a rigid, selfless moral code were abandoned, the underlying elitism of the transformative project survived to take new, perhaps even more potent, forms. The privileged continued to occupy various steps on a ladder above the less advanced and the inherently conflictual masses, and it was they who had the necessary skills, to varying degrees, to act as arbiter of the good of all (Dinerman 2006). A friend described her father's history in the liberation struggle as follows: 'My father did not fight for equality, he fought for development.' Such statements, and the necessity of class privilege they imply, were frequently expressed in a variety of ways. Once, a friend was telling me a quite fascinating story about sorcery. When he saw my interest, however, he suddenly stopped and said, 'Of course, I do not believe in this or even know that much about it. I am an urban person.' By saying this, he drew a firm boundary between himself as a modern urbanite and those who were still supposedly backwards, which was reflected in their belief in things such as sorcery. This sense of cultural superiority was often expressed in racial terms, although there was a rarely a racial difference. The term *preto* (literally the colour black, but very derogatory when used to describe a person) was frequently employed when someone was acting badly, or foolishly, or often for the wider population in general. New inequalities were also justified as simply a matter of interest. Josina, the daughter of a high-ranking family, explained to me that capitalist reforms were necessary for progress and that the job losses and growing social polarisation that were affecting much of the population were not really a problem.

There is a huge difference here that I do not think you understand. You spend all of your time with people like us; we are educated and Westernised. Those of us who are privileged have tastes and desires that are very different from everyone else. It is really a question of interest. Most people in this country are peasants, they have a *machamba* [a small plot of land], and they are interested and satisfied with that. They do not really need education or anything more; in fact, they do not really want it. For instance, my father comes from a poor, rural background. He liked to read, but he was not that interested in education. He did not become interested until he saw the Portuguese and how much they had in comparison to himself. Most people want to be left alone to farm their *machambas*. It is those of us who are privileged that want and need all of these things.

If her father liked to read and had access to books in the colonial period, his background was probably not as poor and rural as Josina thought. Whatever the reality, Josina was referencing a system of signification that remained powerful. The need to submit to an enlightened vanguard as the first step towards transforming society and bringing prosperity for all is a master narrative in Primorac's terms, and one that has recurred in Mozambique in colonial, socialist, and capitalist periods.

In such a context, many members of Maputo's middle class took a rather lackadaisical attitude to the practice of democracy in Mozambique. Once I was speaking with a young man who launched into a litany of abuse against Frelimo. For at least five minutes, he described a catalogue of what he felt to be the ruling party's faults, errors, penchant for corruption, and overall general uselessness. I asked him who his family supported and he said: 'Oh, they vote for Frelimo.' I then asked who he would vote for and he said: 'Frelimo.' I was puzzled by his response and asked why he would vote for Frelimo if he disliked them so much. He replied: 'Because the pockets of Frelimo are already full while the pockets of Renamo are still empty.' He was implying that Frelimo would not have to steal too much more to support the party members in their current lifestyle, while Renamo officials would have to begin from the bottom and work their way up. A vote for Renamo would thus be a vote for even greater levels of corruption. His remarks encapsulate what many people see as the major change brought about by economic reforms; this was often referred to as gangster or savage capitalism, with Maputo as the epitome of the new system.

While the majority of the city's population appeared to be more or less excluded from the economy, Maputo had been at the forefront of the nation's growth during the 1990s and for most of the 2000s. I was told by the president of Mozambique's second-largest bank and the former Minister of Finance that between 70 per cent and 80 per cent of the nation's banking deposits during this period were in Maputo, and the city's purchasing power constituted around 60 per cent of that of the entire nation. Furthermore, the Maputo province absorbed around 70 per cent of the nation's foreign investment. Following the end of the war, Maputo was heavily integrated into the South African-dominated regional economy, especially through the construction of the Johannesburg–Maputo transport corridor that links the two cities (Castel-Branco 2002). Maputo once again operated as a port for the rand while South African goods filled the city. If Maputo had resumed its late colonial economic role, some of the Frelimo leadership saw capitalism as the latest step in a dialectical model, very similar to that of Marxism.

I met Senhor Marques, a former minister, in his offices. After leaving government service he became the president of the Mozambican branch of an international conglomerate. To enter his office one had to go through multiple uniformed secretaries and two armed guards next to the elevator before one was finally ushered into a large room dominated by an impressive desk. We sat at a table seemingly placed there to greet visitors while a secretary brought coffee. I asked Senhor Marques for his thoughts on the country's economic liberalisation process and he replied:

That depends on the criteria you use to judge it by. If you want a degree of economic freedom with people able to conduct their affairs with some room to manoeuvre then it has been a reasonable success. If the objective was to reduce poverty, then no, it has not been a success. One also must ask just how liberal the economy is. In some countries one can open a business in four days; here it normally takes more than 100. Also, the current government's economic agenda is that of the IMF and the World Bank. There is no clear policy towards agriculture, which is the future of this country. Our current situation concerning land and agriculture is basically feudal; we need to move farming to the capitalist stage of development. Peasants all have a right to their land, but production is very low. We need to encourage a kulak class of middle peasants, but they will need labour. Now we have people working on one hectare of land using ancient tools from 500 years ago. We need to create a kulak class, someone with five or six hectares and access to more modern tools, someone who can hire labour. The peasantry can keep some of their land, enough for some basic subsistence while sending family members to work. We need to privatise land, create a rural proletariat, and allow for the concentration of productive capital in the hands of kulaks, who could then be the engine of development.

Senhor Marques was a least interested in agriculture, something that dominated the livelihoods of the vast majority of the country. Few others in the leadership seemed to be, beyond paying lip service to the importance of the peasantry or engaging in land grabs. Maputo remained the economic hub.

However, although the lion's share of the benefits of the new economic system were accrued by a politically connected elite, middle-class Mozambicans also benefited. In addition to the acquisition of the city's housing stock, opportunities opened up in newly privatised businesses and the rapidly expanding NGO sector, where salaries could exceed US $1,000 a month, compared with the US$300 or so that could be had in a government ministry post in 2002–4. Even with the steady rise in prices, this offered a level of financial security beyond the reach of most. Despite this unprecedented prosperity, there was a strong streak of nostalgia for the socialist period. An example can be found in a conversation I had with two young men in their mid-twenties in 2002. They were both students at University Eduardo Mondlane (UEM), the major public institution, and had grown up in Maputo. They complained bitterly of the inequalities they felt had become more deeply manifest after the transition. They remembered the socialist period as difficult and arduous, but also felt that there was a sense of solidarity, with efforts to ensure that everyone received a share of the little that was available: 'There was more equality back then. Sure the government people got better rations, but even the ministers were thin, they did not wear flashy suits and drive Mercedes to their mansions like now.' Another woman claimed:

I liked Samora – he was in control, no thieves, no rubbish and everything was orderly. If people got out of line he would cut their fingers. Since the end of socialism some people have made lots of money, but there has also been a loss of fear and respect. It has been good for some. Even during socialism there was a gap between the rich and the poor, but Samora was hard on the rich. Now it is all these new rich, they made their money from corruption; everything now goes to the fastest.

For reasons such as these, Samora Machel remained an icon of revolutionary nationalism among younger residents in Maputo. One frequently saw young people wearing T-shirts with pictures of Samora Machel on the front and his slogan 'A luta continua' ('The struggle continues') on the back. For many, Samora Machel has become the symbol of the best aspects of the socialist period, the free healthcare and education, the lack of corruption, self-sacrifice, and the commitment to build a nation that would protect and benefit everyone. At public protests against corruption, it was common to see signs emblazoned with 'Naõ havia acontecer se Samora estivesse vivo' ('This could not happen if Samora were alive'). Many of the problems of the period were explained by means of the 'good tsar, wicked ministers' allegory. Such ideas indicate a lack of exteriority, as challenges to the party are made in its own symbolic vocabulary, yet they also discredit Frelimo's claims of continuing legitimacy in its own terms. As many of the 'wicked ministers' continued to play a role in politics, a clear line of demarcation was drawn between what the party once stood for (as symbolised by the quasi-martyred figure of Samora Machel) and the perils of the new capitalist period (as symbolised by the supposed venality of the surviving Frelimo government). It was often hinted darkly that certain current prominent government figures had had a hand in Samora's death.

In the deeply factionalised milieu of the ruling party, it was common even for some Frelimo cadres to speak in these dichotomous terms: counterpoising old/nationalistic/pure against new/involved with international interests/venal. One former cadre said in despair: 'They [the party leadership] are just thieves now. Look at the country now, they are acting like the colonialists used to.' These critiques of the present are firmly based in growing social inequality, yet their nostalgic idealisations appear retrospectively to downplay the existence of status differences during the socialist period. Such differences did exist and became more pronounced as the government became increasingly authoritarian, even while Samora Machel was alive. By the mid-1980s, high-ranking party members were given special rations, special housing, special sections of hospitals, special schools for their children, and access to special stores and restaurants. In Beira, the second city of Mozambique, the leadership was driven in military convoys and passers-by were required to stop, move out of the way, and salute (Hall and Young 1997: 76). Yet, for many in Maputo, whatever status differences existed during the socialist era paled in comparison with what they saw as the starker differences of the 1990s and early 2000s.

Those closer to the top of the social hierarchy, while being aware of the misdeeds of the powerful (and on occasion being complicit), usually felt that their status as being more 'culturally advanced' than the wider population justified emerging inequalities. One woman, the daughter of a high-ranking official, explained that she and her family were still strong Frelimo supporters. She felt that, corruption aside, there was no one else who was capable of running the country. In her opinion, Renamo was simply a group of uneducated peasants. To illustrate her point, she told me a story:

I remember in 1992 when peace was declared and Renamo came out of the bush. They were given houses – at least the big guys in the party were. It was one of the conditions for peace. Dhlakama [the leader of Renamo] said he would not come to the capital because he did not have a house. The government finally had to give him one; it had originally been built for the European Union. When they [Renamo] came here they had no idea how to live in a city; they were fresh from the bush. They used to wash their clothes and leave them on the front lawn to dry! Can you believe that? These people think they could run a country. It's a joke; they had never been out of the bush before.

At the time, I found it remarkable that, after all the horrors of the civil war, this woman disqualified Renamo from political leadership because they displayed peasant habits with their washing. I asked her if members of Frelimo did not act in a similar way when they returned from the bush after the ten-year liberation struggle. She just laughed and replied: 'Are you kidding? Frelimo knew far more than that.' Through her statements, she made use of a trope I often heard among the middle class. The promise of superior civilisational standing – modernity in effect – was monopolised by Frelimo; to be a modern person in Mozambique is to be deeply intertwined with the party.

If the legitimacy of the party leadership rested on the claim that, because they were culturally advanced, they were the only ones capable of transforming the nation and its populace for the better, the question remained as to why this has not yet happened. For some, the fault lay with Mozambicans themselves and the idea that there was an enlightened group that could stand above society and arbitrate between the conflict-ual masses. As Varyna told me:

The problem is we blacks are still 200 years behind. You can see it everywhere. When we get power it just becomes about lining your own pockets. Everything is about who you are and who you know. When something goes wrong we just blame the outside. It's the West or spirits; it's always something. They go and find a *curandeiro* or *feiticeiro* [traditional healer or sorcerer] to find out what it is. It's not just disease, I mean they know something about herbalism and that might work. They do it for stupid things, like relationship trouble. People think magic can stop someone from cheating on them. You would be surprised about the people I am talking about; I mean people who have been to university, they are educated and should know better.

Varyna grew up towards the end of the socialist period, but her com-ments seem very similar to some of the rhetoric of the new man. It is telling that those who bear the brunt of her attack are the people who should be the closest to the ideal citizen, as they are educated and failing by their own terms, whereas one could expect lapses from the wider population. Doubts exist within Frelimo as well. According to one party member, 'What we need is a revolution inside of Frelimo. We just keep recycling old ideas and everything seems to get worse.'

The symbolic vocabulary and underlying system of signification for Frelimo's rule are predicated on the idea that the Mozambican popula-tion is backward and needs to be transformed in order for the nation to develop and become prosperous. Many members of the middle class that I knew shared this system of signification. Such connections are what have historically formed the basis of relationships of dependence between them, the party, and the institutions the party controls. While a shared system of signification creates support, it can also breed dissidence, especially when leading cadres, their family members, and close associ-ates fall visibly short of the ideal as defined in their own terms. During the Chissano era, people I knew often felt that the party elite had given up the moral high ground through their venality. An especially popular target for condemnation was the children of party leaders. It was they who seemed to embody everything that had gone wrong since the end of the war. According to one woman:

There is a system of last names here and the children of ministers think they can do whatever they want because they have powerful names. I blame the parents for giving them the idea that they are better. They just dream of America and they think that life is a hip-hop video and they try and act it. These people have no culture, no identity, and no etiquette. Mozambique is losing its identity after the death of Samora.

Another man expressed similar sentiments:

The powerful here are basically the same as the ones during the socialist era. They used to control absolutely everything, but they have abandoned the obviousness of that, although they have held on to economic power. They did not have to work for it, they were just in the right place at the right time. The worst are the children of the leadership – they have been groomed to rule, to take over, but in actuality they are filthy spoiled brats who could never make it on their own. They have absolutely no discipline; they have had everything handed to them since the beginning of time. They have everything and they have no idea what to do with it.

Widely held contempt for the behaviour of the children of the ruling elite did not stop people from imitating it as a demonstration of authority. Once, when driving with a friend, we were stopped at one of the numerous police checkpoints that litter Maputo's streets. While stopped, my friend turned to me and said in English, 'Oh, these guys, this is all show – you know what they want,' referring to the very likely proposition that the police would find something amiss with his paperwork or car and demand a bribe. My friend must have assumed that the police would not understand his comment, as the police force is generally thought to be staffed by the exceedingly ill-educated who are unlikely to be conversant in English. On this occasion my friend was decidedly incorrect and the leading officer, who was visibly annoyed, responded in perfect English: 'What is it you think myself and my comrades want? As I understand we are not here to want anything, but to enforce the law.' While my friend was reasonably successful and drove a nice car, he did not have sufficient clout to deal with an angry police officer who was ostentatiously fondling a Kalashnikov rifle. My friend then replied with a British-inflected upper-class accent: 'Your job may be to enforce the law but it is not to eavesdrop on private conversations. Please stand over there while I finish speaking to my friend.' The police officer now seemed confused, trying to figure out if my friend was simply mad or was related to someone with a high enough ranking that an overt dismissal of armed men would be a feasible option. Finally, it appeared that the policeman did not think it worth the risk to find out and let us go on our way.

My friend than exclaimed: 'That was really risky, but he had me and I did not know what else to do!' While many were able to mimic the actions of authority, sometimes with a degree of success, few felt that such authority had much of a moral basis.

This point was driven home following the assassination of Mozambique's most respected journalist, Carlos Cardoso, and the allegations that President Chissano's eldest son, Nyimpine, was involved. Carlos Cardoso had been one of the senior managers of the Mozambican state news agency during the socialist period. While he had occasional confrontations with the Frelimo government, he was a strong supporter of Samora Machel. After Samora's death and the transition to capitalism, Cardoso became increasingly critical of government policies, which he felt primarily benefited the wealthy. He left the state-run news agency and formed two independent papers, *Mediafax* and later *Metical*. Although these papers were distributed by fax, they became very influential beyond their limited circulation of a couple of hundred. Cardoso began aggressively to report cases of corruption, especially bank scandals and allegations of money laundering during the 1990s property boom in Maputo (Fauvet and Mosse 2003).

On 22 November 2000, Cardoso was assassinated while being driven home from work. Although the government was initially reluctant to pursue the case, their hand was forced by mounting pressure, both internal and international. Six people were eventually arrested, and the murder was blamed on the Satars, a prominent Mozambican Indian family with alleged mafia ties who were involved in embezzling funds from one of the banks Cardoso was investigating. All six defendants were found guilty and three received sentences of 28 years in prison.[5] During the trial, one of the accused claimed that they were acting on behalf of Nyimpine Chissano, son of then president Joaquim Chissano. Nyimpine had been employed by one of the banks in question as a consultant when its assets disappeared and he was also rumoured to have made immense, if illegal, profits in the property boom.

Cardoso was not the only well-respected Mozambican to be assassinated in connection with the widespread banking scandals. A senior officer at Banco Austral named Siba-Siba was killed after he published the names of approximately 1,500 people who refused to pay back long-standing loans. Many of the names were those of prominent elite families. The Cardoso case was different, though. In addition to the public outrage his death caused within Mozambique, he was white, well

---

[5] However, one of the assassins, who reputedly held key information about the case, managed to escape and leave the country twice, in this instance because his cell was left unlocked. He simply walked out of the prison complex to a waiting car, which contained a passport, and was conveniently parked nearby. He was sentenced in absentia.

connected both internationally and to members of the Frelimo government, and his wife was Danish and involved with Danish aid to Mozambique. The government was under intense pressure from the international community to deal with the case in a manner that demonstrated the donor's particular definitions of good governance and transparency. Accordingly, the trial became the second ever to be televised in Mozambique's history. Internationally, this had the desired effect, and that year Mozambique was awarded more foreign aid from the World Bank than was requested, effectively shoring up the losses from the bank scandal.[6] Domestically, however, the trial just threw up more questions.

The trial was electrifying. Throughout its duration, one could not enter a shop without seeing all of the staff and the customers huddled by the radio listening to its progress (Sumich 2008). When Nyimpine was called to testify, talk in every taxi or bus concerned the possible fate of *o filho do galo* (the son of the rooster, referring to Nyimpine). Many I knew took the day off when Nyimpine was first called before the court and invited friends and family over to watch the unfolding spectacle. I was present at a friend's home and I watched how the audience initially took great joy in watching the heavyset young man in a designer suit, who was rumoured to be wealthy beyond their wildest dreams, uncomfortably mumble answers to the judge's questions. They had finally seen the epitome of the arrogance of the ruling class humbled publicly. The owner of the house delightedly told me a story about Nyimpine being forced to leave a shop because the other patrons started loudly jeering when he arrived.

Yet, as the trial progressed and it became apparent that Nyimpine would survive his encounter with the law with his wealth intact, this joy turned to resentment.[7] Nyimpine had long had a bad reputation and was cast in popular imagination as a gangster and a drug smuggler. As the trial continued, the stories about Nyimpine became increasingly elaborate. Members of the middle class began to tell me how Nyimpine had threatened them with a gun, beaten up police officers for insolence, tried to coerce women to have sex with him using the power of his family name, and been shot in the leg by the presidential security detail when he drew a pistol and tried to attack his father in a fit of rage. The stories began to take on all the elements of a soap opera, with corruption, nepotism, brutality, murder, and a son who raises his hand in anger to his father. It was the antithesis to the claim of the elite holding a special place through a state of cultural advancement. The Nyimpine trial

---

[6] See the AIM Report (Agência de Informação de Moçambique) for 2003, edited by Joseph Hanlon.

[7] Nyimpine Chissano was found dead as result of a heart attack on 19 November 2007. He was 37 years old.

symbolised a wider moral panic for those I knew in Maputo. Many felt at the mercy of a state that veered wildly from venal incompetence to malevolent efficiency. It appeared that its moral basis of power had seriously eroded and any remaining political project was increasingly restricted to the powerful, but few had any idea of what a plausible alternative to this state of affairs would or could actually be.

Conclusion

The political and economic changes that followed the end of the war set the foundations for a hybrid system to develop, where regular elections took place and donors made demands for 'good governance' and were able to oversee political and economic reforms, while the Frelimo party state slowly began to rebuild itself and maintain its monopoly on power. Political freedoms were extended, even as the economic realities for many in Maputo remained dire. Capitalist reforms theoretically intended to create autonomous individuals as the foundations of the liberal order instead created a national bourgeoisie and increased dependence on state power. The great political project of transformation had ended in disaster, and any pretence of mass mobilisation was abandoned. At the same time, the liberation script remained part of the legacy of Frelimo, although instead of being a roadmap for the nation, it was increasingly restricted to the privileged themselves. While the changes that accompanied the abandonment of socialism and the end of the civil war attracted much comment, less attention has been paid to the equally important continuities. The adoption of liberal capitalism is in many ways as messianic as scientific socialism (West 1997). Once again, success depends on an enlightened elite who can lead the nation down this path, guarding against the dangers of narrow sectarianism. While Frelimo now accepts a multiparty system, in practice it seems more a case of the party allowing the margins of power to be divisible in order to keep the centre inviolate.

While the continuities were deeply important, so were many of the more unintended changes. One of the most significant was the fracturing of the remains of the party's transformative project. Under socialism, the political limit dividing a good citizen from a traitor was relatively clear, and the exemplar of the party's vision, the new man, while privileged, was supposed to selflessly dedicate himself to building the nation. This no longer seemed to be the case, and while the dominant classes felt that their role as standing above the nation excused them from the consequences of occasional misdeeds, from the perspective of those below it often seemed that selfish acquisition and venality disqualified them from their status. This was an argument I heard many times from members of Maputo's middle class. The lack of exteriority in the dominant symbolic vocabulary and system of signification also held up a mirror to the system's internal failures. It was not that members of the middle class disagreed that it was necessary to have someone who through background and education could stand above society; it was that the wrong people were doing so. While many members of the urban middle class decried what they saw as the arrogance of the ways in which elites displayed their wealth and interacted with the rest of the population, they often acted similarly in relation to those who lacked their privileges. Like the elite, the middle classes often employed one or more household servants, had cable television, and tried to surround themselves with the attributes of supposedly modern life. They spent time in cafés and discos whose prices made them out of reach for all but a small minority. They had professional, white-collar jobs of varying levels of remuneration, but these were steady, permanent positions. Even the more lowly paid posts in the state ministries allowed one to make connections with powerful officials and gave one the experience necessary to find better offers with NGOs or privatised industries. Furthermore, they could be just as disdainful towards the rest of the population. I was told numerous contemptuous stories by middle-class friends of the 'failures' of recent rural immigrants to adjust to an urban lifestyle. This was shown by the way in which they tried to keep animals on the balcony of apartment buildings and failed to understand the purpose of indoor plumbing. Privilege had been the mark of the vanguard, the first step in a grand transformation that would bring new forms of belonging to all. After the war, though, as factions in Frelimo engaged in populist arguments against their erstwhile comrades and the wealth of the new era was concentrated in a few hands, it was no longer clear whether belonging was to be yearned for, or if it meant 'backwardness' and poverty.

6   Decay, 2005–15

The crisis consists precisely in the fact that the old is dying and the new cannot be born; in this interregnum a great variety of morbid symptoms appear.
(Gramsci 1971: 276)

Introduction

For many in Maputo, the initial post-war period of 1992–2004 seemed a period of both profound transformation and surprising continuity. On the one hand, the war finally came to an end, government was to be decided by multiparty elections, political scrutiny was relaxed, personal freedoms expanded, and deepening market reforms brought dizzying prosperity to some and continuing deprivation to others. On the other hand, the country was still ruled by Frelimo and many of those who held power from 1992 to 2004 had been members of the leadership since the socialist period. Those with the greatest chance of succeeding under capitalism were often those who had been privileged in the revolutionary period (either personally or through links of kinship). In Mozambique, the nationalist project was and is the cornerstone of the social order. If nationalism was based on a project of grand social transformation, though, how does it continue to be relevant when it failed in so many of its original promises?

Throughout this book, I have focused on the ways in which the Frelimo party state and the middle class have been mutually constitutive of each other since independence. My interlocutors have been, for the most part, among the most successful in understanding, shaping, and adapting themselves to the dominant system of signification, to which they lacked exteriority, and they were thus able to secure positions of privilege within the social order. In this chapter, I discuss the years from 2005 to 2015, when, under a new president, Frelimo attempted to institutionalise itself as an elected single-party state. I do this first through an examination of yet another tumultuous process of political transformation, its limits, and the social cleavages it brought to the fore. I then explore how this affected the relationship between the party state and the middle class as the justifications for the social order and the security of the middle class's place in it began to crumble and decay, but little was found to replace it.

In 2005, Chissano was succeeded by Armando Guebuza, former Minister of Transport and the Interior and a party hardliner who had presided over Operation Production. Towards the end of Chissano's time in office, many of those I knew felt that change was needed. Party structures were weak, corruption was seen to be getting out of control, and the overall situation seemed to be stagnating. Some of those I knew were cautiously optimistic about the elevation of Guebuza. He had revitalised Frelimo and strengthened its role as a guardian of the state, he had won staggering electoral victories, and it was thought that he would bring back some of the discipline of Samora. In his inaugural speech, Guebuza, picking up on the feeling of the moment, pledged to put an end to the spirit of *deixa andar* (a reference to the permissiveness of the Chissano era). Guebuza set about institutionalising Frelimo's position as the uncontested centre of power, an elected single-party state, but what was missing in Guebuza's efforts to channel the spirit of Samora was the animating goal of the political project. What would Frelimo do with its power? The ambitious and brutal, all-encompassing transformative vision that was the basis of the new man had been whittled down to a restrictive and often self-replicating mark of status. If Guebuza managed to strengthen the party, the question of what the party stood for still remained.

Yurchak argued that the role of the Leninist party created a distinctive type of state:

> The uniqueness of the Leninist polity lay in the novel way in which the sovereignty of that regime was organized. Sovereignty here was vested neither in the figure (as in the premodern absolutist monarchy or Nazi state) nor in the abstract populace (as in modern liberal democracy), but in the party ... This agent transcended every one of its members, including its current leader – each member could turn out to be wrong and illegitimate, but the party was always already legitimate and right. The correctness and legitimacy of this agent was guaranteed by the foundational truth of Leninism – a truth that was external and prior to the party and to which the party had unique access. (Yurchak 2015: 146)

Unlike the Soviet case, in Mozambique, as with other dominant party states in Southern Africa, Frelimo maintained its hold on power after the introduction of a multiparty system with competing centres of sovereignty. For Coelho, the introduction of a multiparty system creates a paradox in the practices of legitimation: how can Frelimo base its legitimacy – its liberation script, in his terms – as the embodiment of the nation if it exists as one party among many and by definition only represents a fraction, however large, of the population (Coelho 2013: 28)? Guebuza tried to solve this problem by reasserting the primacy of the party (and, paradoxically, himself) while sidelining all other claimants to the voice of the nation. The party could once again claim access to a unique form of knowledge in an otherwise backward nation; only Frelimo had the ability to lead the country on the path of development. Events on the ground seemed to refute this assertion. Guebuza's time in power was marked by growing social polarisation, resurgent authoritarianism, the personalisation of power and wealth, bloody urban riots, widespread labour unrest, a series of strikes in essential services such as healthcare and education, and a resumption of hostilities with Renamo.

If the party leaders were heading in the wrong direction, some still had faith that the party itself could hold the leadership in check (Sumich 2010). Marco, introduced earlier, is a professional whose family has a long connection with Frelimo. He is also a party member and in 2008 he told me about a meeting he had just attended for party cell leaders. Although he had been disillusioned, after this meeting he felt rejuvenated and proud to be a member of Frelimo again.

The meeting was great. They told us that we made a mistake. We were weak and we took all of the best people we had directly into the state. The thing is, though, we do not have to agree with everything the state does. We are the only thing that is powerful enough to check the state and police its actions. We are the source of the state's power and it is answerable to us for its actions. We as cell leaders should monitor our members; if we see somebody doing something wrong we need to speak to them. Starting from there we need to begin policing the state.

Marco believed that the party was the true source of sovereignty, even if, like many members of Maputo's middle class, he had doubts about Guebuza. For Marco, the role of the party was to rekindle a movement and purify a state that had become mired in corruption and cynicism. Many have argued that the middle class is a bastion of liberalism, but the example of Marco complicates such a view. In his view, the concentration of power in a largely unelected body (at least unelected by the wider population) that was superior to official government structures was not the subversion of democracy, but a necessity to secure it. In the initial period of the Guebuza era, many members of Maputo's middle class held widely divergent views of Frelimo, often simultaneously. On the one hand, it was both utterly corrupt and hopelessly incompetent, but also feared and thought to be able to act with ruthless, malevolent efficiency. On the other hand, many still felt a deep attachment to the party's 'heroic' history and its original goals.[1] This attachment demonstrated the lack of exteriority for members of the middle class. Many felt that the party was the problem, but it could still be argued that the party was also

---

[1] Schubert reports similar processes in Luanda, Angola. In this case, some older urbanites may be highly critical of the MPLA and view its current direction with dismay, although they still have a proprietary attachment to the party, viewing it as 'ours', even if it has lost its way (2014).

the solution. If Guebuza was wrong and his state was corrupt, as Yurchak (2015) argued for the USSR, the party could still be right.

As Guebuza consolidated his power, won massive electoral victories, and utterly sidelined the opposition, the party and the nation again became almost indistinguishable in official rhetoric. For a short time, it appeared as if he had managed to restore some of the discipline of the Samora era, although in a brutal manner. After his election, stories swirled about special police squads cruising the city on motorcycles, carrying rifles and wearing balaclavas. According to rumour, these groups were given a free hand to deal with crime and had been rounding up the 'usual suspects' and taking them to the outskirts of town for execution. The degree to which Guebuza centralised power around himself struck many as unprecedented, even in comparison with the Samora era. In some ways, though, Guebuza's very success simply highlighted the decay. Many accounts have focused on how the dominant party states in Southern Africa are feverishly engaged in the creation of official or 'patriotic' histories, narratives that bolster their power and historic role in building the nation while attempting to airbrush inconvenient facts and divergent accounts from the record (Igreja 2008; Primorac 2007; Ranger 2004; Schubert 2015). In Mozambique, this has tended to mean a reification of the liberation script and the heroism of the struggle coupled with deafening silence concerning the civil war (Igreja 2008). Where Guebuza faced severe difficulties, however, was in trying to define the party's grand transformative project for the current era. The party's hegemony of representation was central to attempts to legitimise the social order. The belief was that certain people and social groups are privileged because they are advanced in comparison to the rest of the population. However, as the closely linked signifiers of the new man, the performance of a strict moral code, and the promise of a better world that lay just around the corner had unravelled, it was no longer clear what being socially advanced meant, even to privileged groups such as the middle class who included themselves among the advanced. Under Guebuza, the dominant system of signification was increasingly narrowed to the catch-all phrase 'development'. This narrative trope had been a fundamental facet of the party's system of signification since independence, but if Frelimo was the party of development and the only party that had ever held power, why was the country not yet developed?

During Guebuza's time in office, official slogans exhorting one to develop the nation were everywhere. Even musicians would routinely be asked in televised interviews how their music would contribute to national development. For the members of the middle class whom I knew, the official emphasis on development as the promise of a grand transformative mission simply inspired cynical laughter. The government promoted a 'buy Mozambican' campaign, but that became an exercise in crony capitalism while illustrating how few products such a campaign would actually apply to. Guebuza also initiated a campaign of *Moçambicanidade* (Mozambicanness) that would promote values, identity, self-esteem, and the common destiny of all Mozambicans. Unlike the modernist new man, whose status as being socially advanced grew from its rejection of the past and its rigid moral code, what these values and identities of Mozambicanness were and what common destiny they were leading to were never entirely clear. Instead of developing a moral basis for the social order, a compelling means of legitimation, it seemed that the members of the elite were simply helping themselves to ever more wealth, and even those from outside this charmed circle who prospered in the Guebuza era felt unfairly excluded in comparison. Frelimo's stranglehold on power meant that many members of Maputo's middle class still depended on it and were complicit despite their reservations. This sense of complicit fatalism was demonstrated by a young man who told me that he had recently joined the party, even though he complained bitterly about Frelimo's supposed corruption. When I asked why he joined the party, he looked at me with a bemused expression and replied: 'It is the power, it controls everything, how can one go against the power?'

Citizenship and the political limit

The growing incoherence of Frelimo's system of signification in the capitalist era was manifested in the changes concerning the meaning of citizenship. Since the end of the Cold War, the liberal conception of citizenship, which is based on voting and election rights, the legal status of belonging to a specific nation state, and a political subject being guaranteed certain rights, has become increasingly common across the world (Chipkin 2007; Lazar 2012). What that means in practice is unclear; as noted by Chipkin (2007: 10): 'A distinction must be made between a citizen as such and an authentic national subject. So, even if citizenship is founded on principles of universal human rights … some citizens are more authentically members of the nation than others.' In Chapter 5, I discussed the ways in which the adoption of elements of liberalism had materially strengthened the privileged, while also casting doubts on their degree of so-called true citizenship. During the Guebuza years, this ambiguity became increasingly prevalent for Mozambican whites and Indians. These groups are numerically insignificant, as they make up around 0.06 per cent and 0.08 per cent of the population respectively,[2] yet they often have access to party-dominated networks and occupy places of privilege in the social order.

[2] See the 2012 CIA World Factbook for Mozambique. Available at: <www.cia.gov/library/publications/the-world-factbook/geos/mz.html>.

This ambiguity was demonstrated to me in a café in Maputo by Angelica, who is white. We were speaking about her grandfather, who was a high-ranking member of Frelimo during the socialist period. According to Angelica, he was a hard man who often threatened to have people who displeased him shot, including family members. Although she views her grandfather with considerable ambivalence, she is troubled about his legacy. He devoted his life to the party and the goal of building a new Mozambique for all its citizens, but the present-day reality bears little resemblance to his vision. Instead, she increasingly feels like an outsider. Angelica worries that she will be a target of the growing level of violent crime, and she perceives a general climate of popular hostility towards her. She asked a waiter, who was black, if he had heard of her grandfather, and he claimed that he had not. Angelica then asked if he thought that she was a 'real' Mozambican, like him. Whether out of politeness or conviction, the waiter replied: 'It does not matter what colour you are. If you are born in Mozambique, then you are Mozambican.' Angelica seemed gratified with this response, if not convinced.

One of the major contradictions of liberal democracy is its inability to conceive of its own political limit (Chipkin 2007; Mouffe 2005). Human rights are portrayed as universal, yet paradoxically dependent on national belonging. Democratisation in Mozambique in no way diminished the importance of the political limit, or the consequences of either inclusion or exclusion, but it deeply undermined the forms of categorisation that spelled out what the political limit was. During socialism, Frelimo conflated political opposition, criminality, and social problems into an all-embracing category of enemy (Machava 2011). To belong was to be within Frelimo's orbit; to be outside was to be an enemy (Buur 2010). The figure of the enemy, constituted by a shifting set of antisocial behaviours, drew the political limit. The adoption of elements of liberalism undermined the coherence of social categories, while leaving the structures largely intact. The current hierarchy continues to resemble the hierarchy of the socialist period, while certain groups such as whites and Indians retain levels of material privilege reminiscent of colonialism. However, those who engage in what would have been labelled antisocial behaviours and individualistic greed during the socialist period now prosper. Perhaps we should turn to these modes of categorisation when trying to understand why the adoption of democracy in much of the world has led to such different results from those envisioned by its promoters.

Democratisation reimagined the role of the party state in Mozambique. Its premise was based on an idea of individual rights, but the socialist period's goal of radical transformation gradually evolved into half-hearted efforts to keep the majority out of absolute poverty. Outside the party elite, it is not clear who should be privileged and what the legitimate basis of privilege ought to be. Frelimo has made a bewildering series of alliances with foreign investors, donor countries, Pentecostal churches, Islamic brotherhoods, and other groups that can bolster the position of the party. Perhaps this is why, as mentioned in Chapter 5, the spirit of Samora Machel currently reigns in Maputo as a symbol of the supposed moral purity, egalitarianism, and transformative mission of the early independence period. I have been told by street vendors that sales of copies and recordings of his speeches are brisk, and even fiercely anti-government musicians, such as the former hip-hop star Azagaia, have appeared in concert wearing a uniform based on that of Samora.

A prominent and apparent paradox of democratisation in Maputo is the insidious continuation of the colour line in Mozambique. The party leadership is largely black, while the ranks of the middle class in Maputo are very mixed, consisting of whites, Indians, and *mulatos*, but with a strong black component. Poverty in Mozambique, decades after an independence that promised prosperity, is almost exclusively confined to black citizens, while the tiny minorities of whites, Indians, and *mulatos* are privileged as a matter of course. Such cleavages appear to have deepened more generally with the adoption of capitalism. Whites and *mulatos* tend to cluster in skilled trades and the professions. Indians predominate in the mercantile sector and often have close links to the ruling party. Indian merchants have benefited from political protection and preferential access during the privatisation programme, in turn allowing Frelimo to make use of the capital and transnational connections at their disposal (Pitcher 2002). An obvious example is Mohamed Bachir Suleman, the owner of Maputo's largest shopping mall and a large contributor to Frelimo. He has been named as a major trafficker of heroin by the American embassy but still operates with impunity inside Mozambique. In fact, he publicly claims that his financial support was crucial to Frelimo's 2009 national election victory (Buur, Baloi, and Tembe 2012).

Allegations of corruption, racism, and exploitation of the majority have led to widespread resentment of Indian merchants. People of Indian descent have tended to be structurally over-represented in the mercantile sector in East Africa, and Mozambique is no exception. This economic role has caused conflict with majority populations who often interact with African Indians through a racialised system of debt (Brennan 2013). The rumours of illegal dealings, combined with exploitative practices and supposed social aloofness, make many Indian merchants appear to be the epitome of antisocial accumulation, which, during socialism, placed them outside the political limit. Fatima is of Indian descent. One day, after a particularly unpleasant encounter with

Figure 6.1 Mohamed Bachir Suleman's shopping mall in Maputo.
Source: Margaret S / Alamy Stock Photo.

the police, which she was convinced was solely due to prejudice against Indians, she told me:

Black people are black in their skin and their hearts, and the only way to fix the problem would be to shoot all of them. The problem of racism is very serious in Mozambique, and it is primarily directed at Indians. Someone stole the tyres off my car this weekend; this is the second time it has happened. I go to the police and they just shrug their shoulders. I tell you it is because I am an Indian. They do not care about me.

She recounted conversations in which people had accused her of not having a country or homeland because she, and other Mozambican Indians, even those whose families have been in the country for generations, are not from anywhere else, but they are not from here either. I have heard similar sentiments many times in Maputo. Varyna, a black friend of mine, said: 'I think this is because Indians are insecure. This is not really their home, but they have nowhere else to go.' Members of the grand Indian families, such as Bachir Suleman's, appear to be legally untouchable and to enjoy the full protection of high-ranking party members. Others, whose situation is far more humble, lack such immunity and fear that the party will try to placate popular anger by turning on them.

Many of the promises of the transition to democracy are unfulfilled, causing hostility among the vast majority who have been left behind. According to a white Mozambican professional:

There is a lot of racism towards whites now. During socialism, Samora pretended that race did not exist and the struggle had solved all problems. Everyone knew he was advised by some leftist whites in the party, and the people blame us for what happened during socialism. We did comparatively well while they suffered, and we did not even have to fight in the army during the civil war.

Democratisation in Mozambique promised a new dispensation, although it was to be presided over by former champions of socialism. If citizenship under democracy simply means that rights are bestowed on an individual by virtue of birth, instead of being a process of collective uplift, it is not clear what exactly it is that binds the diverse population together. For the majority, it seems that the primary benefit is grinding poverty and continuing subservience, while theoretically suspect citizens, such as whites and Indians, are supposedly becoming rich.

Since the fall of socialism, the meaning of what it is to be Mozambican has become a floating signifier. While this is most obvious for members of minority groups, as in many other African nations, shifting definitions have been used to attack powerful black politicians as well. In 2008, the *Zambeze* newspaper published a piece calling into question the status of the then prime minister, Luísa Diogo, with the sensationalist headline: 'Is the Prime Minister Mozambican?' Luísa Diogo is married to a foreign-born man, and under a clause of the 1975 constitution (later revoked), women who married a foreigner lost their citizenship. In reality, it turned out that the *Zambeze* journalists had not done their homework: Diogo's husband had become a Mozambican citizen in 1977 before they married. Frelimo took the charges seriously, and state prosecutors not only sued *Zambeze* for libel but also invoked an obscure law dealing with state security to demand that the journalists pay 10,000,000 meticais (around US$400,000 at the time) in damages, a claim rejected by the judges.[3] Accusations that leaders in Africa are in fact from another country have become increasingly common in recent years (Schubert 2014; Soares de Oliveira 2015). This may be a symptom of rising xenophobia, a reaction to growing inequality, an attempt to make sense of how leaders can show such a callous disregard for their own citizens, or a combination of these and other factors, but the anger directed towards the powerful seems quite clear.

Originally relying on Samora Machel's ability to demand loyalty to Frelimo's vision of citizenship by occupying the place of the external editor and defining what a supposedly true Mozambican was, the nation-alist ideal is now vulnerable to political and economic changes. If the party is no longer an enlightened vanguard that monopolises specialist knowledge but is to be a servant of the people, it poses the following

---

[3] See   <www.open.ac.uk/technology/mozambique/sites/www.open.ac.uk.technology .mozambique/files/pics/d100054.pdf>.

question: who are the people? If Frelimo is responsible to its voters, why is the vast majority of Mozambicans so poor? If whites and Indians are a tiny and increasingly unpopular minority, why are they so rich? If the basis of privilege in Mozambique is access to the party state, who is legitimately entitled access to it and why? One of the major changes in Mozambique, following the adoption of democracy, is that a government once obsessed with creating a homogeneous national citizenry as a bulwark against ever-multiplying enemies is now constructing difference. While the poor have long been excluded, privileged groups such as whites and Indians are no longer certain of their place in the social order either. In practice, the implementation of a liberal democratic system appears to focus on holding multiparty elections and writing a constitution. Efforts to create liberal democracy in Mozambique, however, are being grafted onto what came before – in this case, a system that defined itself against a supposed enemy. Universal human rights are never eternal, inherent, or, in fact, universal; rather, they are the products of existing political hegemonies (Mouffe 2005: 4). In Mozambique, as in many places in the postcolonial world, formal democratisation occurred simultaneously with spiralling inequality, rendering many of these rights an abstraction. While the forms of capitalism introduced may be directly responsible for new inequalities, democracy's ambivalence in recognising its own political limit renders these inequalities all the more intense and the future all the more uncertain.

Understandings of the past and an uncertain future

During his period in office, Guebuza tried to strengthen the Leninist structure of the party and revive the spirit of Samora to achieve new goals. The all-encompassing ambition of the new man gave way to the restricted economic opportunities of the national bourgeoisie for the elite, uncertain prosperity for a small party-connected middle class, and the nationalist incoherence of *Moçambicanidade* for the wider population. Frelimo, which under Guebuza was probably more powerful than ever in its history, continued to use the legacy of the liberation struggle and the new opportunities of recent economic growth to claim that its rule served the general good. Despite Guebuza's attempt to craft a new transformative political project, his efforts faltered, further undermining the previous meanings of concepts such as citizenship and belonging and the moral basis of privilege, while offering little of substance to replace them.

If the moral basis of Frelimo's rule was eroding, Guebuza went to great lengths to increase the dependency of key constituencies of the party and spread the restricted networks of access more widely than his predecessor. In 2006, Guebuza started a microcredit programme widely known as '*sete milhões*' (seven million). Each district head of the nation's

128 districts was given 7,000,000 Meticais (roughly around US$300,000 when the programme was introduced) to invest in local development projects (Orre 2010). The grants came with very little oversight, and despite efforts to tighten regulations in 2007, the programme had limited results in terms of rural development (ibid.). The programme did help to entrench Frelimo's rule in the rural areas of the centre and north, where Frelimo had historically been weak. It bound local officials more tightly to the leadership, but created resentment among traditional urban strongholds, which felt that they were being ignored. During Guebuza's presidency, the limited autonomy that existed for the urban middle class was further reduced. Being a member of Frelimo was frequently a necessary, if unwritten, requirement to secure a job in the state sector. Under Guebuza, this requirement became even more entrenched in professional positions more generally.

Nuno had graduated from the nation's best university at the top of his class. His parents were state officials and his uncle had been a high-ranking official. He was not a member of Frelimo and had no desire to join a party he felt was corrupt and ossified. However, he began to rethink this position as he began applying for jobs. Although he was invited to numerous interviews, he was always taken aside and asked if he had a *carta vermelha* (a red card, meaning a Frelimo membership card). When he replied that he did not, his interview invariably ended with a shrug of the shoulders and the phrase 'Deal with that'.

If Guebuza attempted to broaden the base of his regime, it still lacked the heroic ambition of the socialist period, and the poor, both urban and rural, were only sporadically and imperfectly incorporated. In an insightful discussion of personhood in South Africa, Ferguson argues that, in a situation where personhood is often seen as a relational concept instead of an autonomous individual, dependence can create larger relationships and mutual obligations in hierarchical social orders (2013). The problem in much of Africa is that inequality is strikingly asocial, as the poor are increasingly severed from a wider, morally binding membership of society (ibid.: 233).

In the current era, the transformative projects that attempted to frame inequality as a temporary measure have fallen by the wayside, privilege has been divorced from wider social meaning, and many obligations between members of different social groups have long since frayed. Liberal reforms were meant to reinvigorate the moribund nationalist project, and to use capitalist methods to achieve the old socialist dream of modernist prosperity. In her work on post-socialist Hungary, Fehérváry argues that life for her interlocutors was explained as an attempt to achieve normalcy, an idealised imaginary of life in the West, as opposed to the socialist period and its legacy, which served as the epitome of abnormal (2002). Unlike Hungary, Mozambican socialism was an attempt to escape what was widely seen as normal for postcolonial African nations: poverty, chaos, and corruption. For most people I know, this grand attempt was ultimately unsuccessful. As a Frelimo cadre told me in despair: 'After all the hopes and dreams, years of struggle and hardship, now we are just another African country.' Scott (2014) argues that the perception of the present depends on how we think the end of the story will unfold, and the unravelling of Frelimo's hegemony can be traced to the erosion of the party's ability to credibly promise a better future for all.[4]

Despite Frelimo's growing power under Guebuza, the cracks in its foundations were beginning to show. The current political system, despite its liberal pretensions, seems disconnected from the mass of the population. As Senhor Cortês, a former minister introduced earlier in this book, explained to me:

> Our political system does not work. The practice is completely disconnected from the lives and needs of the people. Elections here are simply a formality; they do not represent the people in any meaningful way. I think China is the model for Guebuza. This form of national capitalism is beneficial to his interests and it provides an alternative to the West.

The form of national capitalism Guebuza attempted to build in Mozambique was hugely profitable for a small, increasingly endogamous elite that had less and less contact with the wider population. The benefits for the vast majority of the population were far less obvious. The official rhetoric was constantly upbeat, reminding everyone that development was just over the horizon, especially after discoveries of massive deposits of coal, natural gas, and other minerals. Expectations were raised while costs spiralled and daily life was becoming ever more arduous. Eventually, simmering frustration took a violent turn.

On 5 February 2008, riots broke out in Maputo and the neighbouring city of Matola. The specific causes were blamed on the rising price of transport, forcing many urbanites to spend half or more of their salaries just to get to work. Price hikes in transport and fuel also meant that the cost of food, much of which is imported, soared. As one newspaper editorial put it: 'the inhabitants of the *bairros* [neighbourhoods, or poor suburbs] do not live, they survive' (Serra 2010). While these factors – combined with rising crime, gross inequality, urban poverty, an

---

[4] The disquieting sense among party cadres that, after all these years of effort, instead of ushering in a better future they may actually be presiding over a process of regression shows interesting similarities to a concept in poorer *bairros* called *kuzuma utomi*. According to Nielsen, *kuzuma utomi* refers to a statement about or plan for the future that the speaker acknowledges will most likely never happen (2014: 214). It therefore appears that, at least in contemporary Maputo, temporality is viewed as the possibility of a better future, but one that is always just out of reach.

unpopular president, and internal factionalism within Frelimo – were well known, the violence seemed to catch everybody by surprise. Initially, mobs attacked *chapas*, the minivan taxis that are a ubiquitous feature of urban life, overturning and burning them. Wider frustrations soon came to the fore and rioters targeted luxury cars and burned down a school named after Armando Guebuza. One rumour that endlessly circulated claimed that rioters attacked a convoy of luxury cars, but when they found that the convoy contained the former president, Joaquim Chissano, they started cheering and demanded that he retake power. If Chissano's rule lacked the heroic ambition of Samora, it seems to have at least offered some sense of security. The rioters appeared to be attempting to remind the government of its continuing obligations to its citizens, as demonstrated by one young man who told reporters: 'They [Frelimo] think they can cut us off, well we can cut too.' The rioting continued for two days and paralysed the city. It was only quelled when the government deployed contingents of police who had permission to shoot on sight, and made a panicked agreement to subsidise the cost of transport. Numerous commentators debated in editorials and blogs as to whether the riots were caused by a ruling party that had become ossified and out of touch, the slavish following of the economic proscriptions of the IMF and World Bank, the lack of opportunity for urban youth, or all three. Senhor Marques told me after the 2008 riots:

The future is uncertain. The old leadership of Frelimo has kept its unity even though there are many internal conflicts, but I can't say how long that will continue. There are a lot of big projects coming in, but they don't create jobs. There has been a huge increase in the number of universities, but there is nowhere for the graduates to go. They are becoming increasingly frustrated and, unlike their elders, they are not attached to Frelimo in the same way. Even within Frelimo, the party machine is now just being mobilised for elections; we do not actually listen to the base. Chissano gave people the freedom to do what they want; now the party is becoming increasingly autocratic. Guebuza will win the next election without a doubt, but the party is looking at serious challenges ten years down the line. The 5th of February can easily happen again [a point that proved to be prophetic].

The events of 5 February were a dramatic indication that Frelimo was increasingly unable to symbolically reproduce its legitimacy. This point was emphasised as riots broke out again on 1 September 2010 and in 2012, although in the final instance disturbances were quickly repressed by the security forces. Once again, the ostensible cause of the violence was the high cost of living and the lack of opportunities. A wider sense of relatedness that could unite the population in the face of growing polarisation was also lacking. It appeared that this was felt not only by the rioters, but also by those who had historically been close to the regime and among its major beneficiaries, who saw themselves as being squeezed between the corrupt arrogance of the rich and the potentially violent fury of the poor. The rioters in particular were pointing out that Frelimo's loudly proclaimed goals of unity, progress, and a better life for all were nowhere in evidence. The recurring riots and the government's difficulties in dealing with them were a symbolic challenge to the regime. In a similar manner to Wedeen's discussion of Yemen (2008), in many ways Frelimo is powerful because people believe it is powerful. Cracks in the image of omnipotence not only put the regime at risk, but also threaten the foundations of privilege and the social hierarchy more broadly.

The sustainability of middle-class privilege

During Guebuza's time in office, Mozambique became a significant exporter of natural resources, and finds in mining and natural gas paved the way for the economic boom of 2008–13. Those at the top of the social hierarchy now had access to unprecedented wealth. Guebuza became sarcastically known as *Guebiznes* (Guebusiness) and *Tio Patinho* (Scrooge McDuck) in reference to his extensive business interests and his comments that the source of his empire was a duck farm. In a less spectacular manner, many people I knew in Maputo's middle class also appeared more prosperous than when I first met them in the early 2000s. Small apartments gave way to well-appointed houses in the suburbs of the capital or in the neighbouring city of Matola, older model cars became new SUVs, and several people made steady progress up the career ladder. Despite their apparent upward mobility, though, many were deeply apprehensive about what the future held for them and their children. While they had achieved many of the globally recognised trappings of a middle or upper middle class, there were considerable doubts concerning their sustainability.

In the spring of 2013, I was speaking with Walter, a former high-ranking official and long-time member of Frelimo. I had known Walter since 2002 and, while he had consistently been critical of the government, I had never seen him as despondent as he was that day.

I am worried about the ways things are going. It's bad. I have worked for years and I currently earn US$5,000 a month but it's not enough; I can barely make ends meet. We don't wear fancy clothes or take extravagant holidays; it all goes towards taking care of my family and education for my children. Housing and prices are out of control. I struggle and I am far luckier than most people. There is massive corruption, political uncertainty, and the situation is becoming unbearable. I worry about the future; I think this will all end bloodily.

Walter spoke of his unease as we drove through a city filled with construction sites, ever-present Chinese work crews, traffic jams, new shops and restaurants, and all the other detritus of unprecedented prosperity.

All this in a country that 20 years before was one of the poorest in the world.

While the country and its rulers may have been growing exponentially wealthier, the economic boom was paradoxically adversely affecting many others, even the privileged. Almost everyone I spoke with agreed that prices were completely out of control. The costs of food, clothing, and basic goods were soaring, and nowhere was this more evident than in the housing sector. Maria comes from the nation's revolutionary aristocracy. She has a good professional position and was able to study abroad. Maria is near the top of the social hierarchy in Maputo and she still struggles to make ends meet:

Costs are skyrocketing; even a decent kindergarten costs US$300 per month. Housing is even worse; it is something like US$300,000 for a three-room house, and almost no one can afford to live in the city centre anymore if they are under 65 and did not get a place during the privatisation. Everyone has to move out to Matola or Machava [neighbouring cities and areas] and drive for hours to get to work. I am married, have a child and a good job and we still have to live with my parents.

The minimum wage in Maputo in 2013 was around US$100 per month, and this, of course, only applied to those lucky enough to be employed in the formal sector of the economy, around 30 per cent of the city's population. Most of the people I know are considerably more comfortable. While it is often difficult to gauge exactly, some, like Walter, earn US$5,000 per month and most members of the middle class I know earned somewhere between US$1,000 and US$2,000 per month in 2013. While these are princely salaries by Mozambican standards, price rises, and, especially, rising costs in the housing market mean continuing financial insecurity.

Perhaps this is one of the causes of the 'middle-class revolts' seen across the world. Economic growth and new opportunities empower some, while at the same time they entrench the polarising status quo and few seem to have any idea of what to do about it. In Maputo, this means being permanently enmeshed in relationships of dependence that reproduce the social order but that have lost moral significance and the prospect of security. Instead of a wider societal mission, for those I know, it appears that the nation is presided over by an indolent, corrupt ruling class. Middle-class Mozambicans decry official corruption while at the same time internalising its logic. After a long diatribe against the supposed larcenous proclivities of the government, a teacher at a private secondary school told me that she altered the lacklustre marks of her nephew. When I asked if this was not similar to the behaviour she criticised, she replied: 'No, what they do is corruption. What I do is helping my family, what's wrong with that?' Or, when I asked one young man what the result of the revolution he proposed would be, he told me: 'I will be the one driving the Mercedes.'

Even complicity may not be enough to buy stability and the opportunity of a secure future. Marta is a professional woman from a party-connected family. In her view of the situation:

Everyone is unhappy, the cost of living is spiralling out of control, and discontent is growing rapidly. No one really minds if Guebuza is corrupt; this is allowed. The problem is that he is not letting anyone else eat. Instead he is taking everything himself. It's out of control. We wanted Guebuza to rebuild the party, and he did, but at the same time he has made himself stronger than the party and that has never happened before, not even in the time of Samora. I am worried; I think there could be another civil war or revolt and I will be caught in the crossfire. My family has been privileged since the colonial era; we have done well with every regime. I am not part of the top, but I doubt too many will make fine distinctions if trouble comes.

Marta's ambivalence with regard to the social order, which she and her family are complicit with but simultaneously dependent on, and a regime they fear could be swept away shows the uneasy position of the middle class. Guebuza's current, largely incoherent promise of 'development' can no longer subsume the wider desires of even the party's followers. Instead, there is growing social polarisation.

Even though many people I know are deeply alienated from the Frelimo party state, there is a large degree of complicity. They and their families have benefited from their connection to Frelimo in gaining jobs, access to education, and economic opportunities. Additionally, while they may be extremely critical of the government, they often lack exteriority to Frelimo's systems of signification and symbolic vocabulary. If their implementation has verged on criminal, many of the goals of the revolutionary period that should result in progress and prosperity appear to be self-evidently worthy. However, in recent years, much of the moral basis of Frelimo's rule has been questioned. Some now find themselves under attack as murderers for actions that were previously praised as one's 'revolutionary duty' during the socialist period. Other, younger members of the middle class were shocked to find out the human cost of the transformative project. One man told me that his enthusiasm for Samora took a severe blow when he worked in a programme to help the victims of Operation Production who were exiled to the far north, and understood the senseless suffering it caused. Another, a woman from a Frelimo family, was shocked to discover that her grandfather did not own a bucolic farm where she spent her childhood summers, but was in fact a commandant of a re-education camp and the happy workers of her memories were actually terrified prisoners. Although the party's claims that its cadres had the right to rule as they were socially advanced were now laughable, many middle-class Mozambicans justified their own privilege using similar criteria. They are 'rational', 'modern' citizens who have progressed beyond petty rivalries such as region and ethnicity and are among the few who possess the skills necessary to staff positions of importance and responsibility. Although they may despise the ruling elite, if Frelimo is overthrown it is not clear that things would necessarily improve, but their positions could be in considerable jeopardy. The moral relationship that was the foundation of the transformative project has been severely damaged, and the riots of 2008, 2010, and 2012 underlined just how precarious the foundations of the social order may be.

According to Maria, whom I introduced earlier:

I think another civil war could be coming. Expectations are being raised, but very little is trickling down and there does not seem to be a plan. The government should know the situation is dangerous but they really do not seem to care. There is no plan or overall programme. It is just five or so families eating everything. My generation are still nationalists, we love Mozambique, and while material things are of course important and everyone wants them, we also want to do something for the country, but they don't let us. Instead they [Frelimo] seem to be purposely making things worse and antagonising the population.

Mozambique is nominally a democracy, and there has been an increasingly viable opposition, Movimento Democrático de Moçambique (Democratic Movement of Mozambique or MDM), which split from Renamo. MDM caused considerable excitement in some sectors. Its leader, Daviz Simango, the son of a founder of Frelimo who was executed after being charged as a counter-revolutionary, is too young to have been involved in the civil war or the crimes of the socialist period, and he proved an effective mayor of Mozambique's second city, Beira. There is a concern, though, that the opposition is just as complicit as are my informants. As Maria told me:

My husband just came back from Quelimane [the capital of the Zambezi province in the centre-north of the country]. MDM won Quelimane and it was very embarrassing for Frelimo as their candidate got fewer votes than the city has registered party members. My husband told me that he had spoken with MDM cadres who were saying that the municipality should be buying them houses as they are now the power and they deserve them. It is basically the same logic as Frelimo; it does not seem that there are that many differences. Yes, Frelimo killed Simango's father, but his father was a founder of Frelimo. I do not think much would change if Simango took power; he studied in Frelimo schools and is still tied to many members of the party by old links of friendship. He is part of the system, and he calls Guebuza 'tio' [uncle].

Maria was not alone in her doubts about the MDM. According to Tarson, a university lecturer:

Things are very bad, but there is not much that can be done. We are all too dependent on Frelimo. I do not have much faith in the MDM. They say they are a centre-right party. What does that even mean here? Their MPs also use the state to fill their own pockets. I think they will just do the same as Frelimo if they ever get into power.

Perhaps this is one of the reasons why the MDM lost severely in the national election of 2014. Instead, after nearly two years of low-intensity fighting with the government, Renamo is once again the major opposition party. Voters seemed to appreciate Dhlakama's willingness to stand up to Frelimo, bolstering his party's political comeback after fading to near insignificance in the previous election. Even so, Renamo's inability to win power and its lack of any kind of coherent alternative to Frelimo could entrench the very status quo that causes so much discontent.

Disaffection with the current social order is by no means total. Frelimo claims over two million members, close to 10 per cent of the population (Bertelsmann 2012). The winner of the 2014 election, the Frelimo candidate Filipe Nyusi, garnered around 57 per cent of the vote and was the clear victor despite allegations of fraud and electoral misconduct. While many of the people I know despaired for the future and considered emigration the most viable option, others were being drawn back from abroad by the new opportunities provided during the economic boom. The foreign investments that began as a trickle in the Chissano years became a flood, with new economic ventures being set up by South Africans, Brazilians, Indians, and especially Chinese. These opportunities also tend to fall under the purview of the party. Some of my interlocuters claimed that Frelimo-linked businesses were exempt from the usual taxes and customs duties; instead, they contributed directly to the party, bypassing the formal state. Another Mozambican businessman explained to me that: 'You can set up a corner shop in relative peace, but you need to bring the party in for anything bigger.' Furthermore, the competition between educated Mozambicans and foreigners for the few professional posts outside the state heated up dramatically, especially when the boom slid into economic crisis. The party's crumbling legitimacy and systems of signification faced competition from other sources of meaning and legitimacy, such as the explosion of evangelical churches and Islamic missionary movements. Once again, though, these are being incorporated into a system whose foundations are uncertain.

Housing was one of the major material bases of the post-war middle class in Maputo and became a central component of middle-class self-image. It is not enough to have a cement house that is connected to the water mains and electricity grid; one must also have the right kind of house. Preferably one should own a home in the right part of town (an increasingly difficult feat due to Maputo's escalating property prices), with South African or European-style decorations and appliances.[5] Unsurprisingly, due to the immense social and material importance of

---

[5] One's class outlook and personal cultivation are often expressed through housing and domestic space. There are numerous ethnographic examples, ranging from post-socialist Hungary (Fehérváry 2002) to the *favelas* of Brazil (Holston 1991), to mention just two.

housing for Maputo's middle class, the trials and travails of the housing market provided a topic of almost obsessive interest. Housing was also a productive lens into the contradictions of the capitalist period. If the goal of privatising the housing stock was to banish the legacy of socialism and create a new, autonomous, and entrepreneurial national subject, its success was dubious. As a former minister told me: 'People like to say that socialism destroyed the country. It makes me laugh. If socialism destroyed the country then give up your house and move to the street. How do you think you got your house in the first place?' The political process concerning land rights in urban areas is both top-down and seemingly deliberately confusing, as no reliable register exists (Andersen, Jenkins, and Nielsen 2015a). This allows local officials, such as the *secretario do bairro* (the neighbourhood secretary, a low-level urban party cadre), wide scope in practice to conduct land deals and approve land rights according to their own personal agenda (Andersen, Jenkins, and Nielsen 2015b).

As local officials frequently sell the same plot of land to multiple people simultaneously, it is often considered more expedient to simply stake one's claim to land by building a small thatch or cement house on it, the materiality of an object being worth far more than a dubious paper title. With a dwindling supply of land near the capital, however, the post-socialist system of stratification has become inscribed in the landscape itself. Driving through the outskirts of Maputo, one frequently sees plots of land encircled by concrete walls with a demolished thatch or cement house in the centre. In many instances, this is the result of some powerful or better-connected individual having taken over the former owner's claim to the land – often through informal means – by simply bulldozing their house and building a more permanent, protective structure in its place.

In many ways, housing in Maputo gave one a glimpse of the system of social stratification rendered in concrete. After wild borrowing based on dreams of mineral and natural gas fuelled abundance, the global price collapse for natural resources left the government on the brink of default, with a long list of legally dubious debts it had hitherto hidden from both creditors and its population. While talk of the crisis was on everyone's lips in 2015, Maputo still seemed a boom town under feverish construction. This became clear to me when I went with Marco to pick up his daughter from a private school, so that we could drop her off at her tennis lessons. As we were driving through Costa Del Sol (a wealthy neighbourhood), Marco kept pointing to all the new developments that were springing up everywhere, asking: 'Does it look like there is a crisis?' There were new hotels, houses, shopping malls, and casinos stretching as far as the eye could see. Marco told me that some of what I was seeing were really just scams – housing developments where the developer had sold all the units and had then run off with the money, leaving half-built houses leaning forlornly together, never to be completed. Other areas teeming with newly built developments were on floodplains, and it was likely that the houses would be washed away with the rains. I asked Marco if all the construction – the massive hotels, casinos, and half-finished malls – pre-dated the crisis and whether they would ever be completed. Marco replied:

I don't know. A couple of years ago these were all money-making ventures and would have probably worked. Now, though, it is hard to say; they will probably be half-empty or just close down. I think some of these shops only exist to launder money, though. It is different with houses and land, it does not matter – people are mad for plots, they will buy them no matter where they are or what is going on.

Marco himself was not immune to the 'madness of plots'. In 2012, he was working for an established international company and earning a good salary. His wife was working for the state. They had bought a home in a new development of tract housing on the outskirts of town for the equivalent of US$150,000. It was a very good price at the time, although Marco joked about the development, saying that if one had too much to drink they could never figure out which one of the identical tract houses belonged to them. In 2013, he left his job to start his own business, but the financial crisis had taken its toll. He now made about US$1,500 a month and his wife made about another US$500 or so. The only good thing about the crisis for him was the depreciation of the metical, Mozambique's currency, which lowered the monthly payments for his 24-year lease to around US$80 or US$90 a month. Marco has multiple houses and plots of land in the greater Maputo and surrounding area, and he said that these were becoming his economic mainstay.

Look, the social system here is weak and if something happens I will be on my own. So, what I want to do is turn my plots not just into houses and holiday homes, but businesses that can support me and my family. We have turned one of my plots into a farm; we grow our own vegetables and I raise chickens. With inflation and costs the way that they are, one often has to live on the food that they grow themselves; I am trying to make my family almost self-sufficient. We get a lot of food and it costs us very little. I pay one guy 2,000 meticais [around US$40] a month to clean the plot and another person 400 meticais and some chickens to take care of the animals and crops. As for the houses and land in town, most of them are in the new suburbs. These suburbs are on the outskirts – you have to drive forever to get into town and there is not a lot to do, people just sit in their living rooms. I thought I would turn them into a coffee shop or a bar, some place for people to hang out after they come home from work.

Marco has deftly navigated the precarious social terrain in which he finds himself, making use of his family background, political access, the ability to take control of valued resources, such as houses and plots, and entrepreneurial acumen. As the experiences of Marco and so many others show, the interconnection of political power and personal gain have not lessened in the current era, although in many cases they may have fragmented and become more contradictory. As the following example illustrates, not everyone is able to manoeuvre as dexterously as Marco.

Tarson, who I introduced earlier, has some land outside town and is trying to build a house, but a rich capitalist connected to the *secretario do bairro* is attempting to appropriate it. The land was controlled by a farming association whose leader convinced its members that farming was unprofitable and it would be far better to sell the land. Not everyone really understood the process and they sold the land cheaply or lost control of it to the association. Tarson managed to buy some land from an old woman who was part of the association, but it turned out that, unbeknownst to the association members, their leader had already sold the association's land to a developer. This provoked fury and association members asked the municipality to intervene, a request that was refused. The protests grew, the media took note, and it eventually went to court. As a result of the scandal, the *secretario* offered to trade Tarson's disputed plot for a plot elsewhere. This seemed the easiest solution so Tarson agreed (in fact, the secretary made one of his underlings exchange his own land for Tarson's still unresolved claim). The problems did not end here, though; there are continuing disputes over his new plot. Someone else wants it, and Tarson is living with his sister, waiting to be able to take possession of his land and build a home for his family.

As the example of Tarson shows, the quest to secure land and housing in contemporary Maputo is predicated on both political and entrepreneurial skill. The end result is far from the establishment of the autonomous individual as a basis of liberal capitalism; instead, the system creates greater reliance on a fragmenting state apparatus. Furthermore, the basis and practice of capitalism in Maputo are symptomatic of the structuring of the economy in Mozambique and much of sub-Saharan Africa more generally. According to Senhor Marques:

The city is becoming quite a bit more stratified. However, this created a huge opportunity for many people among the worse off and for the very rich. Quite a few fortunes have been based on acquiring property. The generation coming of age now, though, will not have this opportunity. The base of the economy is not production, but instead it is an economy of rents. Basically, corruption focuses on the commercial aspects of the economy and this penalises overall production, which instead tends to be controlled by foreigners. Mozambique does not really have a tradition of investing in productive enterprises. The way in which the economy is developing now can easily create a social crisis.

While the riots of 2008, 2010, and 2012 and the financial crisis demonstrated the truth of Senhor Marques's words, many members of the middle class I know were also worried that the basis of their current standard of living was a never-to-be-repeated opportunity. Varyna argues that many of the material benefits that came at the end of the war were a one-off gift to the generation above her:

> Our parents fought very hard to get us where we are and they want to make sure we keep this standard of living. That is why they pay so much to send us to good schools. My father is always going on about how we must use the benefits we have been given because he will not always be around to help us. He has some money now, but when he dies all my sister and I will inherit is some property. They earn money from this property now due to the rent but after they are gone we will probably have to sell it to pay the debts.

An emerging middle class in Maputo soon had to come to terms with the danger that the opportunity for dramatic upward social mobility, either through the revolution or the privatisation of housing stock, cannot be repeated. While party connections were and continue to be extremely beneficial if one wants to engage in the property market, the ownership of housing or land held the promise of a form of autonomy. With a house and, ideally, some land, one could engage in the cult of middle-class domesticity. If the transformation of the nation proved to be a failure, one could always retreat behind closed doors and raise a well-educated, modern family. One middle-class woman told me: 'One's own house and children, that is all a woman wants.' This promise, though, is rapidly fading even for relatively privileged members of the middle class. As the economic boom in Mozambique began to grind to a halt following the worldwide drop in commodity prices, property values reportedly began to fall. While housing may become more affordable for some, the possibility of the property bubble finally bursting, coupled with skyrocketing inflation, puts one of the primary material bases of the middle class at risk. While some people, such as Marco, have combined political access (both he and his wife are party members from Frelimo families) with a skilful use of resources – renting houses, turning them into businesses, and even growing their own food – his ability to do this is still dependent on political contacts in a murky legal environment. Instead of privilege leading to social transformation or even autonomous citizens, it remains based on complicity, and there seems to be no end to what Rigi refers to as 'neo-liberal disordered order', where the fetishisation of law and order goes hand in hand with corruption and illegality (2012: 81).

Of course, not all feel themselves to be on the verge of impending doom. I have spent pleasant evenings with friends and their families lounging by the pool, protected by the high, featureless walls of the houses of the privileged. As children run around the yard and guests busy themselves with overflowing plates of food and imported beers, the topic of politics, if it comes up at all, is usually dismissed with amused contempt. Some from higher-ranking political families now say they wish they had paid more attention to what their parents and their parents' friends nattered about at family dinners, as they would have a much better idea about what was currently going on. It all seemed so boring at the time, though, and they have their own children and concerns to worry about. Passionate interest is often aroused by very different subjects, such as work, family life, gossip, current events, holidays, shopping – the subjects that make up the daily texture of life for relatively privileged people across the globe. Their place in the social hierarchy grants a measure of an often unnoticed security, and the slow-motion crisis that appears to be engulfing the country often feels far, far away.

For many other Mozambicans I know, there is still a connection with Frelimo. I attended a small dinner party in one of the new developments on the outskirts of town. Marco and his wife were hosting myself and another couple. As Thelma, Marco's wife, prepared dish after dish, Marco kept our glasses filled and we chatted about work and the news of the day. One of the guests made a dismissive remark about the government, leading to a growing argument between him and Thelma, a Frelimo loyalist. However, even the guest who was the most violently opposed to Guebuza still referred to himself as a 'son of Frelimo' and admitted that he and his family had benefited from the party immensely. That is precisely the bind in which members of Maputo's middle class find themselves. The systems of signification that promised to bring all of the nation's citizens together for the general good have crumbled, even if former hierarchies and power structures remain. The rhetoric and symbolism of the current era do not, as Cohen (1981) argued, mean that relationships of dependence strive for the greater good. Instead, people remain hostage to a system that even many of the privileged feel is unjust.

Conclusion

One day I was asking a friend of mine, Nuno, why the word 'nationalism', once so highly valued, now elicits shrugs and rolled eyes. Nuno said that it was simple: 'Nationalism no longer means love of country, or progress, it simply means Frelimo. They have colonised the word and it is losing its legitimacy, much like "comrade". It just means Frelimo now and I will no longer use it.' Even if many members of the middle class still identify with Frelimo's transformative ideal, it no longer seems that the party is capable or even willing to bring that transformation about. From 2008 to 2014 there were some concrete signs that the promised development was finally coming. During the boom, Mozambique had one of the highest economic growth rates in Africa; businesses were opening; roads, houses, and other buildings were constantly being constructed, at least around the capital and in other major cities; and the prosperity of the elite was increasingly visible. However, much of that new wealth was confined to a small group, and inequality, poverty, prices, and crime were rising. The slogans promising a better future appeared increasingly empty to the urban poor, who use the verb *desenrascar* (to disentangle or unleash, which means to imaginatively get by in any way one can) to describe how they survive. If development occurred during the Guebuza era (2005–15), it rarely seemed to happen for them.

The ever-increasing social polarisation in Mozambique is frequently blamed on the corrupt nature of the ruling class. As noted by Gupta in relation to postcolonial India, 'The discourse of corruption turns out to be a key arena through which the state, citizens and other organizations and aggregations come to be imagined' (2012: 78). There is much truth to this argument: the discourse of corruption is one of the primary ways through which people imagine the various branches of the state apparatus, the basis of the social order, and the foundation of new understandings of citizenship, inclusion, and exclusion. As many Mozambicans have pointed out to me on numerous occasions, it is not corruption itself that is the problem, because in the current era that is simply a regrettable aspect of life that permeates almost every facet of existence. Sometimes many of the quotidian practices glossed over as 'corruption' can make one's day-to-day life quite a bit easier. I found this out myself when, shortly after moving to an apartment, my power was cut off by the state electricity company for non-payment. I was surprised as I had not yet received a bill. However, it seemed that the total amount owed for electricity was connected to the apartment rather than being the amount owed by the individual occupant. When I went to inquire what had happened, I was given a large stack of bills for the equivalent of hundreds of US dollars that went back many years, far in excess of my two-week-long occupancy of the flat. When I asked some of my neighbours how I should deal with the problem, they just laughed and took me to a rather dark bar next to my apartment building. This bar served as the office of a former employee of the electricity company who had been fired after he was electrocuted during a work-related accident. We quickly came to an arrangement and he limped heavily up the seven flights of stairs to my flat, pulled out a screw driver, and reconnected me for the equivalent of around US$2. Such instances were common. I once avoided a three-hour wait at the central hospital to have some stiches removed by acting on the advice of a friend and buying the nurse a can of Coca-Cola.

The ability to access official services was and continues to be based on the informal trade of favours, money, and/or the power of one's family name, which made life far easier for the lucky few, although it also reproduced what was widely seen as a dysfunctional social order. It was, however, the tightening barriers between the ruling class and the rest, the perceived voraciousness of the country's elite, especially during the Guebuza era, that placed the system under such strain. As argued by Yurchak, the basis of Soviet power was that it was not vested in the figure of the leader, or even in an abstract populace, but based on a political party that had unique access to a foundational truth (2015: 146). Frelimo operated in a very similar manner, but, ironically in this case, as the party's power grew, the underlying meaning crumbled.

After the nation's independence in 1975, the relationship between the Frelimo-based ruling class and the emerging middle class became very similar to what Bayart described as the reciprocal assimilation of elites, where a dominant class is produced by its relationship to state accumulation and steadily creates an active inter-penetration of so-called civil society and political society (1993: 176). Under Guebuza, however, the formerly porous barriers between these two groups began to harden. Attempts at creating all-embracing conceptions of citizenship steadily broke down amid soaring inequality. It soon became apparent that policies such as the privatisation of housing, which had served as the post-socialist economic base of much of the middle class, were a one-off, while the new mineral wealth was concentrated in a few hands. Rapidly increasing prices and economic fragility caused the viability of middle-class social reproduction to wane, and matters were far worse for the urban poor, as the riots of 2008, 2010, and 2012 demonstrated.

In Ferguson's discussion of dependence in South Africa, he refers to a political opinion poll in which 'the majority of South Africans agreed with the statement people are like children, the government should take care of them like a parent' (2013: 236). I am not aware if a similar poll exists in Mozambique, but one frequently hears such sentiments. Phrases such as 'the government needs to give me a job' and 'the government needs to take care of us' are common, and, in Cohen's (1981) terms, they provide symbolic legitimacy to the structures of the social order. As I have argued throughout this book, the view of the middle class as a group of autonomous agents who entrench liberal values is reductive at best. Some elements of autonomy have great appeal for those I know; a degree of personal freedom and security are very attractive. Such a view discounts the underlying structures of power that make autonomy possible. Very few people I know believe that the state does not have a large – or even a predominant – role in structuring society. The current problem is not that a paternalistic government is smothering the individual autonomy of its citizens, but that it is acting like a delinquent father; in this case, a father who has burned the house down, forgotten the majority of his children, and is eager to renounce the rest.

7   Concluding thoughts, 2016

> You know how it is, the rich get richer, the poor get poorer and we in the middle just try to stay the same.   (Response of a middle-class woman in Maputo when I asked her how things were going)

In the last decade, Mozambican President Guebuza has attempted to revitalise the party and articulate a new transformative project through appeals to nationalism with slogans such as 'Mozambicanness'. Unlike the 'new patriotic' history in Zimbabwe, much of the post-independence period has been cloaked in stylised recriminations and accusations repeated ad nauseum by the spokespeople of both Frelimo and Renamo, steadily adding fuel to old battles that seemingly can never end. I once heard a Mozambican priest describe it as follows: 'Renamo still thinks Frelimo are a bunch of dictatorial Marxists and Frelimo will never forgive Renamo for the war.' The social consequences of the competing narratives of the civil war and the hollowing out of the liberation script became increasingly apparent after the 2014 election. While Frelimo and Renamo put an end to 17 months of tit-for-tat violence and agreed to contest the election, Dhlakama refused to accept the result and again accused Frelimo of fraud. While it is definitely possible that some form of fraud did occur, it does not appear to have been on a scale sufficient to influence the result. Dhlakama, however, has been adopted by many frustrated Mozambicans as a symbol of defiance against an unjust regime, and he was greeted by huge rallies in areas where Renamo traditionally had little support, including Maputo. Buoyed by his grow-ing popularity, he demanded six provinces in the centre and north as an autonomous republic under his control, despite the fact that he officially won the majority of the vote in only three of them.

By 2016, Mozambique's place as one of Africa's 'cheetah' economies was in doubt, and the financial crisis had grown to staggering proportions thanks to secret loans the state had taken out to finance a strangely heavily armed tuna fleet. The sums that had been borrowed secretly kept growing and the state simply could not pay them back. Donors with relationships with Frelimo that spanned decades were curtailing aid and threatening to cut them off, while the IMF refused to lend any more money until accurate accounts for the tuna fleet were provided. Foreign exchange was becoming scarce, inflation had effectively halved people's salaries as imports became ever more dear, and, on top of all this, the fighting with Renamo simmered on.

Periodic clashes between state security and Renamo militants continued, along with frequent threats from Dhlakama to impose his rule by force if necessary. According to a politically connected friend, Frelimo was initially quite eager for Renamo to return to violence. He told me:

> They [Frelimo] actually wanted a war; they thought they could win it in a week and then they would be free of Renamo. Of course, that is not what actually happened. They became arrogant and simply made a momentously stupid mistake. Dhlakama is a guerrilla, he knows what he is doing and so do his people – Renamo were the ones who really won the last war, at least in military terms, so to think they could beat him now and beat him easily was a catastrophic misjudgement.

Instead of a quick victory over Dhlakama and what was initially reported to be around 500 guerrillas, whose ages, on average, ranged between 40 and 60, the fighting dragged on. By 2016, over 100 rounds of inclusive peace talks had been held, but on the ground the seemingly endless cycle of attacks, ambushes, and assassinations continued. Renamo appears to have strong popular support in many central and northern villages, and rumours swirl about high government casualties and frustrated government troops engaging in wholesale massacres of villagers. Frelimo has tried to assassinate Dhlakama twice; their failures have simply contributed to his legend and his reputed ability to wield supernatural powers.[1] Within Frelimo, it is no longer entirely clear who, or which faction, is in control, and if Guebuza was characterised as brutal and corrupt, his successor, Nyusi, is dismissed as a clueless boy. Many Mozambicans I know told me that the situation had not been this dire since the darkest days of the civil war. There was also growing disquiet among the powerful foreign agencies and investors who had so recently spoken of the investment opportunities in Mozambique in glowing terms, declaring the nation a prime example of a rising Africa.

In 2016, I was invited to speak about the prospects of the Mozambican middle class at an 'economic summit' hosted by the *Financial Times*. The summit, which apparently had been in the works for a few years by then, had originally been intended as a showcase for investors of Mozambique's economic dynamism and tremendous potential. With the crisis well under way, some of the initial optimism had faded and the name of the event was changed to 'Accelerating a return to growth

---

[1] Hostilities abated when Renamo announced the first of a series of ceasefires beginning in December 2016 that were periodically renewed. Afonso Dhlakama announced an indefinite ceasefire in March 2017.

and stability'. The actual summit, though, was impressive. It was held at the Polana, Mozambique's most famous and probably best hotel. It was a blur of 'networking events', where one met the great and the good from government, international investors, and foreign missions over fine wines and sumptuous meals. Amidst the colonial elegance and understated luxury of the Polana, it seemed almost surreal to hear foreign dignitaries claim that Mozambique was speeding towards the abyss and their governments were seriously considering reducing aid or cutting it altogether. Others displayed a newfound enthusiasm for Renamo, wondering if the parliamentary wing of the party, now led by Ivone Soares, Dhlakama's niece, could command the loyalty of the Renamo troops in the field.

The event began with a speech by President Nyusi reminding everyone that, despite the current difficulties, Mozambique still possessed untapped potential. The president left to have his picture taken with some of the highest-ranking visiting dignitaries, and the next speaker, the Minister of Finance, came to the stage to deliver a more subdued presentation. When it came time for the question and answer portion of his presentation, someone asked the question that must have been on everyone's lips: what happened to all the money, now over a billion US dollars, that had been borrowed for the tuna fleet? The minister's reply basically boiled down to the fact that he was also interested to know what had happened to the money, both as a member of the government and as a private citizen, and considering that there were so many knowledgeable and distinguished visitors in the room, perhaps a member of the audience could shed some light on it. Few were convinced by this response. As one foreign dignitary told me afterwards:

God, he knew that question would be coming and they have had months to come up with a party line and that is the best he could do? Either he is a liar and a bad one, or the Minister of Finance really does not know who in the government is borrowing money or how much they are borrowing. Neither option is good.

Not everyone was pessimistic. A Dubai businessman who controls a major portion of the nation's ports gave a rousing speech telling everyone that the people are over-reacting and the fundamentals are fine. 'Who cares how much they borrow as long as they can pay it back,' was his overarching refrain. While he called for less regulation of foreign businesses, he was keen to remind people of the nation's potential, drawing a warm chuckle from the crowd with a statement of perhaps unintentional irony, considering the nation's history: 'People say Mozambique is the new Venezuela; that is silly. Venezuela is run by a bunch of crazy communists, not like here.' The speaker claimed that the current crisis was just a temporary hiccup; soon things would be back to normal and the economy would be booming. Set against the grandeur of the surroundings, such a claim was almost credible, although, after talking to the conference participants, especially those with experience in Mozambique, they felt that such optimism was simply a front, the shiny packaging of something that had long since been hollowed out.

This sense of 'hollowness' has pervaded most of my recent interactions in Mozambique. On the surface, everything is still fine: the city is filled with construction cranes, new shops are opening everywhere, and I meet old friends in packed bars that serve expensive pizza and craft beer, in new wine bars, or in pop-up restaurants hidden throughout the city that can be found only through Facebook. In many ways, life, for them at least, appears to be conforming to the global middle-class ideal. However, while the bars are still doing a roaring trade, most of the shops are empty and many are closing down. I walked by one where the cashier seemed so uninterested she had forgotten to take down the 'We are closed' sign, despite the fact it was 2 p.m. and the door was open. The conversations I had with friends also hinted at serious disquiet, despite the trappings of sushi and South African wines, pizza, and craft beer.

As Marta, who was introduced in Chapter 6, told me:

We are in a difficult situation, everybody thinks Nyusi is an idiot and a puppet, no one takes him particularly seriously. The party is collapsing, it is tearing itself apart. Renamo was nothing, but Guebuza in his single-mindedness brought it back from the brink. While there was always corruption the general attitude was that since I am here and doing my job, I might as well take a bit more. Under Guebuza the idea of actually doing one's job died; now it is just about what you can get your hands on. You can see this with idiotic moves like parliament giving itself a raise while subsidies are cut and teachers are not getting paid for months at a time. Guebuza modelled himself on Samora but without the vision or the charisma. He made the party so obviously dominant that it became responsible for everything that went wrong. Before Guebuza, Frelimo's strategy was to subtly weaken Renamo until it was barely a presence, Guebuza brought it back from the dead. Killing Dhlakama would be a serious mistake. No one seems to realise that the country is full of armed men and only Dhlakama is keeping them under control. Especially as it is Frelimo that is committing atrocities this time; its troops are massacring villages and raping women. Frelimo will probably win the elections again. It seems almost terminally weakened, but Frelimo is far more terrified of losing power than it is of the people, so they will do whatever it takes to try and hang on.[2]

Even Marco, who is still a member of Frelimo, told me:

Everyone is furious, but it is only Renamo who is standing up to Frelimo. My friends keep saying that if it was not for Renamo, there would be no resistance and we need something. Look, I do not think Renamo is doing things the right way, but something must be done; they are the only thing keeping Frelimo in check.

---

[2] Afonso Dhlakama died of a heart attack in 2018. Since his death he has been elevated to an uncontested national hero, with president Nyusi referring to him as a 'brother' and a partner for peace. Dhlakama's successor, former general Ossufo Momade, is supposedly a hardliner and the status of the peace declared in 2017 remains unclear.

Both Marta and Marco have all the outward attributes of what would be recognised as members of a middle class across the globe. That is how they would describe themselves as well. However, little of their current experience echoes the discourse of 'middle-classness', which casts them as bastions of liberalism who will usher in reforms and punish political extremism.

In this book, I have traced the relationship between the state and the middle class in Mozambique and how this group has emerged through its connections with various iterations of the party's grand transformative projects. As mentioned in Chapter 1, the state is not a thing, the unified expression of a singular will, even if it often appears that way to its subjects (Abrams 1988; Welker 2014). This point may be especially apt when discussing Mozambique. In addition to the fact that the state is composed of people who run its sometimes cooperating, sometimes competing institutions, Frelimo has long been a central hub of a governance structure with international dimensions. In the socialist period and during the civil war, there were the *cooperants*, the foreign sympathisers who came to offer their skills. Furthermore, there were the East German advisers, Russian military attachés, Bulgarian agricultural experts, Nordic NGOs, international aid agencies, and Tanzanian and Zimbabwean troops to counter Rhodesian- and South African-funded rebels. After the abandonment of socialism and the adoption of structural adjustment and other economic reforms, the international dimension of governance only increased, with an endless stream of international agencies; the IMF, the World Bank, and NGOs; South African, Indian, Brazilian, and Chinese businesses; mining concerns, contractors, and investors; Portuguese banks; Norwegian and Italian oil and natural gas conglomerates; Christian and Muslim religious groups; and many more.

In her work on a mining corporation in Indonesia, Welker argues that the corporation is continually 'enacted' (2014), not only as an actor with particular goals and rationalities but as a system of material relations and practices (ibid.:4). Thus, the corporation can be a hub of political and economic life, while simultaneously being provisional, always in the process of being made and remade. Frelimo operates in a similar manner, as a nexus of institutions, structures, relationships, and ideas that 'hang together despite tensions and inconsistencies' (ibid.: 4). Privileged subjects, such as the middle class, were formed through their relationships to party structures, the opportunities for advancement that the party provides, and the great transformative projects. In this sense, Frelimo is similar to other 'party machines' in Southern Africa, where the promise of the liberation movement became a mechanism of accumulation, 'state capture', patronage, and social advancement for the chosen few once power was seized (Southall 2013). The central role of access to the party state in shaping the middle class in Mozambique, as well as in other dominant party regimes in the region and more generally, could be seen as yet another example of neo-patrimonialism. The case of Mozambique, though, points to a different conclusion. While vertical relationships linking individuals in clientelist networks surely exist, they can do so alongside broad horizontal solidarities that we must also explore. While power and material benefits may be dependent on the means of access, such a situation can still be structured by systems of signification. For example, for those I have worked with in Maputo, privilege is not solely restricted to a direct relationship with a powerful patron; it is also shaped by one's ability to understand and adapt oneself to symbolic vocabularies and ideas of political and social meaning, ideas that draw on the social background of both the leadership and the middle class. Social status is often related to grand transformative projects, but these projects have always been tentative and incomplete, continually being made, unmade, and reformed yet again. They are processes that have resulted in tremendous social mobility, but often at the cost of continuing precariousness. While Frelimo represents itself as a mono-lithic whole and has historically tried to categorise the population in all-encompassing binaries of citizen or enemy, the reality is far more improvisational and shifting. Even for privileged subjects, security remains elusive, with access to opportunities granted one minute and withdrawn the next. Not only is the middle class of Mozambique tightly bound to grand projects of transformation, it is itself in a process of continuous transformation.

Mozambique, the middle class, and the discourse of middle-classness

In this book, I have discussed the ways in which the formation of a middle class is intertwined with previous projects of transformation. Such projects are continually being enacted, and they do not necessarily lead to a set outcome in an evolutionary manner. The concept of the middle class in contemporary Maputo, much like that of the new man during the socialist period, draws on international discourses to explain and legitimate forms of stratification and positions of privilege. The subjects of this book are primarily members of an older, established middle class. Many come from families who have held privileged social positions since independence, and in many cases since the colonial period, and they have tended to occupy an officially valorised social position, from *assimilado* to *homem novo* to member of the middle class. Despite the revolutionary or transformative rhetoric that accompanies them, each incarnation is built upon layers of pre-existing social sedi-ment, the legacies of which have an important and sometimes contradict-ory effect on the present. This can be seen in the ways in which members of this group engage in what Lentz (2015) calls 'boundary drawing', the expressions of moral and social difference that mark members of a social category as distinct, and the ways in which these have been made and remade for successive projects while also being accompanied by elements of surprising continuity. Examples include, but are not limited to, forms of family and romantic relationships, education and professional achievement, modes of consumption and socialising, housing practices, and world views more generally. Many of the cultural expressions of middle-class difference – its urban character, the emphasis on the nuclear family, changing forms of gender relationships, the disdain (often tempered with fear) of so-called traditional practices, and aspirations to an idea of modernity – were all central to political projects of transformation.

During the socialist period, the ability to draw a boundary between oneself and the party state was rigorously suppressed. No matter what one thought personally, one had to conform to the public performance of a rigid moral code, at least outwardly. While the fall of socialism allowed people to develop a social base that granted them at least some form of autonomy, in practice this autonomy remains limited, even if my interlocutors often wish to draw a firm line between themselves and what they view as a corrupt, incompetent, and malign elite. This continuing connection was expressed in a variety of ways. Examples include a woman who explained the difference between herself and her elders by referring to herself as 'second-generation Frelimo', although she has never actually been a member of the party. Another man once told me that he was considering a career in politics but was hesitant due to his deep misgivings about the ways in which Frelimo is running the country. I asked him if he could run as a candidate for another party. He just laughed and responded: 'How could I? With my family I am genetically Frelimo; no one could take me seriously as anything else.' Even those who do not identify so explicitly with Frelimo are often caught in webs of complicity. While they may lambast Frelimo for its corruption and immorality, they frequently make use of similar logics and practices to navigate the minefield of everyday life in Maputo, thus reproducing the social order. Through a particular relationship with the prevailing political order, the middle class has drawn a boundary, both material and symbolic, between it and the wider population, but that order is increasingly under strain. The political and economic crises Mozambique is undergoing correspond to moral and symbolic crises. The loss of moral certainty about the basis of the social order, and one's place within it, is accompanied by fading security.

The supposed rise of a middle class in Africa has, according to some, the potential to transform Africa's political and economic destiny, entrenching liberal democracy, free markets, and prosperity. Such a view, usually championed by institutions such as the World Bank, the African Development Bank, and the IMF, casts the middle class as an almost evolutionary agent of liberal transformation. Although the collapse of global commodity prices and the resulting economic slowdown has called the Africa Rising narrative into question, the vision of a new middle-class generation, demanding reform and connected to the wider world through mobile phones and social media, retains its allure. This is understandable, and such a vision offers a corrective to the lazy narratives invoking a pathologically corrupt and backward 'heart of darkness' that characterised Africa in the 1990s and early 2000s. It is also a welcome palliative to the cultural determinism of other influential forms of analysis, such as neo-patrimonialism, in order to understand African politics. As argued by Lentz, the designation of the middle class discursively combines the promise of upward mobility with personal merit and achievement, rendering it morally legitimate, even in a context of deepening inequality (2015: 25). This concept of the middle class takes on the aspects of a liberal 'blank slate' ideology, one that will completely reform the dysfunctional politics of the continent.

The irony is that in Mozambique, as well as in many other former revolutionary states, liberalism is simply the latest in a line of 'blank slate' ideologies and political projects, whose legacies have been instrumental in shaping the social order, and thus the middle class. Chipkin (2007) argues that there is a danger in postcolonial studies of privileging the colonial, with everything that occurred after independence being viewed solely as a reaction to colonialism. The legacy and structures of the past help shape the present and the future, but, as I have demonstrated throughout this book, they are often deployed in attempts to achieve very different goals and are imbued with radically different meanings. One cannot understand the formation of a middle class in Mozambique, its material base, and the cultural behaviours that mark it as being distinct from other social groups without understanding its historical relationship with Frelimo.

By focusing on the political underpinnings of a middle class, those that both guide its emergence and perhaps threaten its future, one arrives at an understanding of the middle class that is very different from the international discourse of middle-classness that describes what it is supposed to be. While the social role assigned to a middle class by this discourse is all-encompassing, the criteria determining who belongs to such a group are extremely narrow, reduced to a few, often vague, economic measures, such as a purchasing power of between US$2 and US$20 per day. Such a definition is thoroughly inadequate, according to Lentz: 'Virtually all historical and anthropological studies on the global middle classes agree that economistic definitions of the middle class through its location in the occupational structure or its income and expenditure do not suffice, and can even be misleading' (2015: 25). Economic reductionism omits most of the sociologically significant aspects of middle-class formation, the myriad contested ways in which boundaries are drawn between these social categories and others, and how they change over time (ibid.). Furthermore, the focus on economic metrics and consumption obscures the wider relationships of power and domination that give rise to a middle class.

Kalb (2014) has argued that the major international institutions' current fascination with the role of the middle class stems from the ways in which such a category allows one to speak about progress and development without any overt challenge to the existing politico-economic system. Even if Western Europe and the United States are being eclipsed by new rivals such as China, a global middle class will sustain the liberal project that has been championed for so long by the 'West' (ibid.). The focus on a growing middle class in the Global South is less a challenge to the existing system as it is a means of securing it. The African Development Bank, the IMF, and the World Bank use the term as a less ambitious version of Rostow's 'non-communist manifesto'; prosperity is steadily growing and wealth is trickling down, an ideological formulation that holds obvious appeal for those near the summit of the economic hierarchy. Additionally, the concept of a rising middle class can be very attractive to its would-be members. The failures of previous collectivist and/or nationalist projects may be lamented, but at least the urbane and cosmopolitan members of a middle class can claim equality with the wider world, a source of comfort amidst despair for the nation more generally. In Mozambique, the category of 'middle class' also acts as a more individualised version of the revolutionary political movements of previous decades. The stress on individual merit tends to hide the fact that power is a relationship: for some to have more, others must have less. As Mozambique's political, economic, and military crisis continues, the ability to justify why some have more is increasingly under threat, and the moral basis of the social order decayed long ago.

In Chapter 1, I argued that the central question that must be asked in any exploration of the new middle classes of Africa and globally is the following: what is the basis of the class system and the social order that gave rise to the middle classes and binds them together? In the case of Mozambique, the basis of the class system for my interlocuters is one's degree of access to the Frelimo party state and their relationships to its grand projects of transformation. Many of those I know secured positions of status and privilege through their, or their families', relationships to great, disciplinary projects of social engineering. However, instead of acting as an anchor of the new order, they were often precarious hostages to systems that soon began to crumble. Although Frelimo has managed to stay in power since independence, none of its great transformational projects have been able to address the deep social cleavages in Mozambique – in fact, they have intensified them. Socialism slid into economic crisis and civil war, and it appears as if Mozambique's liberal capitalism may share a less dramatic, slow-motion version of the same fate.

The social order in Mozambique has been based on the distinction – albeit a distinction that has often been oscillating and precarious – between friend and enemy, who is to be included and who is to be excluded. As argued by Mouffe, democracy is also based on relationships of inclusion and exclusion. However, democratic theory is unable to conceptualise its internal 'political limit' (2005). The growing inability to determine what an 'authentic' citizen is, the ultimate goal of so many of Mozambique's grand transformative projects, has severely undermined the party's systems of signification. This has been accompanied by a general loss of vision; brave if brutal attempts to build a new world are reduced to frenzied accumulation and the management of persistent inequality, with no end in sight. The dominant forms of politics over the last 20 years increasingly seem like attempts to, in Somers' (1992) words, add a slightly different ending to an old story: mere cosmetic changes to prop up the foundations of power that offer little security, even to the privileged. If my middle-class interlocuters are exemplars of anything now, it is a complicated web of dependence, alienation, and ambivalence. They have little love for Frelimo, a party that seems hell-bent on putting everything they have managed to acquire at risk. However, a future without Frelimo could be even worse. Unlike the confident vanguard of the global liberal order portrayed by the discourse of middle-classness, many people I know view the future with profound uncertainty. Thus, the Mozambican case destabilises the dominant notion of the middle class as a largely secure and comfortable social grouping, one that promotes growth and political stability.

While, in this book, I have focused on Mozambique, this sense of uncertainty seems to be widespread, especially as the political foundations of the liberal order appear increasingly fragile in many countries across the globe. The discourse of middle-classness in Africa is based on an idealised version of the history of the United States and Western Europe. Ironically, it is being employed in Africa while doubts grow over the material base, self-confidence, and future viability of the middle classes of the West. It is this uncertainty that stands in glaring contradiction to many of the discussions concerning the ability of the middle class to deepen democracy, hold governments to account, and form the foundation of a liberal future. I argue that a recognition of that uncertainty is an essential factor for attempts to analyse the new middle classes of Africa and the Global South more broadly. In such cases, the ability – and perhaps the desire – of a middle class to reshape the political and social system from which it arises is far more limited than many recent commentaries would suggest. Rather, as demonstrated by the case of Mozambique, such groups are intimately linked within the political systems and the systems of signification that gave birth to them, and, like the systems they emerged from, they are an ongoing process that remains in flux and whose future is unknown.

Bibliography

Abrams, Philip. 1988. 'Notes on the difficulty of studying the state', *Journal of Historical Sociology* 1 (1): 58–89.

Adam, Yussef and Peter Gibbon. 1991. 'Post-colonial development in Mozambique (1975–1990): from the people's republic to the republic'. Unpublished seminar paper, Centre for African Studies, Eduardo Mondlane University (UEM).

Agamben, Giorgio. 2000. *Means without End: notes on politics*. Vol. 20. Minneapolis MN: University of Minnesota Press.

Alpers, Edward and Christopher Ehret. 1975. 'Eastern Africa' in Richard Gray (ed.), *The Cambridge History of Africa. Volume Four: from c. 1600 to c. 1790*. Cambridge: Cambridge University Press.

Anderson, Benedict. 2006. *Imagined Communities: reflections on the origin and spread of nationalism*. London and New York: Verso.

Andersen, Jørgen Eskemose. 2012. 'Home space: socio-economic study (research programme "Home Space in African Cities" funded by the Danish Research Council for Innovation 2009–2011)'. Working paper. Copenhagen: Royal Danish Academy of Fine Arts, School of Architecture, Department of Human Settlements.

Andersen, Jørgen Eskemose, Paul Jenkins, and Morton Nielsen. 2015a. 'Who plans the African city? A case study of Maputo. Part 1: the structural context', *International Development Planning Review* 37 (3): 331–52.

2015b. 'Who plans the African city? A case study of Maputo. Part 2: agency in action', *International Development Planning Review* 37 (4): 423–44.

Atmore, Anthony. 1985. 'Africa on the eve of partition' in Roland Oliver and G. N. Sanderson (eds), *The Cambridge History of Africa. Volume Six: from 1870–1905*. Cambridge and New York: Cambridge University Press.

Axelson, Eric. 1967. *Portugal and the Scramble for Africa: 1871–1891*. Johannesburg: Witwatersrand University Press.

Bayart, Jean-François. 1993. *The State in Africa: the politics of the belly*. New York: Longman.

2000. 'Africa and the world: a history of extraversion', *African Affairs* 99: 217–67.

Bertelsen, Bjørn Enge. 2016. *Violent Becomings: state formation, sociality and power in Mozambique*. New York: Berghahn Books.

Bertelsen, Bjørn Enge, Inge Tvedten, and Sandra Roque. 2014. 'Engaging, transcending and subverting dichotomies: discursive dynamics of Maputo's urban space', *Urban Studies* 51 (13): 2752–69.

Bertelsmann. 2012. *BTI 2012: Mozambique country report*. Gütersloh: Bertelsmann Stiftung.

161

Bickford, Andrew. 2011. *Fallen Elites: the military other in post-unification Germany*. Stanford CA: Stanford University Press.

Birmingham, David. 1992. *Frontline Nationalism in Angola and Mozambique*. Trenton NJ: Africa World Press.

Blom Hansen, Thomas and Finn Stepputat. 2001. 'Introduction: states of imagination' in Thomas Blom Hansen and Finn Stepputat (eds), *States of Imagination: ethnographic explorations of the post-colonial state*. Durham NC: Duke University Press.

Bourdieu, Pierre. 1984. *Distinction: a social critique of the judgement of taste*. Cambridge MA: Harvard University Press.

Bowen, Merle. 2000. *The State against the Peasantry: rural struggles in colonial and post-colonial Mozambique*. Charlottesville VA and London: University of Virginia Press.

Brennan, James. 2013. 'Rents and entitlements: reassessing Africa's urban pasts and futures', *Afrika Focus* 26 (1): 37–49.

Buck-Morss, Susan. 1995. 'The city as dreamworld and catastrophe', *October* 73: 3–26.

Buur, Lars. 2010. 'Xiconhoca: Mozambique's ubiquitous post-independence traitor' in Sharika Thiranagama and Tobias Kelly (eds), *Traitors: suspicion, intimacy and the ethics of state-building*. Philadelphia PA: University of Pennsylvania Press.

Buur, Lars, Obede Baloi, and Carlota Tembe. 2012. *Between Pockets of Efficiency and Elite Capture in Mozambique*. DIIS Working Paper Series. Copenhagen: Danish Institute for International Studies (DIIS).

Cabrita, João. 2000. *Mozambique: the tortuous road to democracy*. New York: Palgrave Macmillan.

Casimiro, Isabel. 1979. 'Movimento associativo como foco de nacionalismo – movimento estudantil – NESAM e AAM'. Undergraduate thesis, Universidade Eduardo Mondlane.

Castel-Branco, Carlos. 1994. *Moçambique: perspectivas económicas*. Maputo: Universidade Eduardo Mondlane in association with Friedrich Ebert Foundation.

2002. 'Economic linkages between South Africa and Mozambique'. Unpublished research paper. London: Department for International Development.

Castel-Branco, Carlos, Christopher Cramer, and Degol Hailu. 2001. *Privatisation and Economic Strategy in Mozambique*. Discussion Paper No. 2001/64. London: WIDER, United Nations University.

Chabal, Patrick. 2002. 'Lusophone Africa in a historical and comparative perspective' in Patrick Chabal with David Birmingham, Joshua Forrest, Malyn Newitt, Gerard Seibert, and Elisa Silva Andrade (eds), *A History of Postcolonial Lusophone Africa*. London: C. Hurst and Company.

Chabal, Patrick and Jean-Pascal Daloz. 1999. *Africa Works: disorder as a political instrument*. Indianapolis IN and Oxford: Indiana University Press and James Currey.

Chakrabarty, Dipesh. 1997. 'The difference-deferral of a colonial modernity: public debates on domesticity in British Bengal' in Ann Stoler and Frederick Cooper (eds), *Tensions of Empire: colonial cultures in a bourgeois world*. Berkeley, Los Angeles CA, and London: University of California Press.

Chatterjee, Partha. 1986. *Nationalist Thought and the Colonial World: a derivative discourse*. London: Zed Books for the United Nations University.

Cheng, Yingbong. 2009. *Creating the 'New Man': from enlightenment ideals to socialist realities*. Honolulu HI: University of Hawai'i Press.

Chipkin, Ivor. 2007. *Do South Africans Exist?: Nationalism, democracy and the identity of 'the people'*. Johannesburg: Wits University Press.

Christie, Iain. 1989. *Samora Machel: a biography*. London: Zed Books.

Coelho, João Paulo Borges. 1998. 'State resettlement policies in post-colonial rural Mozambique: the impact of the communal village programme on Tete Province, 1977–1982', *Journal of Southern African Studies* 24: 61–91.

2004. 'The state and its public: notes on state ritualisation in the transition from socialism to neo-liberalism in Mozambique'. Paper presented at the 'Ritualisation of the State' conference, Wits Institute for Social and Economic Research (WISER), Witswatersrand University, Johannesburg, 3–4 June.

2013. 'Politics and contemporary history in Mozambique: a set of epistemological notes', *Kronos* 39 (1): 20–39.

Cohen, Abner. 1974. *Two-dimensional Man: an essay on the anthropology of power and symbolism in a complex society*. London: Routledge and Kegan Paul.

1981. *The Politics of Elite Culture: explorations in the dramaturgy of power in a modern African society*. Berkeley, Los Angeles CA, and London: University of California Press.

Cohen, Michael. 1982. 'Public policy and class formation' in Chris Allen and Gavin Williams (eds), *Sociology of 'Developing Societies': sub-Saharan Africa*. New York NY and London: Monthly Review Press.

Crehan, Kate. 2002. *Gramsci, Culture and Anthropology*. Berkeley CA: University of California Press.

Cruz e Silva, Teresa. 2001. *Protestant Churches and the Formation of Political Consciousness in Southern Mozambique (1930–1974)*. Basel: P. Schlettwein Publishing.

Davidson, Basil. 1984. 'Portuguese-speaking Africa' in Michael Crowder (ed.), *The Cambridge History of Africa. Volume 8: c.1940–c.1975*. Cambridge: Cambridge University Press.

Dinerman, Alice. 1994. 'In search of Mozambique: the imaginings of Christian Geffray in *La Cause Armes au Mozambique. Anthropologie d'une guerre civile*', *Journal of Southern African Studies* 20: 569–86.

2006. *Revolution, Counter-Revolution and Revisionism in Post-colonial Africa: the case of Mozambique, 1975–1994*. London and New York NY: Routledge.

Donham, Donald. 1999. *Marxist Modern: an ethnographic history of the Ethiopian revolution*. Berkeley, Los Angeles CA, and Oxford: University of California Press and James Currey.

Dubow, Saul. 1995. *Scientific Racism in Modern South Africa*. Cambridge: Cambridge University Press.

Ellis, Stephen. 1999. 'The new frontiers of crime in South Africa' in Jean-François Bayart, Stephen Ellis, and Béatrice Hibou (eds), *The Criminalization of the State in Africa*. Oxford, Bloomington, and Indianapolis IN: James Currey and Indiana University Press.

Errington, Frederick and Deborah Gewertz. 1997. 'The Wewak Rotary Club: the middle class in Melanesia', *Journal of the Royal Anthropological Institute* 3 (2): 333–53.

Fanon, Frantz. 1963. *The Wretched of the Earth*. London: Penguin Books.

1967. *A Dying Colonialism*. New York NY: Grove Press.

Fauvet, Paul and Marcelo Mosse. 2003. *Carlos Cardoso: telling the truth in Mozambique*. Cape Town: Double Story.

Fehérváry, Krisztina. 2002. 'American kitchens, luxury bathrooms, and the search for a "normal" life in post-socialist Hungary', *Ethnos* 67 (3): 369–400.

2013. *Politics in Color and Concrete: socialist materialities and the middle class in Hungary*. Bloomington and Indianapolis IN: Indiana University Press.

Feliciano, José Fialho. 1998. *Anthropologia económica dos Thonga do sul de Moçambique*. Maputo: Arquivo Histórico de Moçambique.

Ferguson, James. 2006. *Global Shadows: essays on Africa in the neoliberal world*. Durham NC: Duke University Press.

2013. 'Declarations of dependence: labour, personhood, and welfare in Southern Africa', *Journal of the Royal Anthropological Institute* 19: 223–42.

Finnegan, William. 1992. *A Complicated War: the harrowing of Mozambique*. Berkeley and Los Angeles CA: University of California Press.

Fry, Peter. 2000. 'Cultures of difference: the aftermath of Portuguese and British colonial policies in Southern Africa', *Social Anthropology* 8: 117–43.

Geffray, Christian. 1991. *A causa das armas: anthropologia da guerra contemporánea em Moçambique*. Porto: Edições Afrontamento.

Gómez, Miguel Buendía. 1999. *Educação Moçambicana: história de um processo: 1962–1984*. Maputo: Livraria Universitária, Universidade Eduardo Mondlane.

Gramsci, Antonio. 1971. *Selections from the Prison Notebooks*. Edited and translated by Quintin Hoare and Geoffrey Nowell-Smith. London: Lawrence and Wishart.

Groes-Green, Christian. 2010. 'Orgies of the moment: Bataile's anthropology and the defiance of danger in post-socialist Mozambique', *Anthropological Theory* 10 (4): 385–407.

Gulbrandsen, Ørnulf. 2012. *The State and the Social: state formation in Botswana and its precolonial and colonial genealogies*. New York NY and Oxford: Berghahn Books.

Gupta, Akhil. 2012. *Red Tape: bureaucracy, structural violence and poverty in India*. Durham NC and London: Duke University Press.

Hall, Margaret. 1990. 'The Mozambican national resistance movement (Renamo): a study in the destruction of an African country', *Journal of the International African Institute* 60: 39–68.

Hall, Margaret and Tom Young. 1997. *Confronting Leviathan: Mozambique since independence*. London: C. Hurst and Company.

Hanlon, Joseph. 1990. *Mozambique: the revolution under fire*. London: Zed Books.

1996. *Peace without Profits: how the IMF blocks rebuilding in Mozambique*. Oxford and Portsmouth NH: James Currey and Heinemann.

Hannerz, Ulf. 1980. *Exploring the City: inquiries towards an urban anthropology*. New York NY: Columbia University Press.

Hansen, Anders Sybrandt. 2013. 'Purity and corruption: Chinese communist party applicants and the problem of evil', *Ethnos* 78 (1): 47–74.

Harries, Patrick. 1994. *Work, Culture and Identity: migrant labourers in Mozambique and South Africa c.1860–1910*. London: James Currey.

Harrison, Graham. 1996. 'Democracy in Mozambique: the significance of multiparty elections', *Review of African Political Economy* 67: 19–35.

Hedges, David. 1999. *História de Moçambique volume dois: Moçambique no auge do colonialismo, 1930–1961*. Maputo: Livraria Universitária, Universidade Eduardo Mondlane.

Heiman, Rachel, Mark Liechty, and Carla Freeman. 2012. 'Introduction: charting an anthropology of the middle classes' in Rachel Heiman, Mark Liechty, and Carla Freeman (eds), *The Global Middle Class: theorizing through ethnography*. Santa Fe NM: SAR Press.

Hibou, Béatrice. 1999. 'The "social capital" of the state as an agent of deception: or the ruses of economic intelligence' in Jean-François Bayart, Stephen Ellis, and Béatrice Hibou (eds), *The Criminalization of the State in Africa*. Oxford, Bloomington, and Indianapolis IN: James Currey and Indiana University Press.

2011. *The Force of Obedience: the political economy of repression in Tunisia*. Cambridge: Polity Press.

Hodges, Tony. 2001. *Angola from Afro-Stalinism to Petro-Diamond Capitalism*. Oxford and Indianapolis IN: James Currey and Indiana University Press.

Hoile, David. 1994. *Mozambique Resistance and Freedom: a case for reassessment*. London: Mozambique Institute.

Holston, James. 1991. 'Autoconstruction in working-class Brazil', *Cultural Anthropology* 6 (4): 447–65.

Honwana, Luis. 1969. *We Killed Mangy Dog and Other Stories*. London: Heinemann Educational.

Honwana, Raúl. 1988. *The Life History of Raúl Honwana: an inside view of Mozambique from colonialism to independence, 1905–1975*. Boulder CO: Lynne Rienner Publishers.

Humphrey, Caroline. 2002. *The Unmaking of Soviet Life: everyday economies after socialism*. Ithaca NY and London: Cornell University Press.

Igreja, V. 2008. 'Memories as weapons: the politics of peace and silence in post-civil war Mozambique', *Journal of Southern African Studies* 34: 539–56.

Isaacman, Allen and Barbara Issacman. 1983. *Mozambique: from colonialism to revolution, 1900–1982*. Boulder CO: Westview Press.

Israel, Paolo. 2013. 'A loosening grip: the liberation script in Mozambican history', *Kronos* 39 (1): 11–19.

Jenkins, Paul. 2000. 'City profile Maputo', *Cities* 17 (3): 207–18.

2006. 'The image of the city in Mozambique' in D. Bryceson and D. Potts (eds), *African Urban Economies: viability, vitality or vitiation of major cities in East and Southern Africa?* London: Palgrave.

Kalb, Don. 2014. 'Class: the urban commons and the empty sign of "the middle class" in the twenty-first century' in Donald Nonini (ed.), *A Companion to Urban Anthropology*. New York NY: John Wiley and Sons.

Krohn-Hansen, Christian. 2009. *Political Authoritarianism in the Dominican Republic*. New York NY: Palgrave Macmillan.

Laclau, Ernesto and Chantal Mouffe. 1985. *Hegemony and Socialist Strategy: towards a radical democratic politics*. London: Verso.

Lazar, Sian. 2008. *El Alto, Rebel city: self and citizenship in Andean Bolivia*. Durham NC: Duke University Press.

2012. 'Disjunctive comparison: citizenship and trade unionism in Bolivia and Argentina', *Journal of the Royal Anthropological Institute* 18: 349–68.

Lentz, Carola. 2015. 'Elites or middle classes? Lessons from transnational research for the study of social stratification in Africa'. Mainz: Department of Anthropology and African Studies, Johannes Gutenberg University.

Lévi-Strauss, Claude. 1950. 'Introduction à l'oeuvre de Marcel Mauss' in Claude Lévi-Strauss (ed.), *Marcel Mauss, sociologie et anthropologie*. Paris: Quadridge/ PUF.

Levitsky, Steven and Lucan Way. 2010. *Competitive Authoritarianism: hybrid regimes after the cold war*. Cambridge and New York NY: Cambridge University Press.

Lubkemann, Stephen. 2008. *Culture in Chaos: an anthropology of the social condition in war*. Chicago IL: University of Chicago Press.

Machava, Benedito Luis. 2011. 'State discourse on internal security and the politics of punishment in post-independence Mozambique (1975–1983)', *Journal of Southern African Studies* 37 (3): 593–609.

Machel, Samora. 1974. *Mozambique: sowing the seeds of revolution*. London: Committee for Freedom in Mozambique, Angola and Guiné.

    1982. *The Enemy Within*. Maputo: Department of Information and Propaganda.

Malkki, Liisa. 1995. *Purity and Exile: violence, memory, and national cosmology among Hutu refugees in Tanzania*. Chicago IL and London: University of Chicago Press.

Mamdani, Mahmood. 1996. *Citizen and Subject: contemporary Africa and the legacy of late colonialism*. Princeton NJ: Princeton University Press.

Mann, Kristin. 1985. *Marrying Well: marriage, status and social change among the educated elite in colonial Lagos*. Cambridge and New York NY: Cambridge University Press.

Manning, Carrie. 2002. *The Politics of Peace in Mozambique: post-conflict democratization, 1992–2000*. Westport CT and London: Praeger.

Manuel, Sandra. 2013. 'Sexuality in cosmopolitan Maputo: the aesthetics of gendered practice through the lenses of class' in Brigit Obrist, Veit Arlt, and Elisio Macamo (eds), *Living the City in Africa: processes of invention and intervention*. Schweizerische Afrikastudien 10. Berlin: LIT Verlag.

    2014. 'Maputo has no marriage material: sexual relationships in the politics of social affirmation and emotional stability amongst cosmopolitans in an African city'. PhD thesis, SOAS, University of London.

Marcus, George. 1983. 'Introduction' in George Marcus (ed.), *Elites: ethnographic issues*. Albuquerque NM: University of New Mexico Press.

Marshall, Judith. 1990. 'Structural adjustment and social policy in Mozambique', *Review of African Political Economy* 47: 28–43.

Marx, Karl. 1983. *The Portable Karl Marx*. Edited by Eugene Kamenka. New York NY: Penguin Books.

Mateus, Dalila Cabrita. 1999. *A luta pela independência: A formação das elites fundadoras da FRELIMO, MPLA e PAIGC*. Lisbon: Editorial Inquérito.

Mbembe, Achille. 2001. *On the Postcolony*. Berkeley CA: University of California Press.

Melber, Henning (ed.). 2016. *Examining the African Middle Class(es)*. London: Zed Books.

Metcalf, Thomas. 2007. *Imperial Connections: India in the Indian Ocean arena, 1860–1920*. Berkeley and Los Angeles CA: University of California Press.

Minter, William. 1994. *Apartheid's Contras: an inquiry into the roots of war in Angola and Mozambique*. Johannesburg: University of Witwatersrand Press.

Mitchell, Timothy. 2002. *Rule of Experts: Egypt, techno-politics, modernity*. Berkeley CA: University of California Press.

Mondlane, Eduardo. 1966. 'The struggle for independence in Mozambique' in John Davis and James Baker (eds), *Southern Africa in Transition*. London: Pall Mall Press.

1969. *The Struggle for Mozambique*. London: Penguin Books.

Morgan, Glenda. 1990. 'Violence in Mozambique: towards an understanding of Renamo, *Journal of Modern African Studies* 28: 603–19.

Morier-Genoud, Eric. 2009. 'Mozambique since 1989: shaping democracy after socialism' in A. R. Mustapha and L. Whitfield (eds), *Turning Points in African Democracy*. Oxford: James Currey.

Mouffe, Chantal. 2005. *The Democratic Paradox*. London and New York NY: Verso.

Mubila, Maurice et al. 2011. 'The middle of the pyramid: dynamics of the middle class in Africa'. Market Brief, 20 April. Tunis: African Development Bank.

Munslow, Barry. 1983. *Mozambique: the revolutions and its origins*. London, New York NY, and Lagos: Longman.

Nader, Laura. 1972. 'Up the anthropologist' in Dell Hymes (ed.), *Reinventing Anthropology*. New York NY: Vintage Books.

Newitt, Malyn. 1981. *Portugal in Africa: the last hundred years*. London: C. Hurst and Company.

1995. *A History of Mozambique*. London: C. Hurst and Company.

Nielsen, Morton. 2014. 'The negativity of times: collapsed futures in Maputo, Mozambique', *Social Anthropology* 22 (2): 213–26.

Nilsson, Anders. 1993a. 'From pseudo-terrorists to pseudo-guerrillas: the MNR in Mozambique', *Review of African Political Economy* 57: 60–71.

1993b. 'From pseudo-terrorists to pseudo-guerrillas: the MNR in Mozambique. Part two', *Review of African Political Economy* 58: 34–42.

Norman, William. 2004. 'Living on the frontline: politics, migration and trans-frontier conservation in the Mozambican villages of the Mozambique–South Africa borderland'. PhD thesis, London School of Economics and Political Science.

Nugent, Paul. 2010. 'States and social contracts in Africa', *New Left Review* 63: 35–68.

O'Laughlin, Bridget. 2000. 'Class and the customary: the ambiguous legacy of the *indigenato* in Mozambique', *African Affairs* 99: 5–42.

Orre, Aslak. 2010. 'President Guebuza's own microcredit program: development failure and political success', *Lusophone Countries Bulletin*, May. Available at: www.cmi.no/publications/file/3715-president-guebuzas-own-micro-credit-program.pdf (accessed 24 June 2018).

Opello, Walter. 1975. 'Pluralism and elite conflict in an independence movement: Frelimo in the 1960s', *Journal of Southern African Studies* 2: 66–82.

Paley, Julia. 2002. 'Towards an anthropology of democracy', *Annual Review of Anthropology* 31: 469–96.

Paulo, Margarida, Carmeliza Rosário, and Inge Tvedten. 2007. *'Xiculungo': social relations of urban poverty in Maputo, Mozambique*. Bergen: Chr. Michelsen Institute (CMI).

Pearce, Justin. 2015. *Political Identity and Conflict in Central Angola: 1975–2002*. Cambridge: Cambridge University Press.

Penvenne, Jeanne. 1979. 'Attitudes towards work and race in Mozambique: Lourenço Marques, 1900–1974'. Boston MA: African Studies Center, Boston University.

1989. '"We are all Portuguese!" Challenging the political economy of assimilation: Lourenço Marques, 1870–1933' in Leroy Vail (ed.), *The Creation of Tribalism in Southern Africa*. Berkeley and Los Angeles CA: University of California Press.

1995. *African Workers and Colonial Racism: Mozambican strategies and struggles in Lourenço Marques, 1877–1962*. Portsmouth NH, Johannesburg, and London: Heinemann, Witwatersrand University Press, and James Currey.

Pinsky, Barry. 1982. *The Urban Problematic in Mozambique: initial post-independence responses, 1975–1980*. Major Report 21. Toronto: Centre for Urban and Community Studies, University of Toronto.

Pitcher, Anne. 2002. *Transforming Mozambique: the politics of privatization, 1975–2000*. New York NY and Cambridge: Cambridge University Press.

2006. 'Forgetting from above and memory from below: strategies of legitimation in post-socialist Mozambique', *Africa* 76 (1): 88–112.

2012. *Party Politics and Economic Reform in Africa's Democracies*. New York NY: Cambridge University Press.

Pitcher, Anne, Mary Moran, and Michael Johnston. 2009. 'Rethinking patrimonialism and neopatrimonialism in Africa', *African Studies Review* 52 (1): 125–9.

Primorac, Ranka. 2007. 'The poetics of state terror in twenty-first-century Zimbabwe', *Interventions* 9: 434–50.

Ranger, Terence. 2004. 'Nationalist historiography, patriotic history and the history of the nation: the struggle over the past in Zimbabwe', *Journal of Southern African Studies* 30 (2): 213–33.

Ray, Raka. 2010. '"The middle class": sociological category or proper noun?' in Julian Go (ed.), *Political Power and Social Theory. Volume 21*. Bingley: Emerald Group Publishing Ltd.

Rigi, Jakob. 2012. 'The corrupt state of exception and "law and disorder" in Russia: Putin in the light of Agamben', *Social Analysis* 56 (3): 69–88.

Roberts, Andrew. 1986. 'Portuguese Africa' in Andrew Roberts (ed.), *The Cambridge History of Africa*. London and New York NY: Cambridge University Press.

Rostow, W. W. 1960. *The Stages of Economic Growth: a non-communist manifesto*. Cambridge: Cambridge University Press.

Samoff, Joel. 1979. 'Education in Tanzania: class formation and reproduction', *Journal of Modern African Studies* 17: 47–69.

Saul, John. 1979. *The State and Revolution in Eastern Africa: essays*. New York NY: Monthly Review Press.

Schmitt, Carl. 1985. *The Crisis of Parliamentary Democracy*. Translated by Ellen Kennedy. Cambridge MA: MIT Press.

Schubert, Jon. 2014. '"Working the system": affect, amnesia and the aesthetics of power in the "new Angola"'. PhD thesis, Department of Social Anthropology, University of Edinburgh.

2015. '2002: year zero: history as anti-politics in the "new Angola"', *Journal of Southern African Studies* 41 (4): 835–52.

2016. 'Emerging middle-class political subjectivities in post-war Angola' in Henning Melber (ed.), *Examining the African Middle Class(es)*. London: Zed Books.

Scott, David. 2014. *Omens of Adversity: tragedy, time, memory, justice*. Durham NC and London: Duke University Press.

Scott, James. 1998. *Seeing Like a State: how certain schemes to improve the human condition have failed*. New Haven CT and London: Yale University Press.

Serra, C. 2010. 'Causas e características das manifestações em Maputo e Matola'. Available at: http://oficinadesociologia.blogspot.com/ (accessed 27 February 2011).

Sheldon, Kathleen. 2002. *Pounders of Grain: a history of women, work, and politics in Mozambique*. Portsmouth NH: Heinemann.

Shore, Cris. 2002. 'Introduction: towards an anthropology of elites' in Cris Shore and Stephen Nugent (eds), *Elite Cultures: anthropological perspectives*. London and New York NY: Routledge.

Simone, AbdouMaliq. 2010. *The Social Infrastructure of City Life in Contemporary Africa*. Discussion Paper 51. Uppsala: Nordic Africa Institute.

Sithole, Ndabaningi and Julius Ingwane. 1977. *Frelimo Militant: the story of Ingwane from Mozambique*. Nairobi: Transafrica Books.

Smith, Alan and Clarence Gervase. 1985. 'Portuguese colonies and Madagascar' in Roland Oliver and G. N. Sanderson (eds), *The Cambridge History of Africa. Volume 6: 1870 to 1905*. New York NY and London: Cambridge University Press.

Soares de Oliveira, Ricardo. 2007. *Oil and Politics in the Gulf of Guinea*. London: C. Hurst and Company.

2015. *Magnificent and Beggar Land: Angola since the civil war*. London: C. Hurst and Company.

Somers, Margaret. 1992. 'Narrativity, narrative identity, and social action: re-thinking English working-class formation', *Social Science History* 16: 591–630.

Southall, Roger. 2013. *Liberation Movements in Power: party and state in Southern Africa*. Woodbridge: James Currey and University of KwaZulu-Natal Press.

2016. *The New Black Middle Class in South Africa*. Johannesburg and New York NY: James Currey.

Stoler, Anne. 1997. 'Sexual affronts and racial frontiers: European identities and the cultural politics of exclusion in colonial Southeast Asia' in Anne Stoler and Frederick Cooper (eds), *Tensions of Empire: colonial cultures in a bourgeois world*. Berkeley, Los Angeles CA, and London: University of California Press.

Sumich, Jason. 2008 'Politics after the time of hunger in Mozambique: a critique of neo-patrimonial interpretations of elites', *Journal of Southern African Studies* 34 (1): 111–26.

2009. 'Modernity redirected: socialism, liberalism and the national elite in Mozambique', *Cambridge Anthropology* 28 (2): 1–24.

2010. 'The party and the state?: The ambiguities of power in Mozambique', *Development and Change* 41 (4): 679–98.

2012. 'An imaginary nation: nationalism, ideology and the Mozambican national elite' in Eric Morier-Genoud (ed.), *Sure Road? Nationalisms and nations in Angola, Guinea-Bissau and Mozambique*. Leiden: Brill.

2013. 'Tenuous belonging: citizenship, democracy and power in Mozambique', *Social Analysis* 57 (2): 99–116.

2016. 'The uncertainty of prosperity: dependence and the politics of middle class privilege in Maputo', *Ethnos* 81 (5): 821–41.

Tollenaere, M. 2006. 'Fostering multiparty politics in Mozambique' in J. Zeeuw and K. Kumar (eds), *Promoting Democracy in Post-Colonial Societies*. Boulder CO and London: Lynne Rienner Publishers.

Udelsmann, Cristina. 2007. 'From family solidarity to social classes: urban stratification in Angola (Luanda and Ondjiva)', *Journal of Southern African Studies* 33 (2): 235–50.

Verdery, Katherine. 1991. *National Ideology under Socialism: identity and cultural politics in Ceaușescu's Romania.* Berkeley and Los Angeles CA: University of California Press.

2014. *Secrets and Truths: ethnography in the archive of Romania's secret police.* Budapest and New York NY: Central European University Press.

Vieira, Sergio. 1977. 'The new man is a process'. Speech to the Second Conference of the Ministry of Education, Maputo, December.

Vines, Alex. 1996. *Renamo: from terrorism to democracy in Mozambique?* London: James Currey.

Weber, Max. 1961. *General Economic History.* New York NY: Collier Books.

Wedeen, Lisa. 1999. *Ambiguities of Domination: politics, rhetoric, and symbols in contemporary Syria.* Chicago IL and London: University of Chicago Press.

2008. *Peripheral Visions: publics, power and performance in Yemen.* Chicago IL: University of Chicago Press.

Welker, Marina. 2014. *Enacting the Corporation: an American mining firm in post-authoritarian Indonesia.* Berkeley CA: University of California Press.

Werbner, Richard. 2004. *Reasonable Radicals and Citizenship in Botswana: the public anthropology of Kalanga elites.* Bloomington IN: University of Indiana Press.

West, Harry. 1997. 'Creative destruction and sorcery of construction: power, hope and suspicion in post-war Mozambique', *Cahiers d'Études Africaines* 147: 675–98.

2001. 'Sorcery of construction and socialist modernization: ways of understanding power in post-colonial Mozambique', *American Ethnologist* 28: 119–50.

2005. *Kupilikula: governance and the invisible realm in Mozambique.* Chicago IL: University of Chicago Press.

Whyte, William. 1993. *Street Corner Society: the social structure of an Italian slum.* Chicago IL and London: University of Chicago Press.

Williams, Gavin. 2012. 'Nationalisms, nations and states: concluding reflections' in Eric Morier-Genoud (ed.), *Sure Road? Nationalisms in Angola, Guinea-Bissau and Mozambique.* Leiden and Boston MA: Brill.

Wilson, K. B. 1992. 'Cults of violence and counter-violence in Mozambique', *Journal of Southern African Studies* 18 (3): 527–82.

Wolf, Eric. 1973. *Peasant Wars of the Twentieth Century.* New York NY and London: Harper and Row Publishers.

Yurchak, Alexei. 1997. 'The cynical reason of late socialism: power, pretense, and the "anekdot"', *Public Culture* 9: 161–88.

2006. *Everything Was Forever, Until It Was No More: the last Soviet generation.* Princeton NJ and Oxford: Princeton University Press.

2015. 'Bodies of Lenin: the hidden science of communist sovereignty', *Representations* 129: 116–57.

Zawangoni, Salvador. 2007. *A Frelimo e a formação do homem novo: 1964–1974 and 1975–1982.* Maputo: CIEDIMA.

Žižek, Slavoj. 1989. *The Sublime Object of Ideology.* London: Verso.

Index

Titles in the series

For EU product safety concerns, contact us at Calle de José Abascal, 56–1°,
28003 Madrid, Spain or eugpsr@cambridge.org.

www.ingramcontent.com/pod-product-compliance
Ingram Content Group UK Ltd.
Pitfield, Milton Keynes, MK11 3LW, UK
UKHW020326140625
459647UK00018B/2025